D1338904

MAKING RIGHTS A REALITY?

Making Rights a Reality? explores the way in which disability activists in the United Kingdom and Canada have transformed their aspirations into legal claims in their quest for equality. It unpacks shifting conceptualizations of the political identity of disability and the role of a rights discourse in these dynamics. In doing so, it delves into the diffusion of disability rights among grassroots organizations and the traditional disability charities. It then shows how the diffusion of this model of disability rights can explain how and why disability activists have deployed legal strategies in pursuit of their goals.

The book draws on a wealth of primary sources, including court records and campaign documents and encompassing interviews with more than sixty activists and legal experts. In addition to showing that the disability rights movement has had a significant impact on equality jurisprudence in two countries, the book demonstrates that the act of mobilizing rights can have consequences, both intended and unintended, for social movements themselves.

Lisa Vanhala currently holds a British Academy postdoctoral fellowship at the Centre for Socio-Legal Studies at the University of Oxford. She previously held an Economic and Social Research Council (ESRC) postdoctoral fellowship at the Centre for the Study of Human Rights at the London School of Economics and Political Science (LSE). Her research has been published in the *Journal of European Public Policy, Canadian Journal of Political Science, Common Law World Review*, and *Regional and Federal Studies*.

Disability Law and Policy

The Disability Law and Policy series examines these topics in interdisciplinary and comparative terms. The books in the series reflect the diversity of definitions, causes, and consequences of discrimination against persons with disabilities, while illuminating fundamental themes that unite countries in their pursuit of human rights laws and policies to improve the social and economic status of persons with disabilities. The series contains historical, contemporary, and comparative scholarship crucial to identifying individual, organizational, cultural, attitudinal, and legal themes necessary for the advancement of disability law and policy.

The book topics covered in the series also are reflective of the new moral and political commitment by countries throughout the world toward equal opportunity for persons with disabilities in such areas as employment, housing, transportation, rehabilitation, and individual human rights. The series will thus play a significant role in informing policy makers, researchers, and citizens of issues central to disability rights and disability antidiscrimination policies. The series grounds the future of disability law and policy as a vehicle for ensuring that those living with disabilities participate as equal citizens of the world.

To Aimo, Paula, and Katie

MAKING RIGHTS A REALITY?

Disability Rights Activists and Legal Mobilization

Lisa Vanhala

Centre for Socio-Legal Studies, University of Oxford

CAMBRIDGE
UNIVERSITY PRESS

CAMBRIDGE UNIVERSITY PRESS
Cambridge, New York, Melbourne, Madrid, Cape Town,
Singapore, São Paulo, Delhi, Mexico City

Cambridge University Press
The Edinburgh Building, Cambridge CB2 8RU, UK

Published in the United States of America by Cambridge University Press, New York

www.cambridge.org
Information on this title: www.cambridge.org/9781107616400

First published 2011
First paperback edition 2013

A catalogue record for this publication is available from the British Library

Library of Congress Cataloguing in Publication Data
Vanhala, Lisa, 1979–
Making rights a reality? : disability rights activists and legal mobilization / Lisa Vanhala.
    p.   cm. – (Cambridge disability law and policy series)
Includes bibliographical references and index.
ISBN 978-1-107-00087-2 (hardback)
1. People with disabilities – Legal status, laws, etc. – Great Britain – History.   2. People with
disabilities – Great Britain – History.   3. People with disabilities – Legal status, laws, etc. –
Canada – History.   4. People with disabilities – Canada – History.   I. Title.
K1970.V36   2011
342.4108'7–dc22   2010045638

ISBN 978-1-107-00087-2 Hardback
ISBN 978-1-107-61640-0 Paperback

Contents

Contents

Contents

Figure and Tables

FIGURE

TABLES

Acknowledgments

I must first acknowledge a debt that can never be adequately expressed or repaid. The individuals who participated in the in-depth interviews not only contributed their time and access to organizational documents but also entrusted me with their recollections, perceptions, aspirations, and knowledge. I have tried, where possible, to privilege their voices in the writing of this book, and I am deeply conscious of my responsibility to understand and convey the significance of what they have shared with me. If at times my interpretive skills have fallen short, I have nonetheless made every effort to treat the knowledge they have given me with respect. I thank them for their contribution.

The research conducted for this book, and the doctoral thesis from which it has emerged, were supported by several grants. I am grateful to the British Academy for generous postdoctoral funding and to the Centre for Socio-Legal Studies of the University of Oxford for hosting me during the final stages of my book preparation. I also benefited from a grant from the UK Economic and Social Research Council (award PTA-026–27–2067) and was warmly welcomed by the members of the Centre for the Study of Human Rights at the London School of Economics. I am grateful for an award from the Clarendon Fund that allowed me to take my place in the doctoral course at the University of Oxford. I would like to thank Nuffield College, Hertford College, and the Andrew Smith Memorial Scholarship Committee for support throughout my graduate studies. I thank the Department of Politics and International Relations for funding several trips to Canada and the United Kingdom. The Philip F. Vineberg Travelling Fellowship from McGill University first allowed me to come to Oxford, and I am grateful for that opportunity.

I would also like to thank those who provided accommodation and assistance while I was in the field, undertaking research or attending conferences: Mike McGuire and Jason Bett in Ottawa; the registry staff of the Supreme Court of Canada; Jill Petersen and Guillaume D'Arabian in Vancouver; Colin Barnes, for bringing the Disability Archive at Leeds University to my attention; and Russ Taylor in Oxford.

Panel members and discussants at the following meetings offered helpful comments on individual chapters: Nuffield College Graduate Seminar (2006), the Law and Society Association Graduate Workshop (2008) and Annual Meetings (2008, 2009), Canadian Political Science Association (2008), Political Studies Association (2008), International Studies Association (2009), British Association for Canadian Studies Conference (2009), University of Edinburgh Canadian Studies Centre Research Seminar (2010), and the Initial Colloquium on Disability Law and Policy hosted by the National University of Ireland, Galway (2010). Anonymous reviewers for *Disability and Society, Journal of European Public Policy, Canadian Journal of Political Science,* and *Common Law World Review* provided cogent critiques of earlier versions of some of the ideas contained in this book. I am very grateful for their time and careful attention.

There are many who have intellectually inspired, challenged, and encouraged me. Rob Abercrombie, Nancy Bermeo, Bruce Blain, Betsy Cooper, Victor Evrard, Al Fraser, Carolyn Haggis, Matthew Hennigar, Tim Hicks, Chris Hilson, Chris Hodges, Elisabeth Ivarsflaten, Adrienne LeBas, Dan Lewer, Ravi Malhotra, Frank Munger, Michael Orsini, Patricia Pesquera Menendez, Gwen Sasse, Cindy

Acknowledgments

Skach, Miriam Smith, Dagmar Soennecken, Keith Stanski, Chris Taylor, Russ Taylor, Corin Throsby, Annis May Timpson, and Magdalena Tulibacka have commented on chapters along the way, provided support and encouragement, or both. They have helped me to perform the delicate balancing act of interdisciplinary research.

My intellectual development owes much to two mentors at Oxford. I am grateful for the close and attentive supervision that Katrin Auel provided during my doctoral studies. She engaged herself with my empirical material, helped me to engineer my theoretical approach, and constantly pushed me to refine my thinking and writing. Dan Kelemen provided invaluable feedback on my research and sparked my original interest in law, the courts, and politics early in my graduate studies and, for that, I thank him. I would also like to thank Conor Gearty, my mentor at the Centre for the Study of Human Rights at the LSE. His insights as a scholar and barrister helped me to hone the book at a particularly crucial stage. The book's two anonymous reviewers and the series editors and copy editors, as well as my editor at Cambridge University Press, John Berger, are also owed a wealth of thanks.

I wish to thank the following for permission to use copyrighted material. First, I am grateful to Taylor & Francis for permission to incorporate material from my article "Anti-Discrimination Policy Actors and Their Use of Litigation Strategies: The Influence of Identity Politics," *Journal of European Public Policy* 16:5 (2009), into Chapter 1. Thanks are also due to the Canadian Political Science Association and Cambridge for permission to use material from my article "Disability Rights Activists in the Supreme Court of Canada: Legal Mobilization Theory and Accommodating Social Movements," *Canadian Journal of Political Science* 42:4 (2009), in Chapter 2. Finally, I thank Vathek Publishing for permission to use material from my article "Twenty-Five Years of Disability Equality? Interpreting Disability Rights in the Supreme Court of Canada," *Common Law World Review* 39:1 (2010), in Chapter 3.

Acknowledgments

My sister Katie's adventurous spirit often puts us on opposite ends of the globe, but her generosity and humor have picked me up, even from afar, on countless occasions during the later stages of this project. My parents, Aimo and Paula, have provided endless love, support, and encouragement. It is to them that this work is dedicated.

Abbreviations

ANH	artificial nutrition and hydration
AODA	Accessibility for Ontarians with Disabilities Act
ARCH	Advocacy Resource Centre for the Handicapped (now ARCH Disability Law Centre)
BCODP	British Council of Organisations of Disabled People (now UKDPC)
BOOST	Blind Organization of Ontario with Self-Help Tactics
CACL	Canadian Association for Community Living
CAD	Canadian Association of the Deaf
CAILC	Canadian Association for Independent Living Centres
CAMR	Canadian Association for the Mentally Retarded (now CACL)
CCD	Council of Canadians with Disabilities
CDRC	Canadian Disability Rights Council
CHRA	Canadian Human Rights Act
CHS	Canadian Hearing Society
CMHA	Canadian Mental Health Association
CNIB	Canadian National Institute for the Blind (now using the acronym)
COPOH	Coalition of Provincial Organizations of the Handicapped
CRCD	Canadian Rehabilitation Council for the Disabled
CRE	Commission for Racial Equality
DA	Disability Alliance
DAWN Canada	DisAbled Women's Network Canada
DAWN Ontario	DisAbled Women's Network Ontario
DIG	Disablement Income Group
DPI	Disabled Peoples' International

Abbreviations

DRC	Disability Rights Commission
DWP	Department for Work and Pensions
ECHR	European Convention on Human Rights
ECJ	European Court of Justice
ECtHR	European Court of Human Rights
EDF	European Disability Forum
EHRC	Equality and Human Rights Commission
EOC	Equal Opportunities Commission
ERDCO	Ethno-racial People with Disabilities Coalition of Ontario
FEAT BC	Families for Early Autism Treatment of BC
GMC	General Medical Council
HRA	Human Rights Act
LEAF	Women's Legal Education and Action Fund
LNDP	Liberation Network of Disabled People
LOS	legal opportunity structure
Mind	The National Association for Mental Health
NAACP	National Association for the Advancement of Colored People
NAC	National Action Committee on the Status of Women
NLBD	National League of the Blind and Disabled
ODI	Office of Disability Issues
POS	political opportunity structure
RADAR	Royal Association for Disability and Rehabilitation (now using the acronym)
RM	resource mobilization
RNIB	Royal National Institute of Blind People (now using the acronym)
RNID	Royal National Institute for Deaf People (now using the acronym)
SCC	Supreme Court of Canada
SMOs	social movement organizations
UKDPC	UK Disabled People's Council
UPIAS	Union of the Physically Impaired Against Segregation

1

Introduction: Legal Mobilization and Accommodating Social Movements

THROUGH THE COURTROOM DOORS

In November 1979, Canadians with disabilities met in Ottawa to lobby the federal government on the issue of accessible transport, which, they argued, was crucial to achieving equality and social inclusion.[1] Paradoxically, many activists, who had traveled from across Canada, encountered numerous barriers en route to Ottawa because of the difficulty of finding suitable modes of transport. Some attendees resorted to traveling in freight trains because their personal wheelchairs could not be accommodated in the passenger service cars. The struggle did not stop there. Upon their arrival in Ottawa, they discovered that the inaccessibility of the House of Commons made it impossible for some advocates to carry out meetings with Members of Parliament (MPs). In the late 1970s, such experiences of segregation were common for persons with disabilities. However, the incident was not all bad for the activists meeting in Ottawa; they effectively harnessed their stories to

---

[1] These activists gathered for the second annual "Transportation and the Disabled" conference. The gathering was organized by what was then known as the Coalition of Provincial Organizations of the Handicapped (COPOH), a nascent nongovernmental organization that brought together equality-seeking disability activists. Immediately following the conference, activists presented their concerns at the Canadian Transport Commission Hearings, and many were invited by Members of Parliament to meet at their offices in the House of Commons.

garner media support for their campaign and to stir debate within the political establishment. The government could no longer ignore the voice of Canadians with disabilities.

Almost thirty years later, the Supreme Court of Canada delivered its judgment in *Council of Canadians with Disabilities v. VIA Rail Canada Inc.*, in favor of the Council of Canadians with Disabilities (CCD).[2] At the heart of this case was the decision made by VIA Rail in late 2000 to purchase 139 rail cars ("Renaissance cars") at a significant discount. The train cars were affordable because they were no longer usable for service through the Channel Tunnel; they were inaccessible to persons with disabilities and, hence, violated antidiscrimination legislation in the United Kingdom. Over the next six years, disability activists poured organizational resources – time, money, and energy – into a series of cases challenging this purchase. In *VIA Rail,* activists argued that the objectives of a national transport system must range wider than getting people from point A to point B as cheaply as possible. The Court agreed, finding that accessible transport is critical to enabling persons with disabilities to pursue educational opportunities, gain employment, enjoy recreation, participate in democratic processes, and live independently in the community. The judges ruled that the purchase of inaccessible carriages violated the equal rights of persons with disabilities: transport had moved into the realm of human rights law and policy.

Disability rights activists in Canada were jubilant about the Supreme Court decision in *VIA Rail.* With this decision, they saw the promise of equality established twenty-five years earlier in the Canadian Charter of Rights and Freedoms (1982) fulfilled, and they felt that their message

---

[2] *Council of Canadians with Disabilities v. VIA Rail Canada Inc.*, [2007] 1 S.C.R. 650. CCD was the progeny of COPOH: the organization changed its name in the mid-1980s to better reflect the discursive shift that was occurring in the realm of disability politics at the time. CCD waged a protracted legal campaign against VIA Rail Canada, which operates the national passenger rail service on behalf of the Government of Canada.

about the importance of accessible transportation had finally resonated. However, the final decision was extremely close, and activists were aware of how little it advanced the equality agenda and how difficult it would be to ensure effective enforcement of the Court's decision. Perhaps even more sobering was the realization that the issue of accessible transport – key during the movement's birth – was still capturing the full attention, resources, and energy of the disability rights movement three decades later.

These two examples of relatively small but significant victories for disability rights in Canada shed light on how the social movement has changed in terms of audience and tactics over thirty years. Yet, they also demonstrate those elements that remained the same: the grievances being expressed and the ideas of what true equality for persons with disabilities entails. These examples of the struggle for equality in transport are far from isolated. The campaign for rights and protection from discrimination on grounds of disability has become globalized.[3] The question of disability rights touches on issues ranging from inclusive education, autonomy in end-of-life decision making, and the politics of caregiving. In trying to make disability rights "real," activists rely on a number of tactics and strategies that increasingly include the use of law and courts.

The disability rights movement offers a rich case study of the mobilization of law by social movement actors. The modern disability rights movement has been transformational: over the past twenty-five years, it has engaged a broad spectrum of issues that deeply affect individual and collective identities. For some disability advocacy organizations, the courts have been a primary locus of movement activity; other organizations have completely foregone the judicial route in attempting to achieve their goals. Some activists who were hesitant about participating in litigation in the past have become active players in legal venues.

[3] R. Daniel Kelemen, *The Rise of Adversarial Legalism in Europe* (Cambridge, MA: Harvard University Press, Forthcoming).

Groups that, at certain times, were particularly active in the courts have been completely absent during other periods. This variation across groups and over time presents a puzzle: why do some disability groups turn to the courts as part of their campaigning work, often despite significant resource and procedural hurdles, whereas others, implicitly or explicitly, eschew this approach?

This book addresses this question by telling the story of how and why disability activists have deployed legal norms in their quest for societal equality and by exploring the outcomes of this legal action. Building on the momentum of recent work, I employ a sociological theory of institutions to account for variation in the use of legal action across the population of disability organizations. I offer a distinctive framework that puts the spotlight on two dimensions. First, I look at social movement framing processes: the way in which activists transform their vision and goals into plausible rights claims. Then, I explore the social movement politics surrounding these processes. In developing this framework, I challenge conventional wisdom about what matters most in understanding legal mobilization. Looking at financial resources and political or legal contexts only takes us part of the way in explaining the how, when, and why of legal mobilization. I suggest that, by taking social movement identity politics into account, we may find that there has been a fundamental misunderstanding of the causal mechanisms at play. Only by taking a holistic view of the full range of factors shaping the decision by SMOs to turn to the courts can we truly understand disability rights activism and the evolution of judicial understandings of equality.

Empirically, the disability rights movement provides an illuminating example of the power of the relationship between rights, ideas, and collective identity. This book also highlights the consequences of disability movement politics for legal mobilization and vice versa, engaging with important debates in the disability studies literature. Theoretically, this book contributes to the growing body of research on the judicialization of politics in advanced industrial democracies.

Introduction

It does so by developing an approach to explain why some disability activists – particularly collective actors – are willing and able to use law and legal action to achieve their goals, and why others are not. After a discussion of existing explanations of legal mobilization, I develop a theoretical framework that complements these current approaches. Later in this chapter, I narrow the focus to the empirical subject of the book by exploring why the issue of legal mobilization of disability rights is important and instructive.

UNDERSTANDING LEGAL OPPORTUNITY: BALANCING STRUCTURE AND AGENCY

The term "legal mobilization" means different things to different people; academics, activists, and legal actors conceptualize the use of legal action by social movements in a wide variety of ways.[4] One of the earliest and most cited formulations put forth in the political science literature for the term "legal mobilization" is the basic premise that "the law is . . . mobilized when a desire or want is translated into a demand as an assertion of rights."[5] It has also been used to describe processes "by which legal norms are invoked to regulate behaviour" and a "planned effort to influence the course of judicial policy development to achieve a particular policy goal."[6] Michael McCann adopts an interpretive understanding of legal mobilization; he emphasizes "an understanding of law as identifiable traditions of symbolic practice," legal discourses as "constitutive of practical interactions among citizens," and the inherent

---

[4] Christopher P. Manfredi, *Feminist Activism in the Supreme Court* (Toronto: UBC Press, 2004).

[5] Frances K. Zemans, "Legal Mobilization: The Neglected Role of the Law in the Political System," *American Political Science Review* 77(3), 1983, p. 700.

[6] Robert O. Lempert, "Mobilizing Private Law: An Introductory Essay," *Law and Society Review* 11(2), 1976, p. 173; Susan E. Lawrence, *The Poor in Court: The Legal Services Program and Supreme Court Decision Making* (Princeton, NJ: Princeton University Press, 1990), p. 40.

malleability of legal symbols and discourses that might be mobilized to fight policy battles and advance movement goals.[7] While emphasizing different understandings of the power that law can and does exert in social life, what unifies these approaches is the idea that law has the potential to be an effective instrument for political and social change.[8]

Legal mobilization can include many different types of strategies and tactics, such as raising rights consciousness among particular communities or the public, delivering public legal education or specialized legal education, lobbying for law reform or changes in the levels of access to justice, providing summary legal advice and referral services, and undertaking strategic or test case litigation. I do not make an assessment of the relative benefits and disadvantages of using these various activities to achieve particular goals. Rather, necessitated by scope, this inquiry generally focuses on the use of strategic litigation. The terms "test case" and "strategic litigation" generally refer to those cases in which an organization or individual entreats a court or tribunal to a) look at an issue for the first time or potentially reconsider an issue that has been decided in the past, b) decide an issue that will affect a significant number or class of people, and/or c) consider a particular perspective on an issue that has hitherto not been included in existing jurisprudence.

Whether seeking to create, expand, clarify, narrow, or nullify rights or pursue other goals through the use of litigation, activists and organizations can enter the courtroom in one of several ways. Carol Harlow and Richard Rawlings first developed the distinction between proactive litigation strategies and reactive litigation strategies.[9] For them, proactive litigation describes those situations in which groups act as

---

[7] Michael McCann, *Rights at Work: Pay Equity Reform and the Politics of Legal Mobilization* (Chicago: University of Chicago Press, 1994), pp. 8–9.

[8] Manfredi, *Feminist Activism*, p. 10.

[9] Carol Harlow and Richard Rawlings, *Pressure Through Law* (London: Routledge, 1992).

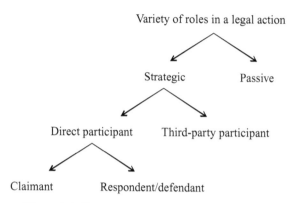

Figure 1.1. Range of Roles in Legal Mobilization.

the litigant, seeking to take their cause to the courts. Reactive litigation is the response of groups that choose to undertake civil disobedience. In these situations, activists purposefully flaunt laws they see as unjust or immoral, with the aim of being arrested and brought before a judge or jury. Activists entreat the judge or jury to overturn or, at least, not enforce the law they see as unjust. Although this framework is a useful analytical contribution, it is also reflective of a relatively simplistic understanding of the range of roles groups can play and the intentions behind particular actions.

To overcome these difficulties, I propose a categorization that hinges the definition of legal mobilization on the identified intentions of the collective actors involved in the litigation (see Figure 1.1). When an organization purposefully turns to the courts to pursue its goals, its action can be classified as strategic. In the strategic category, the type of role played by an organization can be further broken down: the organization can be either a direct participant – the claimant (or supporting an individual claimant) or a respondent (or supporting a respondent) – or a third-party participant. Most studies on the use of strategic litigation have focused on the former – what Harlow and Rawlings referred to as "proactive litigation strategies," whereby groups pursue cases themselves or directly support an individual litigant. Activists can also act strategically so as to be required to appear before the court as respondents or defendants; that is, they will purposefully act unlawfully with the intention of appearing before the court, with the hope that the court will highlight what they see as unjust laws or clarify that the actions of the authorities are not underpinned by law.[10] An organization can also apply for leave to intervene as a third-party intervener. Interveners are not directly involved in the legal dispute of the case but volunteer to offer information – usually in the form of a brief or testimony, or both – to the court on a point of law or to provide other perspectives on the case and the potential consequences of deciding it one way or the other.[11]

In contrast, when an organization is required to appear before the court but prefers not to, and does not use this action as a way of pursuing goals, this strategy can be classified as passive. An organization can be pulled to court as either a respondent or defense in a criminal case. This is most often passive litigation, although, if the organization takes this opportunity to pursue policy or other goals, this type of litigation then falls under the strategic category.[12] The switch from passive to

[10] This tactic can backfire if the court then confirms the existence of a law or power that was controversial until that point.

[11] This is commonly known as *amicus curiae* – a "friend of the court." In Canada, the terminology is slightly different. In addition to interveners, there is another type of third-party participant, an *amicus curiae*, who is requested by the court to appear to provide advice or legal opinion to the Court if the Court feels that a particular perspective is missing from its analysis and there have been no applications for leave to intervene to present a particular perspective.

[12] A recent example is the use of an injunction by the British Airport Authority (BAA) during the Camp for Climate Action protest in August 2007 at London's Heathrow airport. Environmental protection organizations and individuals gathered near the airport over several days to protest the expansion of the airport and the increasing use of aviation and its environmental consequences more generally. The campaigners actually benefited from their opponent's use of the courts to try to stop several individual activists and one organization, Plane Stupid, from attending the protests: the injunction had the unintended effect of generating publicity and public sympathy for the protestors, all at a minimal cost to the campaigners themselves.

strategic litigation is generally not predictable and therefore is difficult to manage. However, if harnessed in an effective way, responses to injunctions and other legal tactics can be very useful in supporting an organization's goals.

What, then, are the conditions under which civil society organizations are likely to rely on litigation strategies to further their interests and advance their goals? What are the factors that shape the decision to turn to the courts, and why do some civil society organizations make this move, whereas others do not? A number of theoretical perspectives have been advanced in existing studies (mainly in the political science literature) on the assertion of legal rights by groups and individuals across a wide range of issue areas; however, three theoretical approaches have dominated the literature: 1) political opportunity structure (POS) approaches; 2) more recently, elements of legal opportunity structure (LOS) approaches; and 3) resource mobilization (RM) theories. Later in this chapter, I develop and deploy a sociological–institutionalist approach to account for why, when, and how some groups are more likely than others to rely on litigation strategy as part of their overall logic of action. I also discuss why the comparative approach taken here, as well as the case study of the disability rights movement, is beneficial in highlighting the theoretical value of my approach.

Insiders and Outsiders: Political Opportunity Structures and Legal Mobilization

Political scientists have often traced the turn to the courts by groups that are "disadvantaged" in traditional political arenas.[13] Early studies,

---

[13] In discussing these groups I tend to use the terms "social movement organization" (SMO), "civil society organization," and "interest group" interchangeably. However, it must be acknowledged that different bodies of literature in sociology and political science vary in their meanings of these terms. For example, the term "social

relying mainly on case studies of the American civil rights movement, argued that groups lacking influence over members of the executive, legislative, or regulatory bodies are more likely to turn to the judicial branch to pursue their policy goals. The literature on the use of European Community (EC) litigation strategies by interest organizations has also identified "political strength" as a factor that conditions the take up of strategic litigation. In more recent debates, political scientists have tended to conceptualize this notion of political disadvantage or strength using the tools of POS approaches, which explore the contextual incentives and constraints that SMOs face in the political environment and which may shape their strategy choices.

The core idea uniting opportunity structure approaches is that the most important determinant of variations in levels and forms of collective action by social movement groups is opportunity, not grievances, resources, or something else. The term "opportunity," as Ruud Koopmans points out, is rarely defined. It generally refers to constraints, possibilities, and threats that originate outside the mobilizing group, but that influence its chances of mobilizing or realizing collective interests.[14] Most POS approaches now consider both an input and an output dimension. Herbert Kitschelt writes that "the capacity of political opportunity structures to implement policies – as well as their openness to societal demands – ought to be seen to determine the overall responsiveness of politics to social movements."[15]

movement" tends to refer to groups advancing a common interest through collective action outside the sphere of established institutions; whereas "interest group" is used to describe groups established to influence political actors. However, many groups (e.g., Greenpeace or the Campaign for Nuclear Disarmament) engage in both protest and political lobbying.

[14] Ruud Koopmans, "Political. Opportunity. Structure. Some Splitting to Balance the Lumping," *Sociological Forum* 14(1), 1999, pp. 93–105.

[15] Herbert P. Kitschelt, "Political Opportunity Structures and Political Protest: Anti-Nuclear Movements in Four Democracies," *British Journal of Political Science* 16(1), 1986, p. 63.

Introduction

Although POS theories have been helpful in understanding the context within which SMOs operate, most POS theories either completely exclude law and legal structures or consider them within the broad definition of "political." P. K. Eisinger, in one of the earliest formulations of POS, makes no mention of the role of the judiciary, reflecting the lack of analytical attention paid by early political scientists to the political dimensions of the law.[16] Only in the 1980s did theorists begin to systematically incorporate the role of the judiciary in POS perspectives.[17] Kitschelt claims that one of the factors affecting the ability of social movement actors to achieve their policy goals is the relative independence and authority of the judiciary. As he notes, "policy implementation becomes more hazardous and cumbersome if courts are forums of political arbitration removed from executive branch control."[18] Hanspeter Kriesi goes one step further and places judicial strength within the definition of POS, on both the input and the output sides, by arguing that a strong judiciary, in providing an alternative access point, can be seen as increasing a polity's openness just as much as it may produce implementation weakness.[19]

Although the inclusion of the judiciary in these formulations of POS is an important acknowledgment of the potentially political role that courts play in liberal democracies, it has resulted in an implicit neglect of some of the key differences between the judiciary and other political institutions. Legal scholars implicitly argue that courts are fundamentally different from other law-producing bodies. Judicial systems and institutions evolve slowly, and courts tend to approach matters in a

---

[16] P. K. Eisinger, "The Conditions of Protest Behavior in American Cities," *American Political Science Review* 67(1), 1973, pp. 11–28.

[17] Chris Hilson, "New Social Movements: The Role of Legal Opportunity," *Journal of European Public Policy* 9(2), 2002, pp. 238–55.

[18] Kitschelt, "Political Opportunity Structures," p. 64.

[19] Hanspeter Kriesi, *The Politics of New Social Movements in Western Europe: A Comparative Analysis* (Minneapolis, MN: University of Minnesota Press, 1995).

backward-looking and reactive manner; that is, they almost exclusively look at how a policy or provision has actually had an impact on the litigants. Legislatures and bureaucracies, on the other hand, tend to be forward-looking, approaching matters on the basis of the likely benefits or cost that a particular policy or provision will produce for various stakeholders. Courts tend not to see themselves as an alternative forum for arguing matters of policy, particularly in the absence of actual instances of policy impact.[20] Eva Rubin summarizes the situation:

> Although courts offer an alternative route to policy change, they have their own institutional peculiarities and idiosyncrasies. The mechanics of the judicial process [are] very different from that of the legislation process, and the approach to judicial institutions must be made in the traditional framework of the lawsuit.[21]

As a result, the activity of SMOs within this realm is fundamentally different (even when the goals are the same) compared with other strategies they might pursue, such as lobbying and protest. The main actors in POS theories are generally assumed to be collective (as in SMOs), whereas the main agent operating within the legal system is generally an individual with a concrete issue that requires a legal resolution. The judicial system is inherently individualistic, and collective bodies interested in using the courts as a vehicle to pursue goals must conform to this. This can be done either through participating via one or several individual proxies as legal claimants or third-party interveners to represent the interests of the organization, or through lobbying to have the legal system changed to accommodate group demands, such as through the liberalization of class action rules or standing rules (regulations on who may take a case before the court). In short, in

---

[20] See *Canadian Council of Churches v. Canada (Minister of Employment and Immigration)*, [1992] 1 S.C.R. 236.

[21] Eva R. Rubin, *Abortion, Politics and the Courts* (Westport, CT: Greenwood Press, 1987), p. 33.

taking legal action, a different type of audience must be addressed, different tools must be employed, and a different language must be adopted. None of this is to say that politics does not play a role in judicial structures and policies regulating legal procedures and the legal profession. However, it does not play as explicit a role, and this must be taken into consideration when developing a theoretical approach to understanding the legal context within which organizations may want to pursue policy goals.

Legal Opportunity Structure Approaches

Scholars interested in legal mobilization have recently begun to develop LOS approaches that explicitly focus on variables both conditioning access to judicial governance and accounting for the role of judges and the judicial system in the policy output process.[22] The LOS approach has been used to examine the variation in activity and to measure the success of this activity by the following groups: gay rights organizations in the United States;[23] the women's movement, gay rights, environmental movement, and animal rights organizations in the United Kingdom and European Union (EU);[24] and gay rights groups and the movement for people living with AIDS in Costa Rica.[25]

One problem with early attempts at applying LOS approaches is their replication of a weakness of POS theories; they tended to be

---

[22] Hilson, "New Social Movements"; Ellen Ann Andersen, *Out of the Closets and Into the Courts: Legal Opportunity Structure and Gay Rights Litigation* (Ann Arbor: University of Michigan Press, 2005); Bruce M. Wilson and Juan Carlos Rodríguez Cordero, "Legal Opportunity Structures and Social Movements: The Effects of Institutional Change on Costa Rican Politics," *Comparative Political Studies* 39(3), 2006, pp. 325–51.

[23] Andersen, *Out of the Closets.*

[24] Hilson, "New Social Movements."

[25] Wilson and Rodriguez Cordero, "Legal Opportunity Structures."

deterministic and ignored actor agency.[26] This had important theoretical and methodological implications for the development of the approach. While lavishing attention on the impact of political and legal opportunities on the choice of strategy, scholars of strategic litigation spent relatively little energy systematically studying the role that collective actors played in reshaping institutional structures and legal procedures.[27] This resulted in a relative lack of exploration of the breadth of law-related goals that collective actors possess and incomplete or misleading measurement techniques in assessing organizational successes.

Ellen Ann Andersen's recent study of gay rights litigation by the Lambda Legal Defense and Education Fund, *Out of the Closets and into the Courts,* overcomes this tendency to privilege structure explanations over agency approaches. Relying on a sophisticated analysis of LOSs, she accounts for the emergence, progress, and outcomes of the principal gay rights litigation organization in the United States. She brings together an understanding of opportunity structures and frame alignment processes to develop an overarching account of "the ways in which socio-legal structures shape movement strategies and are shaped by those strategies in turn."[28] Andersen takes up the argument that opportunity or access can sometimes be the dependent variable: "The political configuration of the state shapes the opportunities afforded to movements; shifts in that configuration can open or close

---

[26] William A. Gamson and David S. Meyer, "The Framing of Political Opportunity," in Doug McAdam, John D. McCarthy, and Mayer N. Zald, eds., *Comparative Perspectives on Social Movements* (New York: Cambridge University Press, 1996), pp. 275–90.

[27] Notable exceptions include the following: Andersen, *Out of the Closets*; Rachel Cichowski and Alec Stone Sweet, "Participation, Representative Democracy, and the Courts," in Bruce E. Cain, Russell J. Dalton, and Susan E. Scarrow, eds., *Democracy Transformed? Expanding Political Opportunities in Advanced Industrial Democracies* (Oxford: Oxford University Press, 2003), pp. 192–221.

[28] Andersen, *Out of the Closets,* p. 8.

'windows' for action. Conversely, social movements can influence the political configuration of the state; through their actions, they can forge opportunities."[29] She also draws on the notion of frames to explain the progress and outcomes of Lambda's claims. In Andersen's conceptualization:

> Successful framing occurs when a speaker's discussion of a subject leads the receiver of the discussion to alter the criteria on which she judges the subject. To succeed in her task, the speaker must package her discussion in a manner that resonates with the beliefs of the receiver . . . the process of frame alignment mediates between opportunity and action.[30]

Andersen's theoretical approach focuses on four dimensions of the LOS. Here, I will briefly discuss those dimensions and make a case for limiting what falls under the term "structure." I then build on the important foundation Andersen has established by narrowing in more closely on social movement framing processes and their organizational implications.

The first dimension highlighted by Andersen is that of access. LOS scholars have noted, with near unanimity, that the extent of access significantly shapes the emergence and progress of legal action. Andersen argues that, in the same way as access to political institutions shapes the emergence, progress, and outcomes of collective action, access to courts shapes the emergence, progress, and outcomes of legal action: "the mechanics of the judicial process shape access in a number of important ways, including what may be litigated, who may litigate, and where such litigation may occur."[31] Most scholars have focused on the liberalization of the standing rules to account for an increase in

---

[29] Ibid., p. 7. See Chris Rootes, "Shaping Collective Action: Structure, Contingency and Knowledge," in Ricca Edmondson, ed., *The Political Context of Collective Action: Power, Argumentation and Democracy* (London: Routledge, 1997), pp. 81–104.

[30] Andersen, *Out of the Closets,* p. 8.

[31] Ibid., p. 9.

the use of litigation strategies by groups.[32] Cichowski and Stone Sweet described this transformation in the institutional incentives to pursue litigation:

> Traditionally, legal systems barred interest groups from taking court action on the grounds that they lacked, by definition, the kind of standing over which courts possessed jurisdiction. Most important, a plaintiff had to be able to show that he or she had been personally injured by state wrongdoing or negligence. Extending standing to sue to groups . . . turns the courts into sites for public-interest lobby activity.[33]

Although access to courts is clearly an important explanatory variable, it is not without problems. The distinction between the different roles that can be played in a legal action (discussed above) challenges implicit understandings of structural determinism in explaining the turn to the courts. If an organization is the object of litigation, it is obligated to appear in court and could feasibly use this as a venue within which to make policy arguments: access questions are turned on their head. Furthermore, social movement theorists increasingly stress that opportunities and threats to limit opportunities are not objective structural features but will only encourage or constrain mobilization if they are perceived by activists.[34] Although the opening of the LOS

---

[32] Cichowski and Stone Sweet, "Participation, Representative Democracy, and the Courts"; Karen Orren, "Standing to Sue: Interest Group Conflict in the Federal Courts," *American Political Science Review* 70(3), 1976, pp. 723–41.

[33] Cichowski and Stone Sweet, "Participation, Representative Democracy, and the Courts."

[34] See also Doug McAdam et al., *Dynamics of Contention* (New York: Cambridge University Press, 2001); Gamson and Meyer, "The Framing of Political Opportunity"; Kathryn Sikkink, "Patterns of Dynamic Multilevel Governance and the Insider-Outsider Coalition," in Donatella Della Porta and Sidney Tarrow, eds., *Transnational Protest and Global Activism* (Oxford: Rowman and Littlefield, 2005), pp. 151–74; Jeff Goodwin and James M. Jasper, "Caught in a Winding, Snarling Vine: The Structural Bias of Political Process Theory," *Sociological Forum* 14(1), 1999, pp. 27–54.

provides opportunities for undertaking legal action, it does not mean that activists will necessarily recognize and exploit those opportunities. Andersen raises this point, arguing that action depends on the capacity of SMOs to identify and act on the opportunities available. However, the one-organization study of a group with inherently high levels of rights consciousness (largely staffed by lawyers) does not provide enough variation to explore the mechanisms that may be at play in explaining the interaction between actor perceptions and LOS.

The second dimension of Andersen's LOS approach is the configuration of elite alignments and the way in which this affects groups' decisions to risk taking legal action. In an LOS understanding of legal mobilization, the elites are generally judges who are presented with a legal dispute they must resolve. Judicial agreement or disagreement, and the sources of it, has indeed spawned a body of literature on the "attitudinal model," which mainly focuses on courts of last instance.[35] The attitudinal model asserts that judicial decision making is shaped by the personal background and experiences of individual judges. It posits that judges sitting on courts of final appeal are, within the confines of legal and institutional constraints, able to make decisions on disputes according to their policy preferences. According to the attitudinal perspective, changes in legal doctrine are generally the product of attitudinal shifts caused by changes in judicial personnel.[36] Andersen correctly points out that "turnovers in the population of judges may open (or close) windows of opportunity for legal action."[37]

---

[35] Jeffrey A. Segal and Harold J. Spaeth, *The Supreme Court and the Attitudinal Model* (New York: Cambridge University Press, 1993); C. Herman Pritchett, *The Roosevelt Court: A Study in Judicial Politics and Values* (New York: Macmillan, 1948). James Gibson, "Judge's Role Orientations, Attitudes and Decision: An Interactive Model," *American Political Science Review* 72(3), 1978, pp. 911–24.

[36] Manfredi, *Feminist Activism in the Supreme Court*, p. 3; Andersen, *Out of the Closets*.

[37] Andersen, *Out of the Closets*. Although judicial preferences certainly matter, they recede into the background in this study because of my shift of focus away from

Here, I question Andersen's categorization of her third and fourth dimensions – "alliance and conflict systems" and "cultural and legal frames," respectively – as part of the concept of "structure." She argues the following:

> The presence of allies and/or opponents is also an aspect of legal opportunity structure. Allies can defray the substantial costs of bringing a case. They can offer assistance with devising legal strategies. They can also file amicus curiae (friend of the court) briefs. These briefs can signal the importance of the case under consideration, provide supplemental legal arguments, and add credibility to claims made by challengers.[38]

Although in the gay rights movement there was relative stability as to who the consistent allies were and who regularly appeared in court as adversaries, other movements face configurations of allies and adversaries that are far less stable. Depending on the specific issue at stake, former adversaries may work together, and allies who see eye-to-eye on one issue may be in opposing camps on another.

With the inclusion of cultural and legal frames as the fourth dimension of her LOS approach, Andersen broadens the notion of structure even further. She argues that "what makes legal opportunity different from political opportunity are the underlying frames that ground them."[39] She suggests that movements seeking to effect change within the legal system are constrained by the availability of cultural stock and legal stock.[40] The difficulty with Andersen's approach is that, by grouping cultural and legal frames together, there is a potential to confuse structural elements with more contingent factors.

---

courts to social movement activists. Instead, what will be explored more concretely (in Chapters 3 and 5) is the development of judicial interpretations of legal frames as they are put forward by organizational actors.

[38] Andersen, *Out of the Closets*, p. 11.

[39] Ibid., p. 12.

[40] Ibid., p. 13.

In fact, the notion that legal stock constrains movements within the legal system has been a key assumption in any framework attempting to explain litigation activity generally and strategic litigation more specifically: groups require relevant legal bases on which to act. Andersen's contention that, in judicial decision making, new decisions are constrained by previous ones is hardly controversial. Legal framing processes means that social movements making claims must articulate them so that they fall within existing legal stock – the categories previously established by an amalgam of constitutional, statutory, administrative, common, and case law. She asserts that these processes will shape the "kinds of legal claims that can be made as well as the persuasiveness of those claims" and the "facts that are considered to be relevant."[41] Although the notion of legal stock can reasonably be classified as structural because legal norms evolve slowly, it is precisely upon this evolutionary nature that actors interested in social change rely. The reality of strategic litigation has been more complex than simply one of actors conforming to constraints in legal norms. There are numerous examples of organized interests that have pursued litigation strategies even when apparently excluded from legal protection. For example, Sebastien Poulter explores how the Sikh turban, an explicitly religious symbol, only came to have protected status in Britain through the back door of ethnicity (discrimination based on ethnicity was legally forbidden, whereas, until 2003, religious discrimination was not); it rests on the House of Lords' legal decision in *Mandla v. Dowell-Lee* that Sikhs are not merely a religious but also an ethnic group.[42] A similar attempt to expand legal provisions to previously unprotected groups (but one that was ultimately unsuccessful) is a case, *Grant v. South West Trains Ltd*, in which Stonewall, a gay rights organization, supported a same-sex couple who were attempting to extend sex discrimination

---

[41] Ibid.

[42] *Mandla v. Dowell-Lee*, [1983] 2 AC 548; Sebastien M. Poulter, *Ethnicity, Law and Human Rights: The English Experience* (Oxford: Oxford University Press, 1998).

protections to sexual orientation in the field of employment rights.[43] In sum, groups are able to pursue litigation strategies even when they are seemingly excluded from specific legal protections by probing and expanding other relevant legal norms. It is precisely these types of opportunities on which organizations using test case litigation rely. They test the waters in terms of judicial support for a shift in understanding of an issue. Using test case strategies often means bringing a series of cases with the expectation of losing. What matters here are the perceptions and priorities of social movement actors, not only of the likelihood of winning a case, but also of the potential benefits even if a case is lost.

Whereas the inclusion of legal frames within a structural approach may be reasonable as long as actor agency is also given attention, the inclusion of cultural frames is more problematic. The danger here is in scholars picking and choosing which elements of culture (frames, symbols, rites, discourse) make their case in explaining any particular social movement's emergence and choice of strategy and incorporating that under the rubric of "structure." Virtually anything that can be seen as having helped a movement mobilize or attain its goals is labeled an "opportunity." The critique of POS made by Goodwin and Jasper can serve as a warning: "process theorists tend to wash the meaning and fluidity out of strategy, agency, and culture so that they will look more like structures."[44]

In short, including a fused understanding of cultural frames and legal stock as an explanatory dimension in LOS is a form of analytical eclecticism disguised as theory building.[45] Gamson and Meyer, critiquing POS, make the following argument:

> The concept of political opportunity structure is in trouble, in danger of becoming a sponge that soaks up virtually every aspect of

---

[43] *Grant v. South West Trains*, [1998] ECR I-621.
[44] Goodwin and Jasper, "Caught in a Winding, Snarling Vine," p. 29.
[45] Koopmans, "Political. Opportunity. Structure," p. 94.

the social movement environment – political institutions and culture, crises of various sorts, political alliances, and policy shifts . . . It threatens to become an all-encompassing fudge factor for all the conditions and circumstances that form the context for collective action. Used to explain so much, it may ultimately explain nothing at all.[46]

Whereas Andersen's conceptualization of LOS demonstrates a sophisticated understanding of the interplay between structure and actor agency, overturning the ritualistic opposition between the two concepts, many recent applications and developments of LOS frameworks do not explore this nuance and are in danger of rendering the concept vulnerable to a similar fate as that described above by Gamson and Meyer.

In this book, I do not undertake a systematic, focused, empirical application of the LOS (or POS or resource mobilization [RM]) approaches. It is already the subject of a burgeoning field of literature, and there is no lack of scholarly attention developing the LOS approach. However, this does not mean that I neglect LOS considerations. LOS effects can be controlled for through careful research design by exploring within national jurisdiction cases as well as cross-national issues. Instead of focusing on structure, I privilege the role of social movement organizational agency and explore how it may influence structural factors. I challenge the assumption in much of the literature on structure that movement activists are passive actors. In doing so, I seek to complement and further develop work like Andersen's.

I argue that the problem with opportunity structure approaches is that they tend to black box organizations in one of two ways. They are single-organization case studies and hence treat the collective actor as *sui generis*. Alternatively, they are multiorganization studies that treat organizations as static, homogenous entities and push characteristics of the groups themselves or the broader social movement environment,

---

[46] Gamson and Meyer, "The Framing of Political Opportunity," p. 275.

which may condition strategy choice, into the background of their analyses. Opportunity approaches tend to ignore the internal and social movement dynamics of organizations, which might exert an important influence on the range of strategy options and the tactics adopted by the group. For example, groups usually possess a variety of goals and ways of developing goals; by taking this variety into account, we can show how some groups might perceive the opportunity structure in different ways (or not at all). Some groups go to the courts even when they are relatively confident that they will not be granted standing, or when they expect to lose the case because they feel that there is something else they may gain, be it highlighting a legislative gap, gaining media attention, or raising consciousness among their own (potential) constituency. I believe that LOS approaches should be understood as just one step along a path to a more synthetic and systematic framework in understanding the turn to litigation by social movement actors.

Resource Threshold Explanations

POS and LOS approaches focus on the legal–political environment to the neglect of the internal dynamics of SMOs. In contrast, explanations that incorporate what could be called RM approaches remedy this somewhat by positing that a SMO's strategy will be largely determined by the resources available to them.[47] Scholars who rely on RM approaches claim that organizations must be able to mobilize resources successfully in order to pursue collective action. The implication for the choice between lobbying and litigation is that the latter is assumed to be far more costly and, therefore, the resource threshold to pursue legal

---

[47] Kitschelt, "Political Opportunity Structures and Political Protest"; John D. McCarthy and Mayer N. Zald, "Resource Mobilization and Social Movements: A Partial Theory," *American Journal of Sociology* 82(6), 1977, pp. 1212–41.

mobilization is generally considered to be much higher.[48] The observable implications of RM theories are that the greater the resources available to an organization, the higher the likelihood that it will rely on a variety of tactics, including strategic litigation, to pursue its policy goals. Conversely, if an organization possesses relatively few resources, it will be less likely to use more expensive strategies, including litigation.

There are, however, several problems with the application of RM theoretical propositions in existing work on strategy choice. First, the assumption that litigation will always be the most expensive route to successfully influencing policy has not been demonstrably confirmed across a wide range of policy fields. Different types of litigation strategies, each with varying resource thresholds, can be employed. Turning back to Figure 1.1, if the organization is acting as the litigant, this is undoubtedly an expensive strategy; submitting third-party participant briefs to influence the court's reasoning is generally less costly and time-consuming. Litigation strategies whereby activists flout a law in order to be arrested and brought before the court render issues of RM and access to justice irrelevant. Questions of standing, forum shopping, and other procedural hurdles (often included in LOS approaches) become moot when the activist is a defendant and is obligated to appear in court. Lumping all forms of litigation strategies together and assuming them to be resource-intensive misses this complexity. I am not arguing that the use of a litigation strategy is not expensive – in most cases, it will be both costly and time-consuming – but different forms of litigation strategies have different resource thresholds, and a more nuanced understanding needs to be developed.

---

[48] Karen Alter and Jeannette Vargas, "Explaining Variation in the Use of European Litigation Strategies," *Comparative Political Studies* 33(4), 2000, pp. 452–82; Pieter Bouwen and Margaret McCown, "Lobbying versus Litigation: Political and Legal Strategies of Interest Representation in the European Union," *Journal of European Public Policy* 14(3), 2007, pp. 422–33; Harlow and Rawlings, *Pressure through Law*; Hilson, "New Social Movements."

Another criticism that can be lodged against analyses that consider resource thresholds purely as independent variables is, again, a lack of acknowledgment of organizational agency. Resources of all types can sometimes be the dependent variable. In other words, the level and types of resources an interest group possesses may be determined by other preferences or values that precede the resource question. For example, a group that has a preference for direct action from its inception may be less concerned with developing resources because protest as a strategy has a lower material resource threshold than lobbying or litigation. At the other end of the spectrum, an organization that develops an in-house legal staff and other legal resources has already expressed an interest and investment in the use of legal mobilization as a strategy. A quintessential study argues that "the resources which private interests have at their disposal have an important impact on the access and litigation strategies they can employ,"[49] but the converse may also be true: the strategy that an organization might like to use may influence the level and types of resources they aim to develop. The relationship between resources and strategy is not necessarily unidirectional, and looking only at the types of resources an organization possesses may be misleading.

ACCOMMODATING SOCIAL MOVEMENTS: FRAMING PROCESSES AND COLLECTIVE IDENTITY

The first three theoretical approaches – resource mobilization theories, POS approaches, and, more recently, elements of LOS approaches – have dominated the literature on the role of SMOs in public-interest litigation.[50] The labels above designate tendencies rather than

---

[49] Bouwen and McCown, "Lobbying versus Litigation."

[50] Studies of social movement litigation, with several notable exceptions, have generally ignored the relevance of transformation in the identity of groups. The most convincing work undertaken that embodies this hypothesis is the research done by Noga

neatly segregated camps, and most recent work has transcended the resources/opportunity structure divide and combined elements of both into frameworks used to analyze the turn to a litigation strategy in specific policy fields or by certain social movements or their organizations. Most recent work has also begun to probe collective actor characteristics other than resources. This has included analyses of organizational structures, membership influence, and relationships with adversaries and allies. However, what the majority of existing explanations of the turn to litigation have in common is that they are underpinned by assumptions of actor rationality and privilege analyses of costs and benefits, barriers and incentives to the exclusion of other potentially important factors. Although RM and opportunity and access considerations are important, they are clearly not the only characteristic of collective actors that might play a role in strategy choice.

I argue here that the theoretical tools of a fourth school of thought are necessary to fully understand why and when some groups are more likely than others to adopt a litigation strategy. The literature in the sociological–institutionalist theoretical camp may be useful in addressing the puzzle of why some organizations that we might expect to use strategic litigation (based on an analysis of resources and opportunities) do not, and why others seem to inherently value litigation as a strategy even when faced with significant material and procedural hurdles. Although elements of a sociological–institutionalist approach to understanding legal mobilization have been incorporated in various formulations of POS, LOS, and RM, I have argued that this is problematic. I will separate them here and introduce new dimensions to this analysis.

Morag-Levine on conservationist organizations in the United States and Israel. She accounts for variation in litigation propensity over time through an examination of the gradual process of transformation within organizations. Noga Morag-Levine, "Partners No More: Relational Transformation and the Turn to Litigation in Two Conservationist Organizations," *Law and Society Review* 37(2), 2003, pp. 457–509.

The relatively recent inclusion of social movement characteristics beyond resources in analyses of strategy choice has begun to remedy a significant lacuna in the literature. There is widespread disagreement, however, regarding which characteristics are the most important. Recent scholarship on interest group litigation in the United States and elsewhere has both unpacked the black-box notion of the interest group and considered the broader multiorganizational environment. A number of explanations have been put forward in recent literature. For example, legal mobilization has been explained by the following:

- the need for elites to please the rank-and-file membership;[51]
- internal, largely intergenerational divisions over attitudes toward cooperation and conflict with state institutions;[52]
- the impact of opposing strategies from counter-interests in particular venues;[53] and
- the population of interest groups within a policy arena.[54]

Summing up the need to move beyond narrow explanations based on opportunity structure and resources, Solberg and Waltenburg convincingly argue that

> a group's assessment of where, and possibly whether, to act is not an easy calculation based on the receptiveness of a venue and the available balance in the bank account. Groups must attend to their

---

[51] Thomas G. Hansford, "Information Provision, Organizational Constraints, and the Decision to Submit an Amicus Curiae Brief in a US Supreme Court Case," *Political Research Quarterly* 57(2), 2004, pp. 219–30; Thomas T. Holyoke, "Choosing Battlegrounds: Interest Group Lobbying Across Multiple Venues," *Political Research Quarterly* 56(3), 2003, pp. 325–36; Rorie Spill Solberg and Eric N. Waltenburg, "Why Do Interest Groups Engage the Judiciary? Policy Wishes and Structural Needs," *Social Science Quarterly* 87(3), 2006, pp. 558–72.

[52] Morag-Levine, "Partners No More."

[53] Holyoke, "Choosing Battlegrounds."

[54] Solberg and Waltenburg, "Why Do Interest Groups Engage the Judiciary?"

members and their competition. Explanations of group advocacy omitting such concerns are inherently flawed.[55]

This book, building on the important foundation laid by the recent work discussed above, employs a sociological theory of institutions to account for why and when some groups are more likely than others to rely on a litigation strategy as part of their overall logic of action. The theoretical approach focuses on factors internal to the organization that might influence strategy choice and those that exert external forces.[56] Although the internal and external pressures are undoubtedly related, for analytical reasons they will be separated in the theoretical discussion below. However, the empirical chapters will strive to understand how these factors interact to influence strategy choice.

Internal Factors: Organizational Identity, Logics of Appropriateness, and Framing Processes

The level of resources available to a group plays an important role in its choice between advocacy strategies – this is the thrust of analyses that privilege resource considerations. However, as discussed above, resources are not the only, and arguably not even the most important, internal interest group characteristic to influence strategy choice. Curiously, while scholars wanting to explain the turn to the courts have regularly adopted elements of social movement theory, they have tended to neglect an important branch of work in the field, where normative values and framing processes have come to be considered key components in understanding the character and course of social movements.[57]

---

[55] Ibid.

[56] Ibid.

[57] Robert D. Benford and David A. Snow, "Framing Processes and Social Movements: An Overview and Assessment," *Annual Review of Sociology* 26, 2000, pp. 611–39;

Organizational identity and institutionalized norms create internal pressures that define the parameters within which strategy decisions are made. For James March and Johan Olsen, institutions are collections of interrelated rules and routines that define appropriate actions in terms of relations between roles and situations.[58] In essence, they argue that organizational norms can possess an inherent legitimacy that commits their members to behave, in extreme cases, in ways that may even violate their own self-interest.[59] March and Olsen use the phrase "logic of appropriateness" to describe this mechanism that exerts a normative influence. From this perspective, if an organization is effective in influencing the behavior of its members, members will think more about whether an action conforms to the norms of the organization than about what the consequences will be for themselves. This appropriate behavior can be contrasted with that assumed by economic models, in which individuals are expected to think primarily about what the objective payoff will be for them. As March and Olsen argue, behaviors will be "intentional but not wilful" when individuals are motivated by institutional values. Individuals will make conscious choices, but those choices will remain within the parameters established by the dominant norms. Donatella Della Porta and Mario Diani have advanced a similar explanation in their exploration of the symbolic dimension of collective action.

> We may think of social action as driven largely by the fundamental principles with which actors identify. According to this perspective, values will influence how actors define specific goals, and identify strategies which are both efficient and morally acceptable. Moreover, values will provide the motivations necessary to sustain the costs of

David A. Snow et al., "Frame Alignment Processes, Micromobilization, and Movement Participation," *American Sociological Review* 51, 1986, pp. 464–81.

[58] James G. March and Johan P. Olsen, *Rediscovering Institutions: The Organizational Basis of Politics* (New York: Free Press, 1989), pp. 21–6.

[59] Ibid., pp. 22–3.

action. The more intense one's socialization to a particular vision of the world, the stronger the impetus to act. The characteristics of a given system of values will shape the components of action.[60]

Although Della Porta and Diani focus more on the bottom-up process of values and bring the individual (rather than the organization) into the center of their analysis, the socialization process and moral acceptability they refer to function in much the same way as March and Olsen's "logic of appropriateness."

March and Olsen's contribution concentrates largely on how the organizational environment influences the behavior of individual members; they neglect the role that individuals might play in shaping organizational structures and also the influence that the broader environment might exert on organizations. I build on March and Olsen's conceptualization by developing a more dynamic understanding of individuals, institutions, and the social movement environment. I see organizations as being situated at a meso-level between the broader social movement above (the macro-level) and the individual members below (the micro-level): they are all mutually constitutive. I discuss the relationship between the social movement environment and organizations in the next section on external pressures. Here, I will focus on the relationship between individuals and organizations.

The focus in the sociological–institutionalist and organizational literature has been on mechanisms through which institutions shape the behavior of individuals. However, individuals are also able to form and reform institutions, and those mechanisms have been relatively understudied. Understanding this dialectical process of change – that institutions can transform individuals and individuals can change institutions – has the added benefit of addressing those critics who have argued that, by placing so much emphasis on the role of institutions and

---

[60] Donatella Della Porta and Mario Diani, *Social Movements: An Introduction* (Oxford: Blackwell Publishing, 2006), p. 67.

the logics underpinning them, March and Olsen have removed human decision making too completely from the process.[61] This structure–agency problem, which I criticized above in early formulations of opportunity structure approaches, can be resolved in two ways in sociological–institutionalist theory. In a top-down manner, individuals can acquire agency by accepting and interpreting the values of institutions. In a bottom-up way, this occurs by exploring how members can challenge and transform those values, either by rejecting them and choosing not to conform or through changes in the individuals who are recruited into the organizations.

To explore this dynamic process of norm change, I combine this notion of "logics of appropriateness" in strategy decisions with an understanding of the power of meaning frames within organizations. From the mid-1980s on, the social movement literature began to pay greater attention to the role of actors as signifying agents actively engaged in the production of meaning. David Snow, in association with various colleagues, brought accounts of subjectivity and culture into analyses of social movement character and action. Drawing on Goffman's ideas to analyze how actors negotiate meaning,[62] they define framing as

> an active, processual phenomenon that implies agency and contention at the level of reality construction. It is active in the sense that something is being done, and processual in the sense of a dynamic, evolving process. It entails agency in the sense that what is evolving is the work of social movement organizations or movement activists. And it is contentious in the sense that it involves the generation of interpretive frames that not only differ from existing ones but that

---

[61] B. Guy Peters, *Institutional Theory in Political Science: The "New Institutionalism"* (London: Continuum Press, 2005); Keith Dowding, "The Compatibility of Behaviouralism, Rational Choice and 'New Institutionalism,'" *Journal of Theoretical Politics* 6(1), 1994, pp. 105–17.

[62] Erving Goffman, *Frame Analysis* (Boston: Northeastern University Press, 1974).

may also challenge them. The resultant products of this framing activity are referred to as "collective action frames."[63]

I am interested in how this framing activity occurs, be it through intraorganization dialogues and/or the diffusion of ideas and frames from other organizations or contexts. In investigating how frames are challenged or affirmed, maintained or overturned, I then link these processes with issues of strategy choice. I argue that a collective actor's framing processes may have an important impact on the type of strategy they will likely choose. Drawing on work on social movement and meaning frame analysis, I show how consensus and contestation over meanings, and their organizational implications, can influence a movement's participation in legal venues.[64] Frames have been defined as schemata of interpretation that enable individuals "to locate, perceive, identify and label occurrences within their life space and the world at large."[65] Meaning frames thus allow individuals and communities to recognize the world: they guide perceptions and expectations and define "logics of appropriateness."[66] These norms limit what is considered acceptable and what is not, within a particular paradigm. The tools of frame analysis allow us to capture the process of the attribution of meaning that groups and individuals give to symbols, events, behavior, and/or discourse.[67] A group's collective action frames and the way it creates meaning and purpose help to define, and in turn are partly defined by, its collective identity. Meaning frames will permeate all aspects of the organization: its membership, its relationships with other actors, its goals, and its strategies in achieving those goals.

---

[63] Benford and Snow, "Framing Processes and Social Movements."

[64] Miriam Smith, "Social Movements and Equality Seeking: The Case of Gay Liberation in Canada," *Canadian Journal of Political Science* 31(2), 1998, pp. 285–309.

[65] David A. Snow et al., "Frame Alignment Processes."

[66] James G. March and Johan P. Olsen, "The Institutional Dynamics of International Political Orders," *International Organization* 52(4), 1998, pp. 943–69.

[67] Goffman, *Frame Analysis.*

In essence, norms and ideas and the way they spread matter. The interpretive frames continuously being constructed, tested, and redefined will be based on shared norms, which may dictate courses of action that are considered more appropriate than others. If this is theoretically sound, we would expect to see that groups are more likely to adopt a litigation strategy when their identity and framing processes define the membership primarily as rights holders and the courts as an appropriate venue within which to pursue policy goals and advance other social movement agendas. Conversely, if an organization's hegemonic ideational frames do not conceptualize their constituency as rights-bearing citizens, it seems unlikely that they will pursue equality goals and actively participate within judicial venues as part of their remit.

External Forces: The Organizational Environment and Social Movement Norms

Interest organizations do not operate within legal–political institutional contexts, such as those described in the POS and LOS approaches, in isolation. They also interact within (and with) multiorganizational fields, defined as "the total possible number of organizations with which the focal organization might establish linkages."[68] The multiorganizational field – or social movement networks – can influence organizational strategy choice. Using a simple understanding of organizational ecology, we can explore how relationships with other organizations and the emergence and disappearance of organizations might shape strategy.[69]

---

[68] Russell L. Curtis and Louis A. Zurcher, "Stable Resources of Protest Movements: The Multi-Organizational Field," *Social Forces* 52(1), 1973, pp. 53–61.

[69] This approach differs from the third dimension of Andersen's LOS approach, focusing on alliance and conflict systems, in its analytical approach. Andersen takes a single organization as a starting point and explores the alliances and adversaries

Introduction

The fundamental premise of organizational ecology approaches is that organizations and their behavior can be understood, in part, through an analogy with populations of biological organisms. In the same way in which the environment provides opportunities for only so many organisms to interact and survive, the social movement environment is only capable of supporting so many organizations, and there may be situations of conflict and cooperation among them.[70] Although there is a danger in taking the analogy too far, the principle contribution of this set of ideas is to emphasize the impact of the environment on organizations and their "embeddedness" in social movement contexts. Research in organizational ecology has focused largely on the emergence and attrition of organizations within the environment. For example, Della Porta and Diani point out that

> few … [SMOs] … actually survive for a significant time spell. Some dissolve because their aims have been achieved. Organizations formed to coordinate specific campaigns, for example, tend to disappear as soon as that campaign is over.[71] Leadership splits during downturns in mobilization and the resultant processes of disintegration and realignment cause others to disappear.[72]

The fluctuation in the population of organizations may shape the types of strategies any one organization might pursue.[73]

of that one group and looks at how each of those relationships, in a static manner, influences the likelihood of mobilizing. An organizational ecology approach takes a number of organizations as its starting point and explores the influence that the multiple and overlapping dynamics between these organizations has on the likelihood of mobilizing. The difference is subtle, and the two approaches should be seen as complementary, simply emphasizing different components of the same phenomenon.

[70] Peters, *Institutional Theory in Political Science*, p. 111.

[71] Louis A. Zurcher and Russell L. Curtis, "A Comparative Analysis of Propositions Describing Social Movement Organizations," *Sociological Quarterly* 14(2), 1973, pp. 175–88.

[72] Della Porta and Diani, *Social Movements*, p. 151.

[73] The population under consideration is highly dependent on analytical lenses. In this book, I have defined this population based on the consensus in the secondary

The content and intensity of relations between organizations might also shape strategy choice.[74] Organizations exist in a situation of potential conflict where they may engage in struggles with adversaries. They are also presented with opportunities to form more or less stable and enduring networks and alliances with other organizations.[75] This constellation of organizational actors across venues, and the dynamics between them, can influence strategy choice in a number of ways. Dynamics can range from cooperative, where organizations provide mutual support for the pursuit of a shared goal while maintaining their autonomy and distinctiveness, to competitive and conflictual, where organizations may differ in their ideological or strategic preferences and develop an interest in their own survival and growth and so clash over policy, audiences, members, and resources. In situations of organizational conflict, that is, when one group's victory in a policy realm necessarily undermines another group's goals, the degree of freedom that instrumental groups have in selecting their strategy may be restricted. They will be more likely to try to engage with their opposition in whichever venue the opposing group is operating to promote their own policy goals and agendas. For example, when pro-life organizations file intervener briefs in the courts, it is highly likely that pro-choice organizations may also try to influence the judiciary's legal reasoning. In situations of cooperation among organizations, a division of labor may emerge, and groups may be freer to choose strategy based on other considerations; however, they do not possess

---

literature on key players within the movement, but the broader organizational movement – beyond just the disability rights movement – could play a role in influencing the course of legal mobilization.

[74] Della Porta and Diani, *Social Movements*, p. 157.

[75] Mario Diani and Doug McAdam, *Social Movements and Networks* (New York: Oxford University Press, 2003); Dieter Rucht, "Movement Allies, Adversaries and Third Parties," in David A. Snow et al., eds., *The Blackwell Companion to Social Movements* (Oxford: Blackwell Publishing, 2005).

total freedom because they may be somewhat constrained by their alliances. If one group has agreed that it will pursue one tactic so that another can operate in a different venue, it may be difficult to change the original arrangement at a future date because of organizational adaptation.

Again, this discussion is underpinned by the notion that social movement norms, and consensus or contestation over them, are a crucial part of the environment. March and Olsen's "logic of appropriateness" can be shifted up whereby the unit under consideration is not the individual member subject to organizational logics but rather is the organization itself subject to social movement logics. Organizations may make choices within the parameters established by the dominant movement values. To understand how meaning frames influence the decision to use a particular strategy, we also need to gain an understanding of how organizations within a movement relate to each other and challenge, or conform to, each other's interpretive frames. I argue that these relations are constitutive and generative: meaning frames will influence organizational relations and vice versa.

By analyzing the evolution of collective meaning frames and interorganizational dynamics in the movement, we can enhance existing theoretical understandings of the conditions under which disability advocacy organizations have relied on the courts to help shape notions of equality. This approach is not incompatible with explanations that focus on RM or POS or LOS in accounting for litigation strategies and outcomes; factors such as funding and structure clearly matter in the decision to use litigation to pursue policy goals. What becomes central are the ways in which movement organizations construct meaning frames and a collective identity both through their own internal struggles as well as through their relations with each other and then how these factors may influence the decision to use strategic litigation and how participation in litigation may shape frames and organizational relations.

REALIZING DISABILITY RIGHTS IN COURT IN CANADA AND THE UNITED KINGDOM

Having laid out the general theoretical approach, I will show that the ideas and meaning frames put forth by the disability rights movement possess a richness and power with wide-ranging effects that are both practical and theoretical. Disability activists and their colleagues in the field of disabilities studies have much to teach scholars interested in legal mobilization theory, as well as those concerned with equality in law and policy.

Disability and Equality

Significant evidence exists that demonstrates both the growth of the population of persons who consider themselves disabled as well as an increase in instances of discrimination based on disability. For example, a recent Statistics Canada survey reveals that one of every seven people in Canada self-identifies as disabled. In 2001, 12.4 percent of the population reported a disability; by 2006, this rate had increased to 14.3 percent.[76] Alongside this growth in the population of persons with disabilities, there are also several indicators demonstrating that discrimination based on disability is a major problem within Canadian society.[77] From 2002 to 2006, experiencing discrimination "on

---

[76] Statistics Canada, "Participation and Activity Limitation Survey (PALS) 2006," http://www.statcan.gc.ca (accessed December 3, 2007).

[77] This high proportion of complaints from persons with disabilities to human rights commissions could be caused by a number of different factors, or, most likely, some combination of factors. Some factors involve levels of discrimination; for example, they may indicate a high level of prejudicial attitudes toward persons with disabilities, or, more likely, they signal a lack of understanding among employers and the public of the concept of the duty to accommodate or the extent of that duty. Other factors concern the discriminated-against population themselves. An ageing

grounds of disability" produced the highest number of complaints to the Canadian Human Rights Commission, ranging from 37 percent to 50 percent of all complaints received among the eleven different grounds covered by the Human Rights Act.[78] The picture at the respective provincial Human Rights Commissions is similar.[79] The fact that experiences of discrimination based on grounds of disability are widespread is indisputable.

Similarly, there remains a high degree of social and economic exclusion experienced by the 8.2 million people with disabilities who are living in the United Kingdom.[80] According to a 2007 government study by the Office of Disability Issues (ODI), among people with disabilities of working age, 43 percent were in paid work. This proportion is slightly higher than that observed in the 2001 "Disabled for Life" survey (39 percent).[81] However, people with disabilities remained significantly less likely to be in paid work than working-age adults in the

---

population could lead to a higher proportion of persons with disabilities in the general population, and/or there could be an increase in rights-consciousness among the population of persons with disabilities – which leads to an increased willingness to self-identify as disabled. Factors also relate to the relationship between the discriminated-against population and the Human Rights Commissions: the degree of confidence that individuals have in the Commission's willingness and ability to successfully resolve an issue will influence the number of complaints made.

[78] Canadian Human Rights Commission, "Annual Report 2007," http://www.chrc-ccdp.ca/pdf/ar_2007_ra_en.pdf (accessed May 28, 2008).

[79] Interviews with legal counsel at Human Rights Commissions on October 26, November 2, and November 6, 2007.

[80] World Health Organization, *Rethinking Care from the Perspective of Disabled People: Conference Report and Recommendations* (Geneva: WHO's Disability and Rehabilitation Team, 2001). According to WHO, disabled people are among the poorest of the poor in developed and developing countries alike. See also Colin Barnes, "Disability, Policy and Politics," *Policy and Politics* 30(3), 2002, p. 311; Gerard Quinn, "The Human Rights of People with Disabilities under EU Law," in P. Alston et al., eds., *The EU and Human Rights* (Oxford: Oxford University Press, 1999).

[81] Ini Grewal et al., *"Disabled for Life"? Attitudes Towards, and Experiences of, Disability in Britain* (London: DWP Research Report No. 148, 2002).

general population, as 74 percent of working-age adults in the general population were gainfully employed.[82] Employers are six times more likely to turn down a disabled person for an interview than a nondisabled applicant with the same qualifications.[83] Perhaps the most striking evidence of disability discrimination is the nature and number of complaints made to the Disability Rights Commission (DRC). The number of complaints of alleged disability-based discrimination made to the DRC nearly doubled – from about 15,000 in 2004 to about 30,000 in 2007.[84]

Ensuring equality for persons with disabilities is a complicated endeavor and one that both Canadian and British lawmakers have undertaken. As Aileen McColgan writes, "this complexity arises both in the concept of 'equality' and in the nature of its absence."[85] Persons with disabilities share their experiences being the target of prejudice with other groups. However, disability discrimination can be considered different from other forms of discrimination, such as sexism or racism, in a number of ways. The definition of who is disabled is highly variable across time and place, and many persons with disabilities do not self-identify as disabled; the population is highly heterogeneous and constantly shifting. Similarly, the experience of disability discrimination is highly contextual and is constituted of both attitudinal discrimination and the existence of barriers – aspects of the physical or social environment that prohibit meaningful involvement in normal life activities by persons with disabilities. The notion of "reasonable

---

[82] One explanation for the high level of unemployment is the impact of an individual's impairment. However, there is also a consensus that discrimination in recruitment and retention is extensive. See Bridget Williams et al., *Experiences and Expectations of Disabled People* (London: Office for Disability Issues, July 2008), p. 100.

[83] Aileen McColgan, *Discrimination Law: Text, Cases and Materials* (Oxford: Hart Publishing, 2005), p. 559.

[84] Disability Rights Commission, *DRC Legal Achievements 2000–2007* (Manchester: Disability Rights Commission, 2007), p. 142.

[85] McColgan, *Discrimination Law*, p. 559.

accommodation" as a remedy is a significant complement to traditional approaches to combating discrimination and requires that efforts be undertaken to render the experience in the environment available to persons with disabilities.

Generally, antidiscrimination provisions create protection for perhaps the most vulnerable individuals who suffer the effects of prejudice and exclusion, yet it appears that antidiscrimination rights are among the least invoked of all laws.[86] David Engel and Frank Munger summarize this paradox between the existence of rights and rights assertion:

> Civil rights differ from other forms of legal entitlement. They concern themselves not only with the legal interests of those who belong to civil society but also with the issue of membership itself. Civil rights are rights of inclusion for the individual whom society otherwise excludes. They go against the grain; they often violate social norms rather than institutionalizing them in legal form; they annoy, they outrage at the very moment when they most effectively insist on an identity and a legal status for the person who invokes them. When civil rights are *not* asserted, the consequences can be profound: invisibility, the erasure of the individual from membership in the community.[87]

On an individual level, enforcement of these measures is important in improving the lot of those diverse, but growing, socially excluded groups. Arguably, individuals who suffer from discrimination are less likely than other citizens to take court action because of various additional hurdles they face. These range from a lack of rights consciousness to financial obstacles to a lack of access to lawyers experienced in the specificities of disability law. The paradox has important

---

[86] David M. Engel and Frank W. Munger, *Rights of Inclusion: Law and Identity in the Life Stories of Americans with Disabilities* (Chicago: University of Chicago Press, 2003), p. 3.

[87] Ibid.

implications on the meso-level, between individuals and state institutions. Collective actors, such as nongovernmental organizations and SMOs, are particularly important when considering questions of litigation because of their ability to be "repeat players" who bring a series of test cases to various judicial venues over an extended period; this allows for coherent enforcement of rights and establishes precedent.[88] For these reasons, socially excluded groups may depend asymmetrically on SMOs to provide support. In turn, if levels of organization-supported litigation are set to rise, this could have important implications for the organizations themselves; for example, by affecting public image and the associated impact (positive or negative) on developing resources and voice on the policy stage.

Purpose and Plan

This book chronicles the way in which activists and lawyers in the United Kingdom and Canada have constructed and negotiated the political identity associated with disability. It reveals that the collective identities constructed by activists shape, and in turn are shaped by, their decisions to enter the courtroom. I do this by showing how judicial understandings of disability and equality have evolved over time. I probe the way in which courts and lawyers have dealt with a range of issues important to persons with disabilities through a close examination of jurisprudence in key cases. This is important in understanding the means and ends of legal mobilization. I also focus on the effects of participating in strategic litigation and the influence resulting decisions have had on the groups themselves and the social movement

---

[88] Marc Galanter, "Why the 'Haves' Come out Ahead: Speculations on the Limits of Legal Change," *Law and Society Review* 9(1), 1974, pp. 95–160; Charles R. Epp, "The Two Motifs of 'Why the "Haves" Come out Ahead' and its Heirs," *Law and Society Review* 33(4), 1999, pp. 1089–98.

within which they are situated. Unlike other studies of impact, which focus on whether strategic litigation leads to social change, I eschew this approach when considering judicial impact and instead follow Engel and Munger in adopting a recursive theory of rights and identity.[89] They argue that the relationship between rights and identity is recursive "in the sense that not only does identity determine how and when rights become active, but rights can also shape identity."[90] Here, I build on their approach, which focuses on individuals, by considering the relationship between rights and "collective" identity. This also highlights why it is important for organizations to be thoughtful about the use of strategic litigation, not just from a policy perspective but also from a movement perspective. These objectives assume that litigation can have consequences that are both intended and unintended.[91] Although this book focuses on activists, their organizations, and the conditions under which they are more likely to mobilize legally, it situates this activity within the broader context of legal and constitutional change and social movement dynamics over a period from 1975 to 2007.

This book relies on a nuanced understanding of the varieties of litigation strategies that can be employed to challenge some of the assumptions underpinning the dominant explanatory approaches to social movement organizational litigation. By focusing on the differing types of roles organizations can take (be it supporting an appellant or respondent or intervening as a third party) and their intentions in becoming involved in particular cases, I do not seek to challenge the importance of RM and opportunity structure approaches. Rather, I aim to help refine them and identify situations where they may be less able to explain variation in the use of strategic litigation by organizational actors across time, across organizations, or across national jurisdictions.

---

[89] Engel and Munger, *Rights of Inclusion*.
[90] Ibid., p. 242.
[91] Andersen, *Out of the Closets*, p. 15.

With some notable exceptions, there has been a modest amount of cross-national and cross-organizational comparative work undertaken on the use of legal mobilization.[92] This may be due to implicit scholarly assumptions of national exceptionalism or the difficulty associated with comparing the variation in abilities to access national or subnational judicial systems. This book contributes to a growing body of comparative work by presenting analyses of legal mobilization activity across different disability organizations in Canada and the United Kingdom.

I overcome the danger of the analysis becoming bogged down in legal procedural technicalities by undertaking this comparative analysis, which operates on several levels. The first is a within-country, cross-organizational comparison. This adds a level of depth to the analysis and mitigates problems associated with instances of studying the "negative case" – those instances where organizations do not mobilize legally.[93] By identifying and exploring the key organizational differences and similarities in approaches to litigation opportunities, I am able to better understand the effects of national LOSs and tease out the factors that may be driving differential approaches toward the use of strategic litigation. Through a second form of comparison – a cross-temporal one – both within select individual organizations and across the movement as a whole, I can again control for changes in national LOSs and their effects over time and understand shifts in other potential explanatory variables, such as resources, ideational frames and intraorganizational dynamics, which may be driving the decision of

---

[92] Exceptions include the following: Rachel A. Cichowski, *The European Court and Civil Society* (Cambridge, UK: Cambridge University Press, 2007); Charles R. Epp, *The Rights Revolution: Lawyers, Activists, and Supreme Courts in Comparative Perspective* (Chicago: University of Chicago Press, 1998); Morag-Levine, "Partners No More"; Miriam Smith, *Political Institutions and Lesbian and Gay Rights in the United States and Canada* (London: Routledge, 2008).

[93] James Mahoney and Gary Goertz, "The Possibility Principle: Choosing Negative Cases in Comparative Research," *American Political Science Review* 98(4), 2004, pp. 653–69.

whether or not to use strategic litigation. A third form of comparison, presented in the conclusion, is cross-national, where country-specific similarities and differences among organizations' propensity to use litigation are identified. The overall approach is chronological, rather than topical, as this is important in exploring the changing nature of meaning frames and social movement politics.

Canada and the United Kingdom were chosen for this study because of their comparable protections against discrimination (although in Canada the protections are a part of a general constitutional equality promise, whereas in the United Kingdom, they constitute a specific statutory mechanism), their similar legal systems, and the fact that they were among the earliest adopters of legal protections, allowing sufficient time scales for comparison. The existence of sufficiently comparable legal systems is crucial as this is where much of the complexity with comparing legal mobilization lies. Both the United Kingdom and Canada have common law legal systems.[94] This means that case law – precedents set by judges in deciding a case – plays an important role. The divisions of the common law – its concepts, substance, legal culture, and procedures – are very different from civil law systems that are predominantly found in continental Europe. Although there are still important variations across borders with respect to the functioning of the different common law legal systems, studying countries that operate under at least similar legal structures, and focusing specifically on courts of appeal and/or final courts of appeal, has the benefit of controlling for key legal system influences.

The groups I discuss here were identified through a review of the academic and policy literature. I conducted more than sixty elite interviews with experienced disability lawyers, policy actors, and disability activists across both countries. I explicitly exclude any analysis of groups whose primary focus is mental health, as this policy domain adds another dimension of complexity and often operates

---

[94] Quebec is the exception, as it operates under a Civil Code.

under different legal mechanisms. My methodological approach to analysis of these cases, like Christopher Manfredi's, is inspired by Lee Epstein and Joseph Kobylka's observation that it is the law and legal arguments as framed by legal actors that most clearly influence the context and direction of legal change.[95] This approach assumes that neither traditional legal analysis nor judicial attitudinal analysis is completely adequate for understanding the development and impact of strategic litigation. Traditional legal analysis masks the politics and social movement context of legal mobilization, whereas attitudinal analysis attributes agency only to some actors within the courtroom: judges. My discussion of judicial policy making in the field of disability equality combines legal analysis with elements of social movement analysis to understand the significance of the full range of actors at play in influencing legal doctrine and judicial influence on social change.

To achieve these objectives, the rest of this book is divided into five chapters. Chapter 2 explores how, in Canada, the social model or civil rights model of disability came to challenge the dominant view of disability as a medical defect or pathological limitation lying with the individual (known as the "medical model"). The chapter then delves into the organizational dynamics of the disability movement. I explain the organizational implications of this paradigm shift – the emergence of radical, grassroots organizations and changes/retrenchment among existing disability charities. The chapter then explores how the main organizational actors of the Canadian disability movement have approached the opportunities and challenges of operating in the legal arena during a twenty-year period, from the mid-1980s to the mid-2000s. It draws on concepts elaborated in the introduction – such as social movement framing processes and the relationships between

---

[95] Manfredi, *Feminist Activism*, p. xix; Lee Epstein and Joseph Kobylka, *The Supreme Court and Legal Change: Abortion and the Death Penalty* (Chapel Hill, NC: University of North Carolina Press, 1992), p. 8.

organizations – to account for the turn to the courts. It focuses specifically on six case studies of some of the most influential disability-related organizations in Canada – ranging from the umbrella organization to a feminist disability organization to a litigation-focused disability group – to highlight the organizational and ideological context within which strategic litigation has been adopted or rejected as a strategy.

Chapter 3 shows how Canadian disability activists have gone to the courts to advance their own conceptions of the appropriate paradigms of disability, discrimination, and accommodation of difference and thereby influenced emerging notions of human rights and equality. By tracing the evolution of the Supreme Court of Canada's jurisprudence on important equality and disability issues, this chapter highlights why it is important that groups have turned to the courts from a policy perspective. I argue that Supreme Court decisions, such as *Eve, Eaton, Latimer, Rodriguez,* and *VIA Rail,* have had important implications in the way human rights of persons with disabilities are interpreted and implemented.[96] In many cases, these decisions have advanced equality, but there have also been some significant policy losses from the perspective of disability rights advocates. The chapter traces the evolution of court-influenced disability policy and equality policy relevant to persons with disabilities and probes how the Supreme Court has defined, clarified, expanded, or retracted policy through key cases. While laying out the key trends in case law, I also discuss how disability rights organizations have approached some of the most controversial and well-known cases, exploring the decisions to go to court, the development of strategies and arguments deployed in the courtroom, and choices groups make about the organizations with which they ally and those they oppose.

---

[96] *E. (Mrs.) v. Eve,* [1986] 2 S.C.R. 388; *Eaton v. Brant County Board of Education,* [1997] 1 S.C.R. 241; *R. v. Latimer,* [1997] 1 S.C.R. 217; *Rodriguez v. British Columbia (Attorney General),* [1993] 3 S.C.R. 519; *Council of Canadians with Disabilities v. VIA Rail Canada Inc,* 2007 SCC 15, [2007] 1 S.C.R. 650.

Chapter 4 compares the emergence of a rights discourse and its organizational diffusion in the United Kingdom with that in Canada, as discussed in Chapter 1. Contention in the early days of the disability movement over disability paradigms and tensions among grassroots organizations helped to establish legal mobilization as an appropriate strategy in the pursuit of policy goals. However, the majority of grassroots groups have not used strategic litigation because of resource constraints. The chapter then turns to a second category of organizations active in the disability sector: the disability charities. It describes which of the main disability charities have used strategic litigation and which have not. It then explores in greater detail the case of two specific organizations, the Royal National Institute of Blind People and Scope (the cerebral palsy charity), in order to illustrate more fully the influence of framing processes on decisions to use or reject legal activity as a campaign tactic. I then explore the unique situation of the Disability Rights Commission – an arm's length agency of government – as a policy actor and key proponent of the use of strategic litigation to enforce and expand disability rights. I explore the evolving attitudes and resistance within and across organizations toward social model understandings of disability and show how this correlates with organizational use of strategic litigation as a policy-influencing tool. The analysis in this chapter highlights the significant variation both among and within the three types of organizations in the disability sector in the United Kingdom regarding the use of (and organizational values on the use of) strategic litigation.

Chapter 5 notes that, in a country that has traditionally been considered averse to the concept of entrenched rights, there has been a remarkable shift over the last fifteen years to a rights-based framework in disability law and policy in the United Kingdom. This chapter includes a jurisprudential analysis of key cases, ranging from those that clarify the meaning of disability and discrimination in domestic and EC law to controversial cases about the right to die, the right to treatment, and discrimination by association. It also reveals some of the unexpected opportunities to pursue changes in levels of access to justice that arise during the course of legal mobilization in pursuit of substantive goals.

The concluding chapter highlights how the monograph as a whole contributes to the growing body of research on the judicialization of politics in advanced industrial democracies. It further develops the theoretical approach to explain why some collective actors are willing and able to use law and legal action to achieve their goals and why others are not. I also show that, by seriously considering the importance of social movement ideas and identities, the way the discipline of disability studies does, we may find that there has been a fundamental misunderstanding of the causal mechanisms linking resources and opportunity structures with the decision to use strategic litigation to achieve organizational goals. The book concludes by arguing that it is only through comprehending the full range of factors shaping the decision by SMOs to turn to the courts that we can better understand the historic development of judicial understandings of disability equality and begin to envisage the future role of civil society in court-influenced understandings of equality.

2

Rights and Political Identity in the Canadian Disability Movement

INTRODUCTION

On November 3, 1980, members of the Coalition of Provincial Organizations of the Handicapped (COPOH) held a protest on Parliament Hill in Ottawa to assert their demands for recognition in a proposed new constitutional Charter of Rights and Freedoms. The protest was the first time that people with a range of disabilities gathered together from across Canada to loudly and publicly claim the right to disability rights. The proposed Charter contained a section explicitly guaranteeing equality rights on some grounds, such as sex and race, but did not accord such protection to the rights of Canadians with disabilities. Previous calls by activists with disabilities to gain a voice in the constitutional process had failed, and the activists' frustration culminated in the demonstration. Yvonne Peters, a long-time activist and human rights lawyer who was both present at the protest and active in the Charter lobby effort, writes, "People with disabilities were just beginning to experience the promise of rights, and we were resolved not to let the architects of the Charter diminish or undermine this potential by ignoring our claim to legally recognized equality."[1] In the end,

---

[1] Yvonne Peters, "From Charity to Equality: Canadians with Disabilities take their Rightful Place in Canada's Constitution," in Deborah Stienstra and Aileen

disability as an enumerated ground was added to the list of grounds protected by the proposed Charter at the eleventh hour in the Constitutional negotiations after a relentless lobbying effort on the part of these activists and their allies. As a result, Canadians with disabilities can now call on the promise of equality contained within the Charter to combat discrimination, exclusion, and marginalization. The equality promise in the Charter is both a cause and consequence of the emergence of a disability rights consciousness. It is also the battlefield on which subsequent wars for equality would be waged.

This chapter paints a picture of the disability movement in Canada and focuses specifically on the role of rights and legal mobilization within the movement. It unearths the roots of a disability rights consciousness on a cross-disability basis in a paradigm shift in the political identity associated with disability. The chapter then delves into the organizational and legal implications of this paradigm shift, although I leave a detailed analysis of jurisprudence to the next chapter. I survey six organizations in the disability community and explore how they have approached the opportunities and challenges of operating in the legal arena during a twenty-year period, from the mid-1980s to the mid-2000s. My aim is two-fold: the first is to understand the organizational and ideological context within which strategic litigation has taken place. The second is to then trace the sometimes subtle relationships among the evolution of the paradigm of disability, the transformation of relations within the disability rights movement, and litigation activity. I draw on sociological–institutionalist theory to account for the turn to the courts. I focus specifically on the two theoretical dimensions presented in Chapter 1 to build my argument: the role of framing processes and social movement organizational ecology.

Wight-Felske, eds., *Making Equality: History of Advocacy and Persons with Disabilities in Canada* (Concord, ON: Cpatus Press, 2003), p. 121.

THE EMERGENCE OF A DISABILITY RIGHTS CONSCIOUSNESS

Until the 1980s, an attitude of paternalism explicitly dominated disability issues.[2] At a societal level, this was expressed through the existence of disability organizations that excluded disabled persons from governance structures and promoted general perceptions of disabled persons as helpless, defined by their impairment, and objects of charity or pity. At a policy level, this paternalism was expressed through a consideration of disability as a social security, welfare, or health policy issue, not a human rights, citizenship, or equality issue.[3]

In the 1960s and 1970s, activists began to transform the political identity associated with being disabled, from a biomedical identity focused on an individual's impairment to an identity based on the quest for equality within a society that is structurally and culturally biased against disabled persons.[4] This has since become known as the "social model of disability." According to the social model, members of society, particularly employers and service providers, have a duty to make reasonable adjustments to accommodate persons with disabilities in order to remedy these biases.[5] Instead of simply requiring conformity to the able-bodied norm, the social model requires some adjustment of that norm to afford genuine equality to people with disabilities.[6] This shift can be at least partially explained through social movement

---

[2] Aldred H. Neufeldt, "Growth and Evolution of Disability Advocacy in Canada," in Deborah Stienstra and Aileen Wight-Felske, eds., *Making Equality: History of Advocacy and Persons with Disabilities in Canada* (Concord, ON: Captus Press, 2003).

[3] Sandra Fredman, *Discrimination Law* (Oxford: Oxford University Press, 2002).

[4] Ibid.

[5] Ravi A. Malhotra, "The Duty to Accommodate Unionized Workers with Disabilites in Canada and the United States: A Counter-Hegemonic Approach," *Journal of Law and Equality* 2(1), 2003, pp. 92–155.

[6] It is important to note that the reorientation of disability policy from a charity model to a rights-based model was a global trend. However, this global trend manifested itself in different ways within national settings. The comparative nature of this book

diffusion processes: several interviewees traced their own adoption of a rights discourse on disability to their knowledge of or participation in other antidiscrimination organizations, such as the women's movement, the trade unionist movement, or the civil rights movement in the United States.[7]

Disability Rights Meaning Frames

The interpretive frames of the social model of disability, now largely shared across the disability rights movement, have three specific components worth discussing. First, in the late 1970s and early 1980s, the prime concern of "impairment-specific" disability organizations "almost invariably was to promote research leading to prevention and/or successful intervention."[8] In contrast, activists' main concern was to influence public policy to achieve the societal inclusion of persons with disabilities.[9] Complementing this policy agenda was the need to empower persons with disabilities through the spread of an understanding of the social model of disability.

Several activists commenting on the early period of the movement described the emergence of a rights consciousness across the community and on a personal level.

> I think people with disabilities in Canada had to learn more generally that disabled people have rights. [And] that the Charter can have an impact on the quality of life for people with disabilities; that certain

---

explores this dimension but focuses specifically on convergences and divergences of the implications of the social model of disability within the national setting.

[7] Interviews, October 5, 2007; October 30, 2007; and November 6, 2007.

[8] Neufeldt, "Growth and Evolution of Disability Advocacy in Canada, p. 24."

[9] There were exceptions to this that are telling. Neufeldt notes that the range of types of disability represented did not generally include persons with cognitive impairments or hearing impairment. Neufeldt, "Growth and Evolution of Disability Advocacy in Canada."

kinds of barriers and resistance or rejection can be understood as discriminatory acts that the Charter would prohibit... So we had a learning curve of re-understanding our disadvantaged position in society on a rights dimension. Because at one time, as a group, we largely accepted that the fault was in us, that we had to change, rather than social attitudes and institutional structures.[10]

I was involved in some women's organizations before I got involved with disability issues... I have to say that it was a growth experience, while I really understood a feminist approach to issues in various aspects of life; it took me a while to come up with a disability analysis. That's partly because my experience was to persevere and overcome and to cope as an individual and not make too much of a fuss about your disability. It took awhile for me to come to terms with [the fact that] it's not just me as an individual but it's also a societal issue and the barriers I'm encountering are not necessarily ones that I personally can solve... I put the two things together; my feminist experience and disability issues and realized they had many things in common.[11]

This consciousness-raising process was the result of, and in turn fed into, a continual evolution in the paradigm of disability: a shift from the medical model to the social model.

A second component of the interpretive frames associated with the social model of disability is the construction of cross-disability membership, meaning frames. The "old guard" of impairment-specific organizations had little in common when disability was viewed through the lens of the medical model: each individual's impairment requires different medical or rehabilitative treatments, research, or services. With the shift to the social model of disability, however, the focus shifted from curing or treating a myriad of impairments to the shared experience of exclusion. As mentioned in the quote above, in "re-understanding the disadvantaged position in society on a rights

[10] Interview, November 6, 2007.
[11] Interview, October 5, 2007.

dimension," persons with disabilities are now able to articulate the exclusion they experience as discrimination.

A third component of the meaning frames of the social model of disability, stemming from the rearticulation of disadvantage as discrimination, is the goal of removing barriers and the associated concept of accommodation. The vision of creating a barrier-free society through the positive duty of accommodation creates an umbrella frame, one that addresses the discrimination faced by persons with different disabilities. The accommodations needed to break down barriers vary widely. For example, the provision of braille or assistive technology for persons who are blind or visually impaired, access to sign-language interpretation for deaf persons, or ramps for persons who use wheelchairs are just a few of the many types of accommodations persons with different disabilities might require. The language and vision of a barrier-free society plays a key role in uniting the disability community. One activist used this as a tactic in protesting for antidiscrimination legislation in Ontario: "I loved when my buddy who is deaf talked about braille. I loved when someone in a wheelchair talked about sign language. I, who am blind and can walk, would talk about ramps. It united us all together and it was very powerful."[12]

Deconstructing the social model of disability in this way, we begin to see that these components – the reunderstanding of disadvantage as discrimination, the heightened rights consciousness among the community, and the shared vision of a barrier-free society on a cross-disability basis – play an important role in explaining why disability activists advocating a social model analysis have developed an implicit consensus on the use of strategic litigation. By framing the common problem and experience as one of discrimination, the establishment of equality rights becomes the most appropriate method of addressing the issue. By extension, enforcing, clarifying, and expanding those rights becomes a major policy agenda. This agenda is, in many ways, best

---

[12] Interview, November 6, 2007.

pursued in institutions that are primarily concerned with the interpretation and enforcement of rights: the courts.

Organizational Implications of the Social Model of Disability

Interpretive frames also influence, and in turn are influenced by, changes in the multiorganizational sphere of a social movement. In the early 1970s, four large disability advocacy organizations in Canada dominated the policy agenda: the Canadian National Institute for the Blind, the Canadian Mental Health Association, Canadian Association for the Mentally Retarded (now known as the Canadian Association for Community Living), and the Canadian Rehabilitation Council for the Disabled. These four organizations developed community services and became increasingly professionalized as the need for services (and hence funding) grew. Neufeldt asserts that "an almost inevitable side effect was that such services became increasingly removed from the direct control and influence of individual disabled people and family members . . . Public attitudes towards disability were still paternalistic and degrading."[13] These service or charity organizations all relied to some extent on a paradigm of pity and sickness to raise money from the public. Although some of these organizations had an embryonic commitment to notions of equality, charitable and rehabilitation intentions remained the dominant drivers.

Although there has been a long history of self-advocacy organizations in some sections of the disability movement – particularly among the deaf community and a number of consumer organizations of blind and visually impaired people stemming from the 1920s – it was in the 1970s that an explosion occurred in the number and memberships of grassroots organizations comprised and led by persons with disabilities

[13] Neufeldt, "Growth and Evolution of Disability Advocacy," p. 23.

themselves.[14] In Canada, the term "consumer organization" began (and continues) to be used to distinguish those organizations politically controlled and/or managed by disabled persons from the older charity-minded organizations.[15] Consumer organizations also began to rely for the first time on rights language in an explicit manner.[16]

The consumer groups distinguished themselves from charity, service-provision, and recreational organizations (which grassroots activists coined organizations *for* persons with disabilities) and claimed a voice of their own on the policy stage, instead of being spoken for by rehabilitation organizations. For grassroots activists, they represented, in organizational form, a medical model understanding of disability issues. However, through the 1980s, the principles of the social model of disability began to spread from these grassroots organizations to both newly emerging groups and some (but not all) of the old-guard charity groups.

The first cross-disability self-advocacy organizations emerged in Manitoba, Alberta, and Saskatchewan between 1976 and 1978 – and subsequently allied with one another.[17] This laid the basis for the founding of the COPOH (now called the Council of Canadians with Disabilities), which has since become the key national cross-disability rights organization in Canada. It was within these groups that Canadians with disabilities began to challenge the then dominant

---

[14] Colleen Watters, "History of Advocacy Organizations of the Blind in Canada," in Deborah Stienstra and Aileen Wight-Felske, eds., *Making Equality: History of Advocacy and Persons with Disabilities in Canada* (Concord, ON: Captus Press, 2003).

[15] A long-time disability rights advocate in Canada explained the use of the term: "We had adopted the word 'consumer' from Nader's movement in the States: a way to have power even though you are reliant on others to produce goods and services." In fact, the movement took ownership of the term "consumer" and has used it as a tool for empowerment (Interview, November 6, 2007).

[16] Neufeldt, "Growth and Evolution of Disability Advocacy," pp. 24–25.

[17] Interview, November 6, 2007.

view of disability as a medical defect or pathological limitation of the individual.[18]

By the mid-1970s, the chasm between the ethos of advocacy and service organizations was growing. Some service organizations also began to question the incompatibility between pity images used to raise funds, on one hand, and attempts to change public attitudes toward disabled persons to perceiving them as equally valued members of society on the other. What was then known as the Canadian Association for the Mentally Retarded (CAMR) was one of the first old-guard organizations to try a different approach to fundraising: it explicitly rejected the use of the pity paradigm in its strategic plan for the 1970s.[19] However, this was relatively rare, and grassroots organizations often emerged out of frustration with traditional organizations.

Consumer organizations grew in part because a groundswell of persons with disabilities began to want a voice of their own on the policy stage, instead of being spoken for by rehabilitation or service-oriented organizations.[20] These organizations lobbied for and received government funding instead of relying on charitable contributions, which they felt posed certain ideological problems for the emerging movement due to its incompatibility with the emerging social model understanding of disability. This rejection of charitable funding raised through campaigns that relied on a pity paradigm of disability is difficult to explain without reliance on an understanding of meaning frames: that is, the growing importance of the rights model of disability to disability activists required the rejection of funds raised on portrayals of disability that the activists found disempowering. Turning back to theoretical explanations of legal mobilization presented in Chapter 1, theorists working in the legal opportunity structure (LOS) or resource mobilization (RM) tradition would have difficulty explaining this rejection

---

[18] Ibid.

[19] Neufeldt, "Growth and Evolution of Disability Advocacy in Canada, p. 24."

[20] Deborah Stienstra and Aileen Wight-Felske, *Making Equality: History of Advocacy and Persons with Disabilities in Canada* (Concord, ON: Captus Press, 2003).

of funding from particular sources. Only through understanding the shifting of meaning frames in the construction of the concept of disability can this be logically explained.

A DISABILITY RIGHTS CONSCIOUSNESS AND THE CHARTER OF RIGHTS AND FREEDOMS (1982)

Although there are several legal mechanisms providing protection from discrimination on grounds of mental and physical disability in Canada, arguably the most significant is the equality guarantee in Section 15(1) of the Charter of Rights and Freedoms.[21] It states: "Every individual is equal before and under the law and has the right to the equal protection and equal benefit of the law without discrimination and, in particular, without discrimination based on race, national or ethnic origin, colour, religion, sex, age or mental or physical disability." The equality guarantee came into effect in 1985, and its protections are meant to be interpreted in a purposive sense, that is, applied in a way that will serve to correct the injustices they were intended to rectify. For more than a decade, Canada remained the only state in the world that specifically granted equality protections to people with disabilities in its constitution.[22] The relationship between the development of the Charter and the spread of a disability rights consciousness is complex.

The evident shift in conceptualizing disability as a social construction among leaders of the emerging movement occurred at roughly the

---

[21] The constitutional protection only applies to federal and provincial government action. This is complemented by human rights protection both on the federal and provincial levels, which includes a range of private actions. Ontario was also the first province to establish disability-specific legislation.

[22] Germany followed suit and made disabled persons a constitutionally protected group in 1996. South Africa also included them in their constitution in 1997. Since then, many other countries have also institutionalized disability rights in constitutional and statutory law. Orville R. Endicott, "Key Trends in Case Law Pertaining to Supports for Persons with Disabilities," Unpublished manuscript, Toronto, p. 56.

same time that the Charter of Rights and Freedoms was being debated and developed by Canadian lawmakers.[23] Yvonne Peters, an activist and lawyer who has been involved in the disability rights movement for thirty years, writes of the period:

> It is important to understand that the struggle to obtain constitutional recognition was more than just another political manoeuvre for people with disabilities. Indeed, it was a watershed event that occurred at a time when people with disabilities were just beginning to construct a new vision and analysis of the disability experience... The disability rights movement rejected the medical model of disability, and argued that it was social barriers and prejudices that created disabilities. The goal of the movement was to secure the right of persons with disabilities to self-determination, individual autonomy, and the opportunity to participate in society as full and equal citizens... This shift to a rights-based analysis therefore, represents a profound and decisive turning point in the history of persons with disabilities.[24]

As discussed at the beginning of this chapter, the disability movement applied constant pressure on the Trudeau government, particularly Justice Minister Jean Chretien, during the constitutional negotiations. One activist recalls the lengths to which they went to capture a politician's ear: "We would lobby Mr. Chretien and others, even to the point of following him to the washroom in the Parliament bathroom and talking to him while he was having a pee. There was a lot of pressure and tactics."[25] Activists also built alliances among themselves, though not without conflicts. A bone of contention arose over whether to push for protection from discrimination on the basis of both physical and mental disability or to restrict the campaign to physical disability. Some activists expressed concern that broadening the definition of disability

---

[23] Sarah Armstrong, "Disability Advocacy in the Charter Era," *Journal of Law and Equality* 2:1, 2003, pp. 33–91.

[24] Yvonne Peters, "From Charity to Equality," p. 122.

[25] Interview, November 6, 2007.

in this way would diminish chances for success. Others emphasized the point that disabilities of all types are largely a construction of social prejudice and systemic barriers. As a result, it was decided that acceptance of the broader definition of disability, including mental disability, would be the goal.

The result of the protracted lobbying effort was the inclusion of disability as one of the enumerated grounds in Section 15 of the Charter of Rights and Freedoms (see Table 2.1). Yvonne Peters identifies three consequences of the successful disability charter lobby:

> First, it solidified the establishment of a national disability rights movement that remains active today. As Laurie Beachell puts it, "The Charter lobby was the coming of age for the disability rights movement." Second, it symbolized the shift from disability as a charity concept to legitimizing disability as a status entitled to rights. Third, it provided a legal framework and another mechanism to enable people with disabilities to continue to fight for justice and equality.[26]

The shared rights consciousness was developing among disability (as well as other other) groups in the late 1970s in the same period that the Charter was introduced, which makes it particularly difficult to disentangle causes and effects and complex interactions among various explanatory factors. The evidence suggests that the process of developing and implementing the Charter of Rights and Freedoms accelerated the rights consciousness of groups highlighting a recursive interaction between change of what some scholars would call the LOS (as discussed in Chapter 1) and framing of group identity. Rights can influence collective identity by altering how individuals and groups perceive themselves or by changing how individuals and groups are perceived or treated by others.[27]

---

[26] Yvonne Peters, "From Charity to Equality," p. 134.
[27] Engel and Munger, *Rights of Inclusion*, p. 242.

Table 2.1. *Equality Protections in Canadian Law for Persons with Disabilities*

Legal protection	Provisions	Scope of application
Charter of Rights and Freedoms (1982), Section 15	Every individual is equal before and under the law and has the right to the equal protection and equal benefit of the law without discrimination and, in particular, without discrimination based on race, national or ethnic origin, colour, religion, sex, age or mental and physical disability.	Applies to federal and provincial government legislation and activity – not to discrimination by private citizens.
Canadian Human Rights Act (1978)	For all purposes of this Act, the prohibited grounds of discrimination are race, national or ethnic origin, colour, religion, age, sex, sexual orientation, marital status, family status, disability and conviction for which a pardon has been granted.	Outlaws discrimination in employment and in the delivery of goods/services in areas within the legislative authority of the federal government.
Ontario Human Rights Code (1962, "handicap" included in 1981)	Every person has a right to equal treatment . . . without discrimination because of race, ancestry, place of origin, colour, ethnic origin, citizenship, creed, sex, sexual orientation, age, marital status, family status or disability.	Outlaws discrimination in employment and in the delivery of goods/services in areas within the legislative authority of the provincial government.
Accessibility for Ontarians with Disabilities Act (2005)	Recognizing the history of discrimination against persons with disabilities in Ontario, the purpose of this Act is to benefit all Ontarians by, (a) developing, implementing and enforcing accessibility standards in order to achieve accessibility for Ontarians with disabilities with respect to goods, services, facilities, accommodation, employment, buildings, structures and premises on or before January 1, 2025.	The act applies to every person or organization in the public and private sectors of the Province of Ontario.

Other Legal Protections for Disabled Persons in Canada

Disability rights activists have lobbied successfully for other legal frameworks providing protection from discrimination on grounds of mental and physical disability in Canada, ranging from the federal constitutional protections discussed previously to provincial statutory laws (see Table 2.1). It is important to note that the constitutional protection only applies to federal and provincial government action. This is complemented by human rights protection on both federal and provincial levels.

The Canadian Human Rights Act (CHRA) was adopted in 1978, and the act also established the Canadian Human Rights Commission. The commission administers the CHRA and ensures the principles of equal opportunity and nondiscrimination are followed in all areas of federal jurisdiction. Each province and territory of Canada has a Human Rights Code or Act (or in Quebec *la Charte des droits et libertés de la personne du Québec*), all with slightly different grounds protected against discrimination. These human rights protections cover areas not included under federal legislation, for example, schools, retail shops, restaurants, and accommodation.[28] A survey of each provincial and territorial code is beyond the scope of this chapter, but a brief look at the provisions within Ontario will serve as an illustration (see Table 2.1). The Ontario Human Rights Code was the first human rights code enacted in Canada in 1962. However, "handicap" as an enumerated ground was not included until a successful advocacy effort resulted in its insertion into the code in 1981. Like its federal counterpart, the Ontario Human Rights Commission, an arm's length agency of the government, was established in 1961 to administer the Code.[29]

---

[28] This is a result of Canada's federal system and the division of powers between different branches of government.

[29] This institution underwent a fundamental reform effective June 2008 and, subsequently, will no longer receive complaints. This is now the purview of the Human Rights Tribunal of Ontario.

Ontario is the only province to date to also have disability-specific rights legislation.[30] After an assertive grassroots lobbying effort by Ontarians with disabilities throughout the 1990s, a conservative provincial government enacted the Ontarians with Disabilities Act in 2001.[31] The act was considered weak, however, as it suggested voluntary action without enforcement, penalties, or deadlines. Critics of the legislation continued to petition the government to pass a stronger, more effective act. In 2005, a liberal government proved receptive to lobby efforts, and a significantly strengthened Accessibility for Ontarians with Disabilities Act (AODA) was passed.[32] The scope of the act is significant in that it covers both the public and private sectors and has adopted a barrier-removal approach, but it has been criticized for its long time frame (full accessibility to be achieved by 2025). David Lepofsky, one of the leaders of the law reform effort in Ontario, successfully and significantly shortened some of these time frames by taking action against the Toronto Transit Commission (TTC). The Ontario Human Rights Tribunal ruled in July 2007 that the TTC had violated the rights of Mr. Lepofsky by failing to call all stops on surface routes and was given 15 days to devise a strategy to train drivers and enforce the new policy. The case received wide media coverage, and public sentiment was overwhelmingly in favor of Mr. Lepofsky.

DISABILITY ORGANIZATIONS AND STRATEGIC LITIGATION

The shift to the human rights approach and corresponding emergence of an increasing number of consumer-led organizations and the

---

[30] The provincial government in Manitoba is currently considering developing a similar piece of legislation.

[31] Ontarians with Disabilities Act, 2001, S.O. 2001, c. 32.

[32] Accessibility for Ontarians with Disabilities Act, 2005, S.O. 2005, c. 11.

growing number of specific legal protections embedded in federal and provincial laws laid the foundation for the adoption of litigation strategies by the movement. It also led to the establishment of a legal center, the ARCH Disability Law Centre in Toronto, which supports many of these organizations in pursuing law reform and test case litigation. In analyzing this paradigm shift in the concept of disability, through the theoretical lens of interpretive frames and its organizational expression, we can begin to understand legal mobilization by the disability rights movement. When the identity associated with the notion of disability is prescribed by the social model of disability, as opposed to the medical model, the expansion of rights becomes the most appropriate public policy tool for addressing the issues persons with disabilities face. By extension, legal mobilization – as collective action based on those rights – becomes a more acceptable method of influencing public policy than it might be otherwise.

This section explores in greater detail how the evolving meaning frames manifested themselves in, what have been identified as, some of the key movement organizations and will also map the organizational ecology of the disability movement to trace how this has influenced the use of litigation over time and the types of cases in which organizations become involved. This includes a number of case studies of some of the main disability organizations, though I make no claim of comprehensiveness or representativeness. The case studies include the Council of Canadians with Disabilities; the development of an organization of feminist disabled women, the DisAbled Women's Network; the evolution of the family-based organization, the Canadian Association for Community Living; an organization focused specifically on test case litigation called the Canadian Disability Rights Council; an older advocacy organization focused on blindness and vision-health, the Canadian National Institute of the Blind; and, finally, a discussion of the role of the ARCH Disability Law Centre, the legal center that emerged as a crucial player in the strategic delivery of legal services to the disability community. The focus in this chapter is on the use of legal action in the Supreme Court in pursuit of policy or social change and the effects this can sometimes have. Chapter 3 focuses on the extent to which the Court has adopted a social model understanding of disability and how this has been applied to other equality issues.

Overview of Participation by Disability Organizations in the Supreme Court

The disability rights movement is highly heterogeneous and dynamic. The contours of the community, the goals of the movement, and the strategies and tactics for achieving the objectives have all been the matter of intense debate. Certainly, the movement loosely grouped under the title of "disability rights" has been less unified, in an organizational sense, in its representation before the Supreme Court than the women's movement or the gay and lesbian rights movement in Canada.[33] This looseness is reflected in legal mobilization activity by a number of actors who claim to have a public policy mandate on issues of concern to disabled persons. I argue here that the disability rights movement has been a major player before the Supreme Court of Canada (SCC).[34]

Table 2.2 demonstrates that the four key disability rights organizations (some have undergone name changes) appeared before the SCC, either as interveners or as appellants, thirty-nine times between 1985 and 2007. Furthermore, this number represents a conservative

---

[33] Christopher Manfredi, *Feminist Activism in the Supreme Court*; Miriam Smith, "Social Movements and Judicial Empowerment," *Politics and Society* 33(2), 2005, pp. 327–53; F. L. Morton and Avril Allen, "Feminists and the Courts: Measuring Success in Interest Group Litigation in Canada," *Canadian Journal of Political Science* 34(1), 2001, pp. 55–84.

[34] Anecdotal evidence suggests that disabled persons have been the most active equality seekers in the lower courts and before human rights tribunals, but this is beyond the scope of this study. Interviews, October 26, 2007 and November 2, 2007.

Table 2.2. *Disability Rights Organizations before the SCC, 1985–2007*

Case name	Year	Key issues	Interveners
Ont. Human Rights Comm. v. Simpsons – Sears (O'Malley)	1985	Unintentional discrimination/adverse effect discrimination and reasonable accommodation.	CAMR/CACL COPOH/CCD
Bhinder v. CN	1985	Balancing exercise between rule creating discriminatory practice and bona fide occupational requirements.	CAMR/CACL COPOH/CCD
E. (Mrs.) v. Eve	1986	Consent to perform a nontherapeutic sterilization of a woman with a mental disability.	Consumer Advisory Committee of the CAMR/CACL
Andrews v. Law Society of British Columbia	1989	A substantive theory of equality.	COPOH/CCD
R. v. Swain	1991	A substantive equality argument applied specifically to disability.	CDRC CACL
Canadian Council of Churches v. Canada (Minister of Employment and Immigration)	1992	The criteria for a public interest group to be allowed to mount a constitutional challenge in court.	COPOH/CCD CDRC
Weatherall v. Canada (Attorney General)	1993	Formal gender equality in treatment of prisoners.	COPOH/CCD
Rodriguez v. British Columbia (Attorney General)	1993	Terminally ill patient seeks assistance to commit suicide.	COPOH/CCD
A. (L.L.) v. B. (A.)	1995	Disclosure of medical and therapeutic records.	DAWN
R. v. O'Connor	1995	Disclosure of medical and therapeutic records by Crown and by third parties.	DAWN

(continued)

Table 2.2 (*continued*)

Case name	Year	Key issues	Interveners
Battlefords and District Co-operative Ltd. v. Gibbs	1996	Distinction between mental and physical disability.	CCD
Eaton v. Brant County Board of Education	1997	Whether placement in special education class absent parental consent infringes the child's Charter equality rights.	CCD CACL
Eldridge v. British Columbia (Attorney General)	1997	Right to sign language interpretation in provision of health care as a form of accommodation.	CCD DAWN
British Columbia (Superintendent of Motor Vehicles) v. British Columbia (Council of Human Rights)	1999	Whether blanket refusal without possibility of individual assessment constitutes discrimination.	CCD
British Columbia (Public Service Employee Relations Commission) v. BCGSEU	1999	Institutionalized discriminatory standards.	DAWN
R. v. Ewanchuk	1999	Implied consent as defense to sexual assault.	DAWN
New Brunswick (Minister of Health and Community Services) v. G. (J.)	1999	Failure to provide parent with legal aid in custody proceedings.	DAWN
R. v. Darrach	2000	Fair trial: revised "rape shield" provisions unconstitutional.	DAWN
Lovelace v. Ontario	2000	Relationship between equality rights and positive discrimination programs.	CCD

Table 2.2 (*continued*)

Case name	Year	Key issues	Interveners
Granovsky v. Canada (Minister of 2000 Employment and Immigration)	2000	Accommodation requirements for permanently disabled persons but not for temporarily disabled persons.	CCD
R. v. Latimer	2001	Defense of necessity to justify mercy killing of disabled daughter.	CCD CACL DAWN
Auton (Guardian ad litem of) v. British Columbia (Attorney General)	2004	Whether Province's refusal to fund treatment violates equality rights.	CCD CACL DAWN
Newfoundland (Treasury Board) v. N.A.P.E.,	2004	Whether a fiscal crisis can be the basis for justifying a violation of rights.	CCD
Blackwater v. Plint	2005	Students from former Indian residential schools claiming damages.	DAWN
Hilewitz v. Canada (Minister of Citizenship and Immigration); De Jong v. Canada (Minister of Citizenship and Immigration)	2005	Individualized assessments when considering whether the "excessive demands" provision regarding children with intellectual disabilities is applicable in immigration residency applications.	CACL
Nova Scotia (Minister of Health) v. J.J.	2005	Family Court's jurisdiction to impose terms and conditions on plan proposed by Minister of Health for vulnerable adult's care.	CACL
Council of Canadians with Disabilities v. VIA Rail Canada Inc.	2007	The duty to accommodate passengers with disabilities. Duty to not create new barriers.	CCD (as appellant) CACL DAWN

estimate of the disability rights movement's role in the Court. The analysis focuses only on a sample of main organizations in the disability rights movement as identified in the secondary literature and through interviews; it excludes other organizations that are both explicit in their equality objectives and have intervened on one or several occasions. Also excluded are organizations that may not have the advancement of disability rights as their primary objective, but have it as a secondary priority or advance arguments that indirectly support a disability rights analysis.[35]

Council of Canadians with Disabilities

The Council of Canadians with Disabilities (CCD) has been the main consumer-led cross-disability national organization since its founding (under its previous name, the Coalition of Provincial Organizations of the Handicapped [COPOH]) in the late 1970s. CCD brings together both disability-led provincial and territorial cross-disability organizations as well as single-impairment and single-focus disability consumer

---

[35] Organizations advancing an equality agenda for persons with disabilities that have intervened at least once (and in some cases more regularly) include Disabled People for Employment Equity; Persons United for Self Help in Ontario (P.U.S.H.); The Quebec Multi Ethnic Association for the Integration of Handicapped People; British Columbia Coalition of People with Disabilities; The Learning Disabilities Association of Ontario; The Down Syndrome Association of Ontario; The Confédération des organismes de personnes handicapées du Québec; People First of Canada; the Canadian Association of the Deaf; the Canadian Hearing Society; The Queen Street Patients' Council, later known as Empowerment Council – Centre for Addiction and Mental Health, and Social Benefits Tribunal; the Saskatchewan Voice of People with Disabilities; People in Equal Participation Inc.; Ontario Network of Injured Workers Groups, Transportation Action Now; Alliance for Equality of Blind Canadians; Canadian Hard of Hearing Association; Canadian Association of Independent Living Centres; and Ethno-racial People with Disabilities Coalition of Ontario (Factums, Supreme Court Records, 1985–2007).

organizations. The organization has a national office based in Winnipeg, Manitoba. CCD's agenda, from its founding, was to pursue changes in public policy to achieve the inclusion of people with disabilities in society:[36]

> With CCD's emergence, volunteers with disabilities challenged the legitimacy of doctors and therapists to intervene with government on the citizenship issues of persons with disabilities . . . Canadian politicians impressed by new disability models advanced by CCD began to realize that room at policy tables had to be made for the disability rights movement.[37]

The organization's motto, "a voice of our own," and the governance structure exemplify the "nothing about us without us" ideology. CCD's mandate and vision have remained consistent over the last twenty-five years. For instance, in 1983, CCD's then-president, Ronald Kanary, laid out the organization's objectives as follows:

> COPOH believes that disabled Canadians should have the right and responsibility to present their needs and concerns in all areas of our society. Its objectives are as follows: a) to promote full integration of disabled Canadians by creating an environment of equality; b) to establish an open forum where disabled people will freely voice their concerns regarding issues that affect their lifestyle; and c) to act as a monitoring body, to ensure that all rights and freedoms, once acquired, are maintained.[38]

In comparison, Marie White, CCD's chairperson, wrote the following in the 2007 annual report: "We seek protection of our rights, recognition of our status as citizens and elimination of those entrenched

---

[36] Neufeldt, "Growth and Evolution of Disability Advocacy in Canada."

[37] Council of Canadians with Disabilities Web site, http://www.ccdonline.ca/about-us/index.htm (accessed October 7, 2007).

[38] Affidavit accompanying the motion requesting intervention by CAMR and the COPOH in *Bhinder v. CN*, [1985] 2 S.C.R. 561.

systemic barriers which block our path to equality."[39] The interpretative frames and ideology, shared among the organization's members, are reflected in the explicit consensus within the organization that the rights model of disability should be infused through all policies and practices related to disabled persons. The interpretive frames have also influenced the organization's relations with other organizations in the sphere of disability policy.

In its early days, CCD was relatively radical in its refusal to cooperate with non-consumer-led groups. One CCD activist highlighted the changing nature of interorganizational relations:

> We have that history and we remember it well, but I think CCD has become a little more pragmatic and will work with organizations that have the capacity and an interest in promoting disability rights. So we work with CACL [Canadian Association for Community Living], which is differently formed: it consists of parents, caregivers and educators, so it's not a disability-only organization, but they do a similar kind of work so it makes sense to collaborate. I think there is always a healthy cautiousness of how the two organizations work together because of structure and the different perspective but certainly there is lots and lots of good work done between those two organizations and others that CCD has worked with. But each time you go into some kind of collaboration it is with an eye to making sure that the voice of people with disabilities is strong and listened to. The bottom line is that in the early 1980s we were adamant, it didn't matter what work you did, if you weren't disability-led and run then forget it – I think we've changed quite a bit.[40]

The group's meaning frames strongly dictated which types of organizations could serve as allies and which could not. The evolution in relations between CCD and the Canadian Association for Community Living (CACL) is significant. CCD changed and their interpretative

---

[39] CCD Annual Report, 2006–2007.
[40] Interview, October 5, 2007.

frames incorporated elements of pragmatism. Although CCD's growing pragmatism is one cause of the changing nature of relations, what may be even more important is the adoption by CACL of meaning frames compatible with those advanced by CCD. As will be shown below, CACL was one of the first organizations *for* disabled persons to undergo an internal transformation: its focus on equality became a key part of their mandate. This frame alignment process between the two organizations allowed for the evolution in relations between them.

Framing the mandate and mission of the organization primarily in terms of rights has laid the foundation for the use of strategic litigation to influence disability and equality policy. Since the early 1980s, CCD has participated in twenty-five legal challenges at all levels of the justice system. Of these, the organization appeared sixteen times before the SCC between 1985 and 2007. Although the Council of Representatives sets general organizational policy, it is CCD's Human Rights Committee that has a mandate of overseeing any test case litigation. This process includes the following: considering whether to intervene in particular cases of significance to people with disabilities; selecting legal counsel to represent the case; assisting counsel in the development of legal arguments and the factums for cases; undertaking legal analyses once cases have been decided; participating in information-sharing and letter-writing campaigns to influence policy on access to justice issues; and conducting research on issues of access to justice for disabled persons.[41] Cases come to the attention of the Human Rights Committee in a variety of ways: they use their own organizational network or rely on lawyers who regularly represent them to approach them with cases.[42] When a case comes to CCD's attention, the Human Rights Committee determines whether or not to support or intervene in the case by asking the following questions: "Will the case advance disability rights in a broad way?" "Will it set a precedent?"

---

[41] CCD Annual Report, 2006–2007.
[42] Interview, November 7, 2007.

"Does the case concern a new issue or an issue that has not been well developed or well understood by the courts?" "Does CCD have the resources to support this case?" "Is there another way for the issue to be addressed?" "Could the case be taken on by another organization or institution?" "Is this the right case to advance the issue in question?"[43] Because CCD places the use of litigation within its broader objectives and strategic choices, the ability to win a case, although important, is not the sole, nor even the most important, criterion in choosing whether to support a case. Significantly, the resource question is but one among a series of considerations. One member of the Human Rights Committee stated the following in an interview: "Sometimes a case may be risky, in that we know that the courts may be a long way from deciding in our favour, but it may be a good opportunity to get some publicity for the issue. Sometimes losing can be winning in a way because it raises the issues with the public."[44]

CCD has a hands-on approach when it comes to working with legal counsel to develop legal arguments. A former member of the Human Rights Committee described the nature of this process.

Once we find a case, and we decide to go into it, we try to find some funding. We used the Court Challenges program largely until its recent demise. We then gather . . . a sub-committee or working group to advise our counsel on the case. Within that working group we have lawyers who have an area of interest and track record and we'll bring them together with persons with disabilities who have the most at stake in the case . . . We review the factums; we re-write them with the lawyers, we instruct the lawyers as carefully as can be done given our legal expert volunteers and our disability strategists. Finally we try to show up with credible disability spokespeople when the decisions come down so that we can interpret the decisions to the public via the media.[45]

[43] Interview, October 5, 2007.
[44] Ibid.
[45] Interview, November 7, 2007.

This interactive process ensures that grassroots understandings of the issues faced by people with disabilities can filter up. As long as legal counsel is receptive to potentially radical perspectives, and is able to advance them in a credible way before the Supreme Court, this process allows for shifts in meaning frames to influence judicial understandings.

The use of litigation and intervention in the courts is just a small part of the organization's work. CCD complements its participation in important court decisions with law reform and advocacy campaigns.

> You can put a lot of time and energy into litigation, and at the end of the day you have a really good precedent but there is still a lot more work to be done to make that precedent turn into something useful. Never underestimate the value of law reform and advocacy and the kind of initiatives that you need to make change, but I do think the two things go hand-in-hand. Litigation is needed because people with disabilities just don't have a strong enough voice within government. If we get a good court decision it's a great ally, it's a great tool and it does kind of wake the government up, and you can certainly use that as perhaps a stronger weapon to get them to do what they need to do. [But] it's not the answer to achieving equality – it's just one of the tools in our basket that we use.[46]

There is a growing awareness (and associated frustration) that success in the courts does not automatically translate into social change; follow-up work is usually required. The focus on monitoring enforcement of court victories was identified by a number of interviewees as an area of weakness across the disability movement.

> It's important to have those victories and to use them. I think, we as a disability rights movement have to be more effective as to how we use those gains that we make in litigation . . . I'm not sure we've done that as well as we could. But at the same time I don't think

---

[46] Interview, October 5, 2007.

the governments have taken the victories very seriously, [they] just interpret them very, very narrowly.[47]

There is an implicit consensus within the CCD about the use of litigation as an advocacy strategy. When asked during an interview whether CCD membership is unanimously supportive of the use of litigation as a strategy, a member of the Human Rights Committee responded: "Yes. I've never heard of any disputes about it... We might debate the issues and the arguments and how they should be put forward but never the idea of litigation."[48] Similarly, one of the previous quotations hints at the importance of pursuing cases by suggesting that the process of funding the case and deciding to participate in the case is not necessarily a unidirectional causal relationship: "Once we find a case and we decide to go into it, we try to find some funding."[49] This consensus is interesting and important in the face of an organizational recognition of the many limits of litigation: the risks involved with litigation and the perceived unwillingness of governments to implement key victories.

CCD and some of the other consumer organizations examined here have relied on the Court Challenges Program, a federal program that provides funding to nongovernmental organizations specifically for the use of litigation. The program was established by the federal government in the late 1970s and grew during the early years of the Charter to support litigation by groups that have been "historically disadvantaged."[50] During the early phase of political activism, the government was receptive to the empowerment of disabled persons and willingly funded their organizations and encouraged them to work on a cross-disability basis rather than competing for funding on a

[47] Ibid.

[48] Ibid.

[49] Interview, November 7, 2007.

[50] Ian Brodie, "Interest Group Litigation and the Embedded State: Canada's Court Challenges Program," *Canadian Journal of Political Science* 34(2), 2001, pp. 357–76.

74

disability-by-disability basis.[51] However, the program was cut by conservative governments between 1992 and 1994 and again in September 2006.

Since the funding cuts for the Court Challenges Program, CCD's opportunities to use legal mobilization have been constrained. One activist pointed to the importance of the Court Challenges Program for the ability to defend and build on equality gains.

> What will be interesting now that the program has been dismantled, is how much litigation we can undertake. I think there will be a significant difference. I think the number of times we will get involved will be reduced unless we can find other ways to get the resources we need because it's not cheap to go to court.[52]

An analysis of the organization's financial situation, in terms of project funding for legal mobilization activity and the corresponding expense of that activity, supports that claim. Table 2.3 breaks down the various sources of revenue and indicates that the main source of CCD's revenue has been government funding. Table 2.4 illustrates that some of the funding used to support participation in cases came from the Court Challenges Fund; this means the funding is specifically earmarked for certain test case litigation or related projects. It also highlights that even when the Court Challenges funding was available, CCD spent a significant amount of additional revenue on supplementing public funding in taking its cases.

There is little doubt that cutting the Court Challenges program has dealt a significant blow to the ability of the CCD to defend and define equality rights for persons with disabilities.[53] This reliance on a single source of funding, which is susceptible to highly politicized decisions,

---

[51] ARCH Disability Law Centre, *ARCH Celebrating 25 Years* (Toronto: ARCH Disability Law Centre, 2005).

[52] Interview, October 5, 2007.

[53] Interviews, October 26, 2007; November 2, 2007; November 6, 2007; and November 20, 2007.

Table 2.3. *CCD Revenue by Source, 2005–2007*

Year	Total revenue (CAD)	Federal funding	Donations	Memberships	Project revenue	Project income	Miscellaneous
2005	$1,468,447	$1,203,000	$922	$13,000	$185,633	$27,574	$10,744
		81.9%	0.1%	0.9%	12.6%	1.9%	0.7%
2006	$1,724,166	$1,256,500	$2,022	$13,000	$375,063	$34,220	$9,141
		72.9%	0.1%	0.8%	21.8%	2.0%	0.5%
2007	$1,411,954	$1,019,000	$16,187	$13,000	$319,829	$18,290	$7,358
		72.2%	1.1%	0.9%	22.7%	1.3%	0.5%

Sources: CCD Annual Report, 2005–2006; CCD Annual Report, 2006–2007.

Table 2.4. *Examples of Court Challenges of Canada Funding and Legal Expenses for CCD by project, 2005–2007*

Year	Totals (CAD)	Intervention in McKay-Panos	Transport act – One person one fare	VIA rail
2005				
Funding	$32,545	$2,655	$3,640	$26,250
Expenses	$79,829	$2,655	$3,640	$73,534
2006				
Funding	$99,437	$16,925	$22,512	$60,000
Expenses	$101,437	$16,925	$22,512	$62,000
2007				
Funding	$41,713	n/a	$34,713	$7,000
Expenses	$70,768	n/a	$60,313	$10,455

Sources: CCD Annual Report, 2005–2006; CCD Annual Report, 2006–2007.

can be problematic for the use of litigation as a strategy to pursue equality, particularly as legal mobilization often relies on medium- and long-term horizons. In response, the organization is being proactive about RM. Jim Derksen, a long-time activist, undertook a research project focusing on the development of the Disability Rights Defense Fund; in June 2005, the Council of Representatives approved the plan to develop a fund that would be ring-fenced for the use of legal action.[54]

Turning back to a consideration of theoretical explanations of legal mobilization, the acknowledged importance of funding sources also points to the explanatory power of RM approaches in accounting for variations in the types of litigation strategies used (discussed in Chapter 1). The breakdown of expenses in Table 2.4 highlights the resource thresholds required for different types of litigation strategies. The costs in the *VIA Rail* case, in which the organization was the appellant, were much higher compared with the costs in the *McKay-Panos* intervention before the Court of Appeal, in which the organization was acting as a third-party commentator. Although

[54] CCD Annual Report, 2006–2007.

this conforms to the expectation of RM approaches that groups will be more likely to adopt a litigation strategy if the level of resources available to them is greater, it also illustrates the need to refine these theories to better reflect the variety of options available to groups based on different resource thresholds. Furthermore, as the previous discussion highlights, other factors may be equally important in the decision to support a case. Several interviewees pointed out that if the organization had lost the *VIA Rail* case, it is likely the organization would not have survived.[55] It is telling that the organization was willing to risk financial ruin in the *VIA Rail* case in order to articulate its principles on an issue important to persons with disabilities.

DisAbled Women's Network Canada

Although the CCD is, in many ways, considered the national voice on disability rights issues, the hegemony of its interpretive frames as representative of the disability community across Canada has not gone unchallenged. Within the disability community, there is a great deal of heterogeneity of identities and experiences. Some interviewees found that, in the early days of the movement, these diverse identities and differing agendas were less accommodated in the mainstream movement than they are today. For example, one activist commented on her feminist leanings and the sexism she experienced in the disability rights movement:

> My first involvement with advocacy and promotion of rights was through the women's movement. Most of the early leaders of the disability rights movement were men: and they were men who, I think at that point, really didn't understand the women's movement or women's issues. They didn't have any kind of connection or affinity with it. And so I found that there was a very strong current of sexism within the movement. Which at times was discouraging,

[55] Interview, October 5, 2007 and November 20, 2007.

frustrating, but as I said I was really pulled by the idea of working with like-minded people to bring about change and I didn't want to let go of that. Fortunately for me, I did meet other women. There weren't that many involved early on, but I was able to meet other like-minded women who shared my frustration and we supported each other in raising feminist issues at the table.[56]

Within social movements, there are two strategies for advancing the agendas of those who may not feel they are represented by the key organizations. As the previous quote illustrates, activists can work within existing organizations to produce change from within. Another strategy is to produce change from without by establishing separate organizations to advance the particular perspective that activists feel is lacking or weak. The creation of a feminist disability rights organization in Canada is an example of the latter.

In the mid-1980s, disabled women began organizing to identify and discuss the issues important in their lives and their experiences as women with disabilities. Another early activist within the feminist disability rights movement echoes the frustration of the activist cited previously. She was pushed by her experience of exclusion in both the feminist sphere and the disability community to mobilize on the basis of that experience of exclusion in a different way.

> I had learned that most of the political work that I had done before was suddenly not accessible to me. I didn't stop being a feminist and a trade unionist, but I did start using a wheelchair; and my former world had too many stairs and was suddenly closed to me and beyond my reach. The women's movement didn't really "get it" about access and was suddenly also pretty much inaccessible to me. I turned to the disability community to do my political work and, soon after, I realized that the disability community just didn't "get it" around women's issues. I turned there because I figured that at least it would be accessible. It seemed that these organizations, which were mostly dominated by men weren't interested in doing – or didn't have

---

[56] Interview, October 5, 2007.

enough time or money to do – anything about an issue like mothering as a woman with a disability or about the violence in our lives.[57]

At an early meeting held in Ottawa in 1985, six areas of major concern to disabled women were identified: self-image, employment, violence, health, sexuality, and mothering.[58] This meeting, and a founding conference held in 1987, signified the birth of the DisAbled Women's Network Canada (DAWN Canada) and the establishment of their mission to end the poverty, isolation, discrimination, and violence experienced by disabled women. DAWN Canada is comprised of, and controlled by, women with disabilities and is a member of CCD and the National Action Committee (NAC) on the Status of Women.[59] The organization has ebbed and flowed in its composition, activity, and output. It has been highly susceptible, at both national and provincial levels, to government funding levels and, as such, experienced a downturn in the late 1990s and early 2000s.[60]

In terms of legal mobilization, DAWN Canada has been involved in two ways. First, the organization developed a number of research papers on topics of importance to disabled women related to legal issues or questions regarding access to justice. This included collaborative research with the Canadian Disability Rights Council (CDRC) on access to justice issues, for example, the report *Domestic Violence: Accessibility of Legal Information to Women with Disabilities*.[61] Second, DAWN Canada has also used strategic litigation and has appeared as an intervener in twelve legal cases, including eleven before the Supreme Court. In all of these cases, DAWN Canada intervened with

---

[57] Joan Meister, "An Early DAWNing (1985–1994)," in Deborah Stienstra and Aileen Wight-Felske, eds., *Making Equality: History of Advocacy and Persons with Disabilities in Canada* (Concord, ON: Captus Press, 2003), p. 227.

[58] Ibid.

[59] Ibid.

[60] Ibid.

[61] Ibid.

the Women's Legal Education and Action Fund (LEAF), with whom they are very closely ideologically aligned. In fact, it was often leaders of LEAF who approached DAWN Canada about the opportunity to intervene in cases and offer a disability analysis to questions of gender discrimination.[62] This alliance has proved important in DAWN Canada's litigation activity, as it was generally LEAF that had funded and undertaken most of the legal analysis presented to the Court, supplanting the need for DAWN to develop independent resources to pursue litigation.

In turning to an analysis of the meaning frames developed within DAWN Canada, we can see how both the meaning frames shared with CCD, as well as divergent ones, pull DAWN to the courtroom. DAWN Canada's values are similarly underpinned by the social model of disability; this is unsurprising given that many of the leaders of DAWN are also involved in CCD, and the organization as a whole is a member of the umbrella organization. The interpretive frames defined previously – the understanding of disadvantage as discrimination and the importance of rights and their effective enforcement – exert a similar type of influence on DAWN as that exerted on CCD and result in perceiving the Court as an appropriate venue for the influencing of public policy.

However, not all interpretive frames are shared across the disability rights movement. DAWN Canada largely emerged out of the exclusion some women felt within the mainstream disability rights movement, and the organization has distinguished itself as a feminist organization. This has led to some ideological differences with CCD. In one of the organization's documents recounting the history (or "herstory") of the organization, the authors describe the relationship between the two organizations in the following terms:

Working with the Council of Canadians with Disabilities (CCD) has been a challenge in many regards. We have, I think, worked hard

---

[62] Interview, November 16, 2007.

together to strengthen our common voice as people with disabilities on the issue of funding to disability groups and other issues related to social policy in Canada such as transportation, etc. We continue to value this process of working together as important in our development as a culture and as a movement. As DAWN Canada, however, we find ourselves at odds with this very patriarchal (male, top-down, hierarchical) model of a group which is not used to the feminist process of consensus and coalition building . . . Discrimination against and ignorance of feminist principles is systemic (wide spread) and I think we must continue to fight where it is necessary.[63]

DAWN Canada's meaning frames assign importance to the unique experiences of exclusion that women with disabilities face precisely because of their gender. This ideological divide has played out in terms of participation in legal cases before the SCC in several ways. First, a substantive division of labor among the two organizations has been established: CCD and DAWN Canada agree that the latter will work on issues directly related to disabled women. Second, the different emphases mean that, generally, when CCD goes to court to speak on behalf of disabled persons, DAWN Canada will also want input into the factum or the opportunity to present a feminist voice on the same issues. For example, in the *Auton* (2004) case, both CCD and DAWN urged the Court to adopt a social model understanding of autism issues; however, DAWN intervened with the Women's LEAF to highlight the uniqueness of gendered disability discrimination:

Although autism is more common amongst boys than girls, girls with autism, particularly as they grow older, may experience compounded and extreme discrimination because of their gendered disability . . . the negative effects will be compounded for girls with autism. For example, women with autism who are institutionalized are liable to experience the most serious forms of gendered disability discrimination – the physical and sexual abuse that is prevalent in

[63] Joan Meister and Shirley Masunda, DAWNing Manual 1998, http://www. dawn canada.net/ENG/ENGspecial.htm (accessed December 12, 1997).

institutions. Because of their gendered disability, women with certain disabilities are in some circumstances vulnerable in ways that neither non-disabled women nor disabled men would be vulnerable. Gendered disability discrimination is not the additive experience of sex plus disability discrimination; it is a distinct experience, more than the sum of its parts.[64]

Similarly, when an issue of importance to the women's movement is being considered, DAWN strives to bring a disability analysis to bear. For example, DAWN has done this in cases dealing with sexual assault and gender discrimination, such as *A. (L.L.) v. B. (A.)*, *R. v. O'Connor*, *R. v. Ewanchuk*, and *R. v. Darrach*.[65] In sum, it is both shared frames across the disability rights movement and contested ones within it that have led DAWN Canada's intervention activity before the Court.

Canadian Disability Rights Council

While DAWN Canada and CCD have established a substantive division of labor, CCD also participated in a tactical division of labor in the late 1980s and early 1990s with the CDRC. The CDRC was a national nonprofit advocacy organization with the goal of securing disability rights through the use of legal mobilization. It was founded in 1987 and collapsed in 1994. CDRC's mandate included 1) promoting the human and civil rights of people with disabilities by sponsoring selective litigation and, in particular, securing the enforcement of the Constitution Act, 1982, including the Charter; 2) undertaking and promoting research on the rights of people with disabilities; 3) assisting people with disabilities to exercise their rights by developing legal skills

---

[64] Factum of the Intervener, Women's Legal Education and Action Fund and Disabled Women's Network Canada, *Auton v. British Columbia*.

[65] *A. (L.L.) v. B. (A.)*, [1995] 4 S.C.R; *R. v. O'Connor*, [1995] 4 S.C.R. 411; *R. v. Ewanchuk*, [1999] 1 S.C.R. 330; *R. v. Darrach*, 2000 SCC 46, [2000] 2 S.C.R. 443.

and leadership among people with disabilities and providing opportunities for people with disabilities to participate in legal education, research, and litigation; and 4) educating people with disabilities, legal professionals, and the public about the rights of people with disabilities and the significance, interpretation, and enforcement of the Charter as it affects the rights of people with disabilities in Canada.[66] CDRC was created

> [b]ecause of the immediate and pressing need for a national organization which is specifically dedicated to representing the interests of disabled persons in key legal cases. It was observed that in the absence of such an organization disabled persons in all parts of Canada would not have an effective means of exercising their Charter rights, nor would the Canadian courts have the assistance of disabled people in interpreting the provisions of the Charter which directly affect their lives. In addition, the representatives at the founding meeting expressed the conviction that this is a crucial time in the development of the law for disabled persons.[67]

Founded by representatives of a number of social movement organizations, including the Advocacy Resource Centre for the Handicapped (ARCH), the Blind Organization of Ontario with Self-Help Tactics, the Canadian Association of the Deaf, COPOH, DAWN, On Our Own (an Ontario organization of persons who have been institutionalized because of mental illness), and People First (a national organization of persons labeled with mental disabilities), the group grew significantly. By the early 1990s, the organization had thirty-three full member organizations and seven associate member organizations.

Closely aligned meaning frames across the two organizations meant that, during its existence, the CDRC focused on strategic litigation while the CCD turned its attention exclusively to lobbying and related

---

[66] CDRC Annual Report, 1993–1994.

[67] Affidavit of Henry Vlug, Board Member of the Canadian Disability Rights Council in *R. v. Swain*, [1991] 1 S.C.R. 933.

activities. The two organizations cooperated closely; before it secured sustainable funding of its own, CDRC was based in the CCD's office, and the two organizations even shared photocopiers.[68] Understanding the relations between the two organizations can help explain the litigation propensity of CCD over time; the division of labor by strategy is crucial in understanding why CCD was relatively inactive for a period of time when it came to strategic litigation activity. Because the CDRC existed to perform the task of legally mobilizing in pursuit of disability rights, the CCD could focus on its lobby activity instead. Although this is not evident in Table 2.2 because of the brief period this division of labor was in operation, it is significant that CCD was absent from the *R. v. Swain* case, which was the first opportunity to apply a substantive equality argument specifically to disability. CDRC underwent a demise in 1994 due to internal conflicts and a subsequent loss of confidence on the part of funders.[69] After the CDRC's demise, the CCD took on the organization's work and mandate (without the funding) and began participating in strategic litigation again.

Canadian Association for Community Living

CACL, formerly known as the Canadian Association for the Mentally Retarded (CAMR), was founded by parents of disabled children in 1958. It is a family-based, community-living organization that advocates advancing the rights of intellectually and developmentally disabled persons with a focus on ending segregation and supporting disabled persons to leave custodial institutions and live improved lives in the community. CACL strives to ensure that intellectually or developmentally disabled persons 1) have the same rights and access to choice, services, and support as all other persons; 2) have the same

---

[68] Interview, November 6, 2007.
[69] Ibid.

opportunities as others to live in freedom and dignity and have the needed support to do so; and 3) are able to articulate and realize their aspirations and their rights. In 1979, a Consumer Advisory Committee was formed in order to advise the organization's president and board. This committee ensured that the concerns of consumers were taken into consideration and was further responsible for making recommendations as to the involvement of consumers in the activities of the association. The organization has changed dramatically over the last thirty years in both its internal identity and activities and its relations with other key organizational actors in the sphere of disability advocacy. Legal mobilization is now part of the organization's strategy – it has intervened in or supported appellants or interveners in nine cases before the SCC. The organization's involvement in one particular case (the first use of strategic litigation by the organization) will be discussed here.

At the heart of the organization's transformation was a group of self-advocates who made up the consumer advisory committee. Their participation in an important legal case, *E. (Mrs.) v. Eve*, which addressed the issues surrounding the wish of a mother to sterilize her intellectually disabled daughter (the substance of the case is discussed in detail in Chapter 3), had a profound and lasting impact on the organization.[70] When the *Eve* case came to the organization's attention, the board of CACL (then CAMR), made up of parents and professionals, considered whether it should apply for leave to intervene before the SCC. The emerging rights model of disability began to influence thinking within the organization. In the words of one activist,

> It was the time of the Charter. So the rights framework was really beginning to take hold and was the subject of much debate. And certainly the association was totally behind the Charter and did really impressive work to get mental disability as a prohibited ground in

---

[70] *E. (Mrs.) v. Eve*, [1986] 2 S.C.R. 388.

section 15. But, when it came to the *Eve* case, [the organization] couldn't reach a real consensus on whether to proceed.[71]

Despite this growing rights consciousness within the organization in the early 1980s, the board was sharply divided on the issues in the *Eve* case, namely, whether consent over sterilization should be exercised by Eve herself or whether the power to make the decision should fall to her mother.[72] In the face of indecision by the board, the persons with disabilities who made up the Consumer Advisory Committee developed a strong rights-protection perspective on what should be argued in *Eve*. At a meeting of the board of directors in 1981, the chairperson of the committee, Barbara Goode, presented a motion, which was unanimously approved, to gain funding required to enable the consumers to retain counsel and represent the interests of citizens with intellectual disabilities as interveners in the case.[73]

Thus, the Consumer Advisory Committee retained counsel and applied for leave to intervene on its own behalf. The committee's participation and eventual victory had a profound effect on the organization and on the movement. A senior staff member described it in the following terms:

I think that was a really important moment for the organization. First, to recognize that people with intellectual disabilities themselves had a clear voice and that voice should be supported right up to the Supreme Court of Canada. And also the idea, that this isn't just about an organization; it's about a movement and there's a difference, and ultimately for the movement this was an important case and if this organization couldn't take the lead it could support another group to do that.[74]

---

[71] Interview, November 12, 2007.
[72] Interview, November 7, 2007.
[73] Interview, January 23, 2008.
[74] Interview, November 12, 2007.

One member of the legal team representing the committee in the *Eve* intervention pointed out the interactive nature of the process and the way in which the consumers asserted their perspective in the development of the legal factum:

> It was a big move for the self-advocates... The board was split right down the middle, with parents wanting the status quo not even conceiving of how to be strategic and litigious. And it was the self-advocates who took the lead on that and they hired us. And it took years for the self-advocates to convince me, or teach me what the heck they were talking about. And I wrote the factum and the factum really was almost the decision. And the factum was really written by the self-advocates, I was simply the pen. Because I didn't get it. I said "oh you know we should put down when therapeutic sterilization might have to occur, to give the court some guidelines" and the self-advocates were adamant and said "absolutely never, no and not" and 9–0 of the Court agreed with the self-advocates. It was the first time in the history of Canada, that people with intellectual disabilities were representing themselves in court.[75]

Barbara Goode, then Chair of the Consumer Advisory Committee, describes the victory and its importance:

> It was the first time ever that people with mental handicaps have taken a case to the highest court in Canada. It took a long time to get there – seven years we were waiting. I am very glad we had a long time to understand the case really well. Before people were just given the operation. We were not always given the choice. It is now against the law to be sterilized without you saying whether you want it or not... The nine judges agreed with us that Eve should not be sterilized without her saying her own decision or choice.[76]

---

[75] Interview, November 16, 2007.

[76] Barbara Goode, quoted in Peter Park et al., "People First: The History and the Dream," in Deborah Stienstra and Aileen Wight-Felske, eds., *Making Equality: History of Advocacy and Persons with Disabilities in Canada* (Concord, ON: Captus Press, 2003).

The *Eve* case had a number of radiating effects within the organization and the movement. First, it empowered the consumers within the organization and reinforced the legitimacy of their voices within the governance processes. While the consumers were developing their case in *Eve*, they also began pushing the local, provincial, and national associations to change their names; they found the name "Association for the Mentally Retarded" offensive and wanted the organization to adopt a "nonlabeling" name. This was initially resisted, but at the annual general meeting in 1985, a group of consumers and their allies walked out in protest. In addition, their claims were bolstered by the victory in *Eve*, and the name was changed in 1986.[77] The adoption of a new name was more than just a superficial change: the ideology of the organization began to change as well. One activist describing the case highlights this change: "That win probably helped the new board, especially after the name change, to start looking at themselves differently and to start listening to self-advocates."[78] Second, there was a broader impact on levels of rights and legal consciousness: new legal battles emerged out of participation in the case. One of the members of the *Eve* committee went on to be a leader in a legal battle in Alberta, on behalf of persons who had been sterilized against their will at the Michener Centre Institution. Third, there were multiorganizational field effects: a group of self-advocates involved in the *Eve* intervention went on to found People First, a consumer organization made up of "people who have been labelled intellectually disabled."[79] The goals of People First are to promote equality and to speak on behalf of people "who have been labelled."

The *Eve* case thus had a lasting impact on CACL and the broader disability movement, as it led to the emergence of a new organization and the growing recognition that legal tactics could be used to

[77] Park et al., "People First."
[78] Interview, November 16, 2007.
[79] Park et al., "People First."

influence social change. In the 1980s, the organization saw a lull as the disability rights agenda championed by disability self-advocates took the national spotlight, but a reinvigorated association in the 1990s pursued new directions consistent with the rights agenda with a focus on deinstitutionalization and the integration of persons with intellectual and developmental disabilities in all spheres of society.[80] In terms of relations with other organizations, CACL has asserted itself as a key partner and player in the sphere of disability rights policy. A senior staff member noted,

> There has been, for a number of years, a real divide between the family-based, community living, intellectual disability movement and the independent living movement which has seen the family movement as patronizing, paternal etc. So we have taken a very clear initiative over the last four or five years to build those bridges.[81]

One indication of improved relations between CCD and the Canadian Association for Independent Living Centres (CAILC), on one hand, and CACL, on the other, was their close cooperation in 2006 and 2007 to launch a large, national event called End Exclusion.[82]

Understanding the transformation of the CAMR into the CACL in terms of evolving interpretive frames can help to explain why the organization is now keen and able to build bridges with others in the disability rights movement and the organization's use of strategic litigation. Similar to CCD, there seems to be an implicit consensus within the organization regarding the use of strategic litigation. CACL has intervened in or supported interveners in nine cases before the SCC, often

---

[80] Neufeldt, "Growth and Evolution of Disability Advocacy."
[81] Interview, November 12, 2007.
[82] Ibid.

closely cooperating with other disability rights interveners.[83] When the organization's former in-house counsel was asked whether there was any criticism within the organization about the use of litigation, he responded: "I was more likely to hear people say 'why aren't we pursuing this case?' I frequently found myself in a defensive position about why the organization wasn't litigating."[84]

From the Canadian National Institute for the Blind to CNIB

CNIB (formerly known as the Canadian National Institute for the Blind) is a national, community-based, registered charity that undertakes research, public education, and advocacy on issues of vision health and provides services and support for persons with vision loss. The organization was founded in 1918, largely to meet the basic needs of blind Canadians, particularly blind veterans returning from World War I, by providing food, clothing, and residences. Since then, CNIB has continued to provide rehabilitation and other services to blind and visually impaired Canadians. Based in Toronto, CNIB is one of the largest organizations operating in the sphere of disability issues. Although CNIB does not claim to speak on behalf of blind persons, it possesses influence on the policy stage as a service provider and charity organization with significant resources.[85] The organization's emphasis is on medical research, rehabilitation, and service provision.

A study that the organization commissioned in the mid-1970s, *Vision Canada: The Unmet Needs of Blind Canadians*, and public consultations on the report led to the emergence in 1975 of the

---

[83] See, for example, *Eaton v. Brant County Board of Education*, [1997] 1 S.C.R. 241; *R. v. Latimer*, [1997] 1 S.C.R. 217; *Council of Canadians with Disabilities v. Via Rail Canada Inc*, 2007 SCC 15, [2007] 1 S.C.R. 650.

[84] Interview, November 7, 2007.

[85] Interview, October 29, 2007.

Blind Organization of Ontario with Self-Help Tactics (BOOST), an advocacy group of blind Canadians. BOOST criticized CNIB on a number of fronts. First, they argued that the agency lacked mechanisms for consumers to have a meaningful voice in the policies, programs, and decision-making processes of the organization. Second, they criticized that the majority of the organization's directors were not blind or visually impaired.[86] In many ways, the Canadian National Institute for the Blind represented a classic *for* organization guided by the charity model of disability rejected by the disability rights movement.

In 2006, the organization underwent a rebranding; the organization is now known solely by its acronym, CNIB. In their 2005/2006 annual report, CNIB's president Jim Sanders wrote:

> By now you've probably noticed our new appearance. Fresh, modern and welcoming, our new look reflects more than just an aesthetic change – it is a sign of an organization that has entered a whole new era. Today's CNIB is vastly different from the CNIB that was founded in 1918. But we are also worlds apart from the CNIB of 10 years ago. And that's because in 2006, we took a bold step and challenged conventional views of what CNIB does and whom it serves. We challenged ourselves, and then you, to think of CNIB in an entirely new way. We also dared to see vision differently: as a spectrum, from full vision to no vision, with most of us falling somewhere in between. We reached out and became much more inclusive. The CNIB of today is committed to the vision health of all Canadians.[87]

Despite rebranding and the "transformation" discourse used in the previous quote, the CNIB continues to focus on rehabilitation, service provision, and charity fundraising rather than rights promotion

---

[86] Colleen Watters, "History of Advocacy Organizations of the Blind in Canada."
[87] CNIB Annual Report, 2005–2006.

or antidiscrimination advocacy.[88] In internal discussions on the organization's rebranding, there was debate over whether the organization name should be changed to Canadian National Institute *of* the Blind, instead of *for* the Blind. The president argues that this was rejected "because our expertise is technical, CNIB does not speak for persons with vision loss, we don't speak for them. We speak for ourselves. We speak on the professional side. We believe that persons with vision loss should speak for themselves."[89]

There are some signs, however, that the organization has the potential to become more active in equality advocacy in the future. First, the organization is establishing an advocacy network while also, according to the president, being careful to "respect that membership groups, consumer groups, or the so-called *of* the blind, rather than *for* the blind, still have an important role to play."[90] Second, the research agenda, although largely concentrated on medical research for vision health, has also focused at times on the barriers that persons with vision loss face in society.[91] The significance of these steps should not be ignored, nor should they be overemphasized. In contrast to the substantial resources the organization possesses (see Table 2.5), the activity on the advocacy and rights agenda is limited.[92] This contrasts with the fundamental paradigm shift in the conceptualization of disability among the grassroots and its influence on other, traditional organizations, such as the CACL.

To date, the CNIB has not participated in any cases before the SCC, nor has it taken legal cases to lower courts or Human Rights

---

[88] An analysis of the CNIB Annual Report, 2006–2007 showed that 55 percent of funding was spent on rehabilitation services, and this represented the single largest expenditure.

[89] Interview, October 29, 2007.

[90] Ibid.

[91] CNIB Annual Report, 2006–2007.

[92] These figures do not include CNIB's capital assets, which are substantial (over $100 million CAD); CNIB Annual Reports, 2004–2008.

Table 2.5. *CNIB Revenue and Expenditure, 2004–2008*

Year	Revenue (CAD)	Expenditure
2004	$57,562,000	$62,683,000
2005	$59,699,000	$47,098,000
2006	$68,560,000	$63,154,000
2007	$93,001,000	$92,682,000
2008	$82,109,000	$94,001,000

Sources: CNIB Audited Financial Statements, 2004–2008.

Commissions. The president feels that this is because legal challenges are fundamentally an individual endeavor, as opposed to a collective one: "My understanding is that human rights cases have to be brought by individuals, not by organizations, which is why you don't see CNIB there."[93] The organization has provided informal support to particular individuals who have launched actions regarding discriminatory practices against persons with visual impairments. This has included the provision of transportation services and secretarial support. And, although CNIB has not provided financial support for legal actions, they have not completely ruled this out for the future.[94]

Although it is difficult to attribute causality in negative cases (that is, accounting for the reasons why the CNIB has never used strategic litigation) due to the myriad of possible explanations, we can nonetheless make some tentative claims based on the discussion above about the correlation between the lack of "rights talk" in the organization's public-facing services and the eschewing of litigation. The CNIB is one of the oldest, most well-established and well-resourced disability organizations in Canada; it is a charity and service organization and focuses mainly on rehabilitation activities and services. There is little to

[93] Interview, October 29, 2007.
[94] Although there is no policy and no fund for this, the president of CNIB stated that it would be strictly ad hoc based on circumstances (Interview, October 29, 2007).

no mention in the organization's main publications of human rights or the barriers faced by persons with vision impairments.[95] Despite being situated within the same LOS as the other organizations discussed here, and being significantly better financed than most of them, the CNIB has never used strategic litigation to pursue its objectives: this goes against the expectations of RM and LOS theories. However, the correlation is consistent with the argument I have put forward on interpretive frames and their role in shaping the decision to use strategic litigation, or at least consider it as an appropriate method of advocacy.

ARCH Disability Law Centre

An organization that has been a key player in strategic litigation with a disability rights perspective is the ARCH Disability Law Centre based in Toronto. This section focuses less on interpretive frames because the very existence of the organization already signals a focus and willingness to use strategic litigation. Instead, I explore the role that ARCH plays in supporting and advancing the strategic delivery of legal services for disabled persons. ARCH participated in twenty-one cases before the Supreme Court between 1985 and 2007 (see Table 2.6).[96]

ARCH is a specialty legal aid clinic with a mandate to defend and advance the equality rights of disabled persons. Despite a provincial mandate, ARCH's work often entails significant engagement at the federal appellate level. ARCH was founded in 1979 under its previous name, Advocacy Resource Centre for the Handicapped, by David Baker, an equality lawyer who served as its executive director until 1999. He then left and established a law firm which is also

---

[95] I am referring specifically to the Annual Reports and CNIB's Web site.

[96] This figure may be an underestimation; it groups together cases that may have been argued separately.

Table 2.6. *ARCH Disability Law Centre Participation before the SCC, 1985–2007*

Case name	Year	ARCH Participation
Ont. Human Rights Comm. v. Simpsons-Sears (O'Malley)	1985	Intervened on behalf of the CAMR and COPOH
Bhinder v. CN	1985	Intervened on behalf of the CAMR
Andrews v. Law Society of British Columbia	1989	Intervened on behalf of the Coalition of COPOH
Canadian Council of Churches v. Canada (Minister of Employment and Immigration)	1992	Intervened on behalf of the COPOH and the Quebec Multi Ethnic Association for the Integration of Handicapped People
Central Okanagan School District No. 23 v. Renaud	1992	Intervened on behalf of Disabled People for Employment Equity and Persons United for Self Help in Ontario (P.U.S.H.)
Weatherall v. Canada (Attorney General)	1993	Intervened on behalf of the COPOH
Rodriguez v. British Columbia (Attorney General)	1993	Intervened on behalf of the COPOH
Battlefords and District Co-operative Ltd. v. Gibbs	1996	Intervened on behalf of the Canadian Mental Health Association
Eaton v. Brant County Board of Education	1997	Represented the appellants throughout the process: from the Special Education Tribunal to the Supreme Court
Eldridge v. British Columbia (Attorney General)	1997	Intervened on behalf of the Canadian Association of the Deaf, the Canadian Hearing Society, and the CCD
British Columbia (Superintendent of Motor Vehicles) v. British Columbia (Council of Human Rights)	1999	Intervened on behalf of the CCD
Bese v. British Columbia (Forensic Psychiatric Institute)	1999	Intervened on behalf of the Canadian Mental Health Association

Table 2.6 (*continued*)

Case name	Year	ARCH Participation
Orlowski v. British Columbia (Forensic Pychiatric Istitute)	1999	Intervened on behalf of the Canadian Mental Health Association
R. v. LePage	1999	Intervened on behalf of the Canadian Mental Health Association
Winko v. British Columbia (Forensic Psychiatric Institute)	1999	Intervened on behalf of the Canadian Mental Health Association
Lovelace v. Ontario	2000	Intervened on behalf of the CCD
Nova Scotia (Workers' Compensation Board) v. Martin; Nova Scotia (Workers' Compensation Board) v. Lasettr	2003	Intervened on behalf of the Ontario Network of Injured Workers Groups
Auton (Guardian ad litem of) v. British Columbia (Attorney General)	2004	Intervened with co-counsel on behalf of the CACL and the CCD
Newfoundland (Treasury Board) v. N.A.P.E.	2004	Intervened on behalf of the CACL, the Canadian Hearing Society, and the CCD
Nova Scotia (Minister of Health) v. J.J.	2005	Intervened on behalf of People First of Canada and CACL
Hilewitz v. Canada (Minister of Citizenship and Immigration); De Jong v. Canada (Minister of Citizenship and Immigration)	2005	Intervened on behalf of the CACL and Ethno-Racial People with Disabilities Coalition of Ontario
Tranchemontagne v. Ontario (Director, Disability Support Program)	2006	Intervened on behalf of the Empowerment Council – Centre for Addiction and Mental Health
McGill University Health Centre (Montreal General Hospital) v. Syndicat des employés del' Hôpital général de Montréal	2007	Intervened on behalf of the Ontario Network of Injured Workers Groups
Council of Canadians with Disabilities v. VIA Rail Canada Inc.	2007	Intervened on behalf of Transportation Action Now, the Alliance for Equality of Blind Canadians, the CACL, and the Canadian Hard of Hearing Association

heavily involved in rights litigation. ARCH is a nonprofit, charitable, membership-based organization primarily funded by Legal Aid Ontario.[97] There are eleven staff members working at the clinic, a number that has remained largely consistent over the course of the organization's history.[98] Legal Aid Ontario funds the organization for nine and a half positions (one and a half support staff, one office manager, two community legal workers, four lawyers, and one executive director). ARCH also raises money independently to fund another two to three positions, which is rare among the specialty legal clinics.[99] Among interviewees there was general agreement that ARCH plays an important role in the disability community but also suffers from a lack of resources. For example, one former ARCH board member said, "I think one of the most challenging issues is they are underfunded, it's extremely hard to retain the expertise they require in a lawyer, it's extremely hard to retain the skill set that they need."[100]

The membership of ARCH consists of over sixty disability consumer and service organizations, and the staff reports to a consumer-controlled volunteer board of directors. ARCH is one of the few umbrella organizations in the disability movement to straddle organizations *of* persons with disabilities and organizations *for* persons with disabilities (generally service organizations or agencies). David Baker, reflecting on ARCH's twenty-fifth anniversary, commented on this:

> Often overlooked was the generosity of spirit and vision demonstrated by the "old guard" of voluntary organizations. Rather than attempt to stifle the voices of the emerging disability organizations,

---

[97] Legal Aid Ontario is a public agency with a mandate to promote access to justice throughout Ontario for low-income individuals.

[98] ARCH Disability Law Centre Strategic Plan, 2007–2010.

[99] Interview, November 9, 2007.

[100] Interview, October 26, 2007.

some charities encouraged and supported them. Like the government, many of these organizations recognized the need for change, and therefore welcomed the critical voices of their "consumers" as they moved to de-institutionalize and de-stigmatize the way they served persons with disabilities.[101]

Among these organizations, the Canadian Hearing Society, the Canadian and Ontario Associations for the Mentally Retarded (now the CACL and Community Living Ontario), and the Canadian Mental Health Association joined with grassroots organizations to establish ARCH's coalition structure.[102] Through this network and a summary advice and referral service, ARCH manages to stay connected to the grassroots. This provides an overview of the issues important on the ground:

What we have is summary advice and referral, that's basically how we stay grounded and connected to the community so we know what's happening out there and what kind of issues are important to the community on a day-to-day basis and the one we hear of most frequently is discrimination in employment, failure to accommodate.[103]

We have new groups coming up all the time [and] we have groups that don't self-identify as persons with disabilities. For example, persons with mental health issues do not necessarily self-identify as persons with disabilities. And we have things like the ageing population, and we know statistically elderly persons are more likely to have disabilities . . . So the whole population continues to change, and you want to be active in the community and connected with these groups to have a feel for what the context is on an ongoing basis.[104]

[101] ARCH Disability Law Centre, "*ARCH Celebrating 25 Years.*"
[102] Ibid.
[103] Interview, October 30, 2007.
[104] Ibid.

In terms of organizational ecology, the executive vice president of the CACL pointed out the benefit of the model of a specialist legal center working for the community as a whole:

> The [relationship with ARCH] works out really well for us. In terms of a model, it's really good. They have a specialist expertise. They're building a theory, disability rights theory and understanding, and I think it does a much better job of serving the whole community rather than everyone doing their own little bits and pieces.[105]

The benefit of this model for the whole community is that ARCH, as long as it maintains its credibility within the disability rights movement, can select the best cases to take forward on any given issue. In many instances, ARCH has heard about a case and then reached out to their membership to identify a party, which the organization has then served as counsel to. One ARCH staff member identified this as a key component of effective strategic litigation:

> If a case raises a number of issues that are important for the disability community, one of the first things you would be doing is going through your membership list and saying who do we have who is really engaged in this issue, who can add a great deal to it, bring a lot of knowledge to it and would be an ideal party before the court. That's just good strategic litigation . . . What I envisage is becoming more and more and more strategic. I would have to say at this point it's less proactive and more reactive; and I would have to add as well, if we succeed in becoming a real powerhouse of strategic litigation, there are still going to be cases from time to time that aren't on our shortlist but we will just get pulled into them because we have to, we simply have to.[106]

This model is preferable to individual organizations taking weaker cases or making less robust legal arguments on their own, on an ad hoc basis, because it may lead to unfavorable precedents. However, it

[105] Interview, November 12, 2007.
[106] Interview, October 30, 2007.

is not without its own difficulties. ARCH often finds itself at the crux of many of the tensions within the disability community.

> Sometimes you will have very strong divisions, and one of ARCH's constant challenges is to reach some kind of consensus or to develop a position that is not going to send some of our membership in another direction. There is a need to balance all of those factors out . . . As lawyers it is our job to build consensus. We have the tools to develop a position that is acceptable.[107]

ARCH has also identified the enhancement of access to justice for disabled persons as one of its two main priorities in its most recent strategic plan.[108] This includes orienting the organization back toward the legal clinic system and a desire to stay connected with them. It also includes looking at the processes at the different tribunals and encouraging them to become more accessible.[109]

> Access to justice is a grave concern for us and we are very aware of it because we are on the frontline. There are a lot of cases that just don't get picked up because they don't fall within ARCH's mandate . . . We do what we can when it comes to access to justice, and it will be one of our focuses in the future.[110]

ARCH fulfills its mandate in many ways: through law reform initiatives, community development and information, a telephone summary advice and referral service, public legal education, and test case litigation. The litigation strategy and access to justice goals are the main focus of this book, but these are understood to be situated in a context where the other activities are all happening in parallel. Phyllis Gordon, former ARCH executive director, strongly emphasizes the range of activities that ARCH undertakes in trying to enhance the equality

---

[107] Ibid.
[108] ARCH Disability Law Centre Strategic Plan, 2007–2010.
[109] Interview, November 9, 2007.
[110] Interview, October 30, 2007.

and inclusion of persons with disabilities in society. Acknowledging the limits of test case litigation, she argues:

> We're here to get the task done... It's not always the courts that are going to solve something and it takes forever to get a decision actually followed. So we just try to keep working all the different avenues... Because while you do have the AODA [Access for Ontarians with Disabilities Act] and you have *Eldridge* and various cases... it's not trickling down. Our board is pretty interested in it trickling down.[111]

Baker noted this has been a guiding principle all along: "The basic approach of test cases at ARCH... was litigation as a last-resort. There was an incredible amount of success with law reform through the 80s and early 90s, so it really didn't make a lot of sense to be in court on very many issues anyway."[112]

ARCH considers test cases to be "those cases where a court or tribunal is looking at an issue for the first time, where an appellate court is deciding an issue that will affect a large number of people, or where there is a disability analysis that should be brought to the litigation."[113] After a difficult period when leadership difficulties hampered the organization's work, ARCH has, in the 2000s, again become a crucial player in the disability movement's use of litigation.

The organization adopted in July 2001, for the first time, test case selection criteria to manage the intake of potential cases to be used for strategic litigation. This has been refined several times, and the most recent test case selection criteria were adopted by the board of directors in November 2005. The selection criteria consist of a series of questions broadly addressing a range of organizational and legal issues. A significant concern, reflective of past tensions, is how a

---

[111] Interview, November 9, 2007.

[112] Interview, October 25, 2007.

[113] ARCH Disability Law Centre Web site, http://www.archdisabilitylaw.ca (accessed October 7, 2007).

case might impact the community. The organization considers whether there would be a disadvantage to the movement taking the case and poses this question: "Are we really going so far out on a limb that the community would be horrified?"[114] One member of ARCH's staff summed up the case selection process in the following way: "essentially what we are looking for are cases that are going to make a difference on a systemic level for the disability community. So all of the factors that we have in our long list are aimed at that one core question."[115]

The organization has actively considered how to be most effective in litigation, and this necessarily addresses the balance between being reactive and proactive. Strategic considerations involve two key issues: one is whether to support cases from the early stages versus intervening only at the appellate level.

> We have to do some strategic thinking about when we want to go by way of action or application and get in on the ground floor and appear before a tribunal when an issue appears for the first time . . . And when it is safe to wait until the issues have completely gelled and the evidence is in and you know what the specific issues are that are going to have a day-to-day impact on the community of persons with disabilities. So there is some trading off.[116]

The advantage of taking a case from the beginning is that the organization can largely control the creation of the record and develop law from the ground up. This also gives ARCH a much bigger role in how the case turns out.[117] However, the cost and risk involved in such cases are also very high. Although intervening in cases that have reached the appellate court level is generally less costly and time-consuming over the long run than taking a case from the administrative court level, it also has the disadvantage of the argument being diluted. In many key

[114] Interview, November 9, 2007.
[115] Interview, October 30, 2007.
[116] Ibid.
[117] Ibid.

cases in the Supreme Court, more than ten groups or individuals were granted leave to intervene, which makes it extremely difficult to know how any single legal argument made by an intervener may influence a case. By taking a case from the beginning, "you will have a much bigger role in how the case turns out at the end of the day than if you are simply one of many voices who turn up at the Supreme Court of Canada and offer a disability analysis or some other analysis that hopefully will be of assistance to the Court.'[118] A number of interviewees felt the route of taking a case from the lower levels may become increasingly important, as anecdotal evidence suggests there is a trend to cut down on the number of interveners that the Supreme Court grant leave.[119] The other advantage of being a direct participant in the case is that a lot more time is granted in appearing before the Supreme Court than as an intervener.[120]

The other strategic consideration is whether to focus resources on several priority issues or to accept that the organization will be pulled in to cases that may not be identified as priorities, but would remain unaddressed from a disability perspective if ARCH did not get involved. This hijacking of an agenda often seems an unavoidable reality. When asked about the selection of cases, one ARCH staff member had this to say:

> Well it depends on what's going on and what needs our attention because there are some cases where ARCH just absolutely has to be

---

[118] Ibid.

[119] At least four interviewees raised this point independently. There was some speculation as to why this may be the case. Theories included 1) growing confidence on the part of the Court in handling Charter issues, 2) a desire within the Court to streamline the court's functioning and use resources more strategically and hence limit the amount of scientific evidence relied on, and 3) response on the part of the Court to the writing of right-wing academics on the "activist" nature of the Court. On the other hand, one interviewee wondered whether perhaps this was instead simply anecdotal and impressionistic as opposed to a documented trend.

[120] Typically 60 minutes as an appellant versus approximately 10 or 15 for an intervener.

there – provided we can get intervention status – so we're going to have to drop everything and do up our application to intervene.[121]

Through much of ARCH's efforts, the Supreme Court has become an important site of disability rights activism. Although this activism has often been more passive and defensive than the movement might have originally preferred, the organization has also begun to approach cases in a more strategic manner and, in general, has enjoyed relatively broad judicial support for disability perspectives on equality.

CONCLUSIONS

In deconstructing the shift from the medical model of disability to the social model, we begin to see that various ideational components of the social model's meaning frames have played a crucial role in establishing the legitimacy of the use of strategic litigation within the disability rights movement. The reunderstanding of disadvantage as discrimination, related heightened levels of rights consciousness across the community, and the shared vision of a barrier-free society on a cross-disability basis resulted in the use of law reform and litigation strategies possessing great legitimacy among adherents of the movement.

Because the shared rights consciousness was developing among disability groups (as well as others) in the late 1970s – around the same time that the Charter was introduced – it is difficult to disentangle causes and effects and complex interactions among various explanatory factors. There is an ever-expanding body of sociolegal scholarship, which emphasizes the mutually constitutive relationship between law and society, and the case of disability rights and legal protections in Canada seems quintessential of this type of relationship. The evidence presented here supports Engel and Munger's recursive theory of rights and identity.

[121] Interview, October 30, 2007.

The shift to the human rights approach, the expansion in the population of consumer-led organizations, and the adoption of the Charter of Rights and Freedoms laid the foundation for the adoption of litigation strategies by some of the key consumer organizations. When the identity associated with the notion of disability is prescribed by the social model of disability, as opposed to the previously existing medical model, the expansion of rights becomes the most appropriate public policy tool for addressing the issues that disabled persons face. By extension, legal mobilization – collective action based on those rights – becomes an acceptable method of influencing public policy, and the likelihood that it will be used as such increases. This does not mean that lobbying or protest is less appropriate, just that the use of legal mobilization becomes more appropriate than it was before the paradigm shift. The paradigm shift also led to the establishment of a legal center (ARCH Disability Law Centre) that works to support law reform and test case litigation.

The findings here also demonstrate that collective actors do not operate within political opportunity structures (POS) and LOS in isolation: they are presented with opportunities for competition, conflict, and cooperation with other actors in a multiorganizational field. These opportunities can be ephemeral or enduring. As this chapter shows, implicit or explicit divisions of labor may emerge within the movement that can explain the litigation propensity of particular organizations over time. The division of labor can be substantive, which influences the issues and cases in which groups become involved. Examples of this are DAWN's focus on disabled women's issues in its legal interventions and CCD prioritizing its disability analysis. Otherwise, the division of labor could be tactical, with one group focusing on lobbying and another on legal mobilization – the alliance between CCD and the CDRC exemplifies this, with the former concentrating on law reform and the latter on strategic litigation during its existence. This dynamic also highlights the influence that the emergence and attrition of organizations has on strategy choice: CCD leaders felt compelled to take up the use of strategic litigation again when the CDRC collapsed.

The theoretical approach adopted here, which accommodates the social movement variables, is not incompatible with explanations that focus on the mobilization of organizational resources or POS or LOS in accounting for litigation strategies and outcomes. As the empirical examples demonstrate, factors such as funding for litigation, the availability of legal "support structures," favorable judicial reception, and support from political elites clearly matter in the decision to use litigation. However, these approaches need to be complemented by an understanding of the ways in which movement organizations construct meaning frames both through their own internal dialectical processes as well as through their relations with each other. Only then can we begin to understand causality; for example, resources and structures can also be analyzed as dependent variables. Collective actors, if their meaning frames encourage them to value strategic litigation in and of itself, may take action to change structures and develop resources in order to pursue legal mobilization; the case of CCD developing a funding pot specifically for test case litigation is just one example of organizational agency.

In Chapter 3, I explore some of the outcomes of this legal mobilization. Through tracing developments in the judicial treatment of disability issues by analyzing several key cases, we can assess whether or not the SCC has adopted a similar rights discourse and analysis on disability issues in the post-Charter era.

3

Disability Equality and Opportunity in the Supreme Court of Canada

INTRODUCTION

Achieving constitutional recognition of disability rights was an enormous legal and political victory for disability activists in Canada. Rights on paper, however, are simply the first step on a long journey toward true equality on the ground. As shown in Chapter 2, disability advocacy organizations in Canada have been among those that have seized the potential of the equality rights contained within the Charter, and they have relied, to a large extent, on the Supreme Court and lower courts and tribunals to do so. Organizations within the movement have influenced emerging notions of human rights and equality, and they have legally mobilized to advance their own conceptions of the appropriate paradigms of disability, discrimination, and accommodation of difference. Here I address the following questions: What has the Charter provided to Canadians with disabilities in terms of equality? How has the Supreme Court of Canada (SCC) interpreted what equality means? Have the aspirations been met of disability rights activists who campaigned so vigorously for the inclusion of disability as a protected ground in Section 15 of the Charter?

The fact that the Court has the power to shape understandings of constitutional and legislative rights and protections is beyond doubt. By tracing trends in case law on equality and disability issues, we can understand why it is important from a policy perspective that groups have turned to the courts. The incremental character of judicial policy making means that the ultimate legal objectives of strategic litigation activity can be reached only through the gradual development of discrete rules that eventually form the basis of a new, overarching constitutional doctrine. Because traditional legal analysis can downplay (or ignore) the political environment of legal mobilization, this chapter moves beyond a focus simply on arguments made before the Court and resulting legal doctrine to explore the interaction between organizational agency and judicial decisions.

In this chapter, I argue that by participating, both proactively and reactively, in cases before the SCC, disability activists have sought to influence the way human rights of persons with disabilities are interpreted and implemented. I find that, in many cases, judicial decisions have advanced equality policy, but there have also been some significant losses of important cases and policy battles from the perspective of disability rights advocates. While laying out the key trends in case law (summarized in Table 3.1), I broadly discuss how key disability rights organizations have approached the opportunities and complexities of undertaking legal strategies. I begin by describing the immediate post-Charter period and the role of legal strategies in formulating an approach to equality that avoided the pitfalls of formal definitions of equality as neutral provisions. I also explore the first post-Charter disability-specific cases. I then assess the extent to which the potential of the first proactive disability cases was realized in the 1990s and show how difficult it is to remain in control of a strategic litigation agenda. Next, I turn my attention to a series of immigration cases that illustrate this. The analysis culminates with the important 2007 decision *Council of Canadians with Disabilities v. VIA Rail Canada Inc.*, an important legal win that nonetheless has left some activists concerned about the future of disability equality in Canada.

Table 3.1. *Key Disability Equality Cases before the SCC, 1985–2007*

Case name	Year	Key issues
Ont. Human Rights Comm. v. Simpsons-Sears (O'Malley)	1985	Unintentional discrimination/ adverse effect discrimination and reasonable accommodation.
E. (Mrs.) v. Eve	1986	Consent to perform a nontherapeutic sterilization of a woman with a mental disability.
Andrews v. Law Society of British Columbia	1989	A substantive theory of equality.
Rodriguez v. British Columbia (Attorney General)	1993	Terminally ill patient seeks assistance to commit suicide.
Eaton v. Brant County Board of Education	1997	Whether placement in special education class, absent parental consent, infringes the child's Charter equality rights.
Eldridge v. British Columbia (Attorney General)	1997	Right to sign language interpretation in provision of health care as a form of accommodation.
R. v. Latimer	2001	Defense of necessity to justify mercy killing of disabled daughter.
Auton (Guardian ad litem of) v. British Columbia (Attorney General)	2004	Whether Province's refusal to fund treatment violates equality rights.
Hilewitz v. Canada (Minister of Citizenship and Immigration); De Jong v. Canada (Minister of Citizenship and Immigration)	2005	Individualized assessments when considering whether the "excessive demands" provision regarding children with intellectual disabilities is applicable in immigration residency applications.
Council of Canadians with Disabilities v. VIA Rail Canada Inc.	2007	The duty to accommodate passengers with disabilities; duty to not create new barriers.

FORMULATING A SUBSTANTIVE APPROACH TO EQUALITY: LAYING THE FOUNDATION

In the immediate post-Charter period, the mid- to late 1980s, the key equality-promoting nongovernmental organizations sought to ride the wave of antidiscrimination protections implemented in the Charter and Human Rights Codes. This incorporated a much broader spectrum of groups than just those concerned with discrimination based on disability. One disability rights activist highlights the explicit effort made to coordinate litigation strategies across these groups.

> There were a lot of groups in Canada that felt like they had a lot of affinity for each other. And we called our type of group "equality-seeking groups". There was LEAF [The Women's Legal Education and Defence Fund], Women and the Law, Multi-ethnic council, Aboriginal organizations, and we had EGALE [the national organization advocating for the Lesbian, Gay, Bisexual and Transsexual (LGBT) community]. We felt we had a lot in common. We all wanted protection from discrimination by law and the Charter was the means by which we hoped to achieve this. We realized that whatever jurisprudence we developed for one of our groups would affect the others ... and very fundamental things would have to be decided by the Supreme Court in the first cases ... So we were together on the phone constantly with the equality-seeking groups. When the others found an opening to develop jurisprudence ... we all jumped in. That's the reason we were involved in the non-disability type cases. It was very deliberate and very strategic.[1]

It is significant that such a wide variety of groups coordinated their approaches to strategic litigation; a shared agenda emerged in terms of laying the foundation for a constitutional understanding of substantive equality. In brief, substantive equality anticipates differential treatment of disadvantaged groups. It acknowledges that, although norms, rules, and laws may appear neutral on their surface, they are in fact often

---

[1] Interview, November 6, 2007.

constructed in favor of a dominant group to naturalize and maintain its privilege. For Anna Kirkland, the novel element in a substantive equality analysis "[i]s the turn to accommodations for difference and the acceptance that difference may be insoluble, and that ignoring it may be the height of oppression rather than the best hope for seeing past it."[2] A substantive equality approach is also an important component of what Ruth Colker has coined an antisubordination approach. According to this perspective, social and legal policies should help groups, such as women, gay men and lesbians, racial minorities, and persons with disabilities, overcome a history of oppression. For Colker, an antisubordination perspective

> allows one to talk about "different treatment" such as affirmative action or reasonable accommodations as a remedy to inequality without being accused of having created inappropriate discrimination through remedies. Under an anti-subordination perspective, different treatment is only problematic when grounded in a context of lack of power or subordination.[3]

In addition to this broader cross-social movement strategizing to advance this substantive equality perspective, disability-specific issues were also debated within the movement. One explicit decision that came out of these discussions between leaders of the disability movement and their legal counsel was the desire to avoid taking a disability-specific case before a substantive equality approach was established by the SCC. The reasons for this were two-fold: First, by laying the foundation for substantive equality jurisprudence, equality-seeking groups were able to assert broad principles that would protect against the creation of a hierarchy of equalities among the different equality-seeking

---

[2] Anna Kirkland, *Fat Rights: Dilemmas of Difference and Personhood* (New York: New York University Press, 2008), p. 127.

[3] Ruth Colker, *When is Separate Unequal? A Disability Perspective* (New York: Cambridge University Press, 2009), p. 14.

groups. Second, activists and their counsel recognized that the disability discrimination cases often require remedies that are more complex and/or have higher costs than remedies for discrimination on other grounds, such as race or gender. Activists felt that without a broad legal precedent of substantive equality, the Court might be unwilling to order the types of remedies required in disability discrimination cases.

> Essentially the strategy involved having the first cases in the Supreme Court of Canada not be disability cases because it would have scared the living daylights out of the Court... The strategy that was developed around litigation involved recognition on the part of the disability community that there were huge dollar signs attached to major issues. The decision that was made was to not go in with disability cases right off the bat. So for example *Simpson-Sears [O'Malley]* and *Bhinder*, were not disability cases, [but] both of them were hugely important for the disability community and the arguments, of course, largely focused on disability, which was great.[4]

For these reasons, it was a decade before the first active, direct-participant test case, *Eaton*, reached the Court in 1996. However, concepts such as "reasonable accommodation," which are crucial for the achievement of disability equality, were raised in cases brought by other equality-seeking groups.

A first common cross-movement goal was to expand the concept of discrimination beyond just intentional discrimination. The notion of indirect discrimination is based on the idea that an action that is seemingly neutral can be discriminatory if it results in inequality.[5] This understanding of discrimination underlies the barrier-removal and reasonable accommodation approaches to achieving equality for people with disabilities. Yvonne Peters writes, "while people with disabilities often encounter attitudes that are blatantly and intentionally discriminatory, they are more likely to encounter barriers that are

---

[4] Interview, October 25, 2007.
[5] Endicott, "Key Trends in Case Law," p. 5.

unintentional, but that discriminate against them because of a world based on able-bodied norms."[6] The first Charter case in which groups representing persons with disabilities intervened in the mid-1980s, *Ontario Human Rights Commission and Theresa O'Malley v. Simpsons-Sears Limited*, made explicit the prohibition of unintentional and indirect discrimination.[7] The appellant, Theresa O'Malley, alleged that her employers at a department store violated the Ontario Human Rights Act's protection against discrimination based on creed: she was periodically required to work Friday evenings and Saturdays, which required her to act contrary to the tenets of her Seventh Day Adventist beliefs. The crux of the case was whether her employer's demand, imposed on all employees for business reasons, discriminated because compliance required her to act contrary to her religious beliefs but did not affect her colleagues. Two of the key disability organizations, the Canadian Association for the Mentally Retarded (now Canadian Association for Community Living [CACL]) and the Coalition of Provincial Organizations of the Handicapped (COPOH; now Council of Canadians with Disabilities [CCD]) intervened to advance their understanding of indirect discrimination:

> Protection against practices creating discriminatory effects is crucial for disabled people because the individuality of their impairments makes them vulnerable to a wide range of superficially neutral obstacles ... As a practical matter a narrow interpretation of the word discrimination will expose disabled people and members of other protected classes to unreasonable and arbitrary barriers to equality, in cases where malicious motive cannot be proven.[8]

---

[6] Yvonne Peters, "Twenty Years of Litigating for Disability Equality Rights: An Assessment by the Council of Canadians with Disabilities," January 26, 2004, p. 10, available at http://www.ccdonline.ca/en/humanrights/promoting/20years (accessed September 23, 2007).

[7] *Ont. Human Rights Comm. v. Simpsons-Sears*, [1985] 2 S.C.R. 536.

[8] CAMR and COPOH, "Factum of the Interveners," *Ont. Human Rights Comm. v. Simpsons-Sears*, [1985] 2 S.C.R. 536.

In 1985, the SCC issued concurrent judgments in *O'Malley* and another discrimination-on-grounds-of-religion case, *Bhinder*, which addressed the balance between accommodation of religious requirements (in this case, the wearing of the Sikh turban) and occupational requirements.[9] The Court ruled that human rights law, at both the provincial and federal level, implicitly includes both direct and indirect (or "adverse effect") discrimination and promoted the concept of the "duty to accommodate."[10] In the *O'Malley* judgment, the Court held:

> An employment rule, honestly made for sound economic and business reasons and equally applicable to all to whom it is intended to apply, may nevertheless be discriminatory if it affects a person or persons differently from others to whom it is intended to apply . . . In the case of adverse effect discrimination, the employer has a duty to take reasonable steps to accommodate short of undue hardship in the operation of the employer's business.[11]

Although these cases dealt explicitly with issues of discrimination on religious grounds, disability and other groups also seized the opportunity to influence the Court's reasoning on these issues. This laid an important foundation for disability-specific cases in the future. The concept of unintentional discrimination and the corresponding duty to accommodate is a central implication of a social model understanding

---

[9] *Bhinder v. CN*, [1985] 2 S.C.R. 561.

[10] In *Bhinder*, the Court affirmed the importance of the concept of accommodation: "the duty to accommodate, which is so essential an aspect of human rights law (see *O'Malley, supra*), is necessary for ensuring protection of the individual under the Act from adverse effect discrimination." However, in *Bhinder*, the Court went on to put limits on the duty to accommodate, and in the end Mr. Bhinder lost his case. The judgment laid out the principle that when an instance of adverse effect discrimination could be characterized as a bona fide occupational requirement or qualification (BFOR/Q), there was no duty to accommodate. A BFOR/Q is a limitation that is imposed by the employer in good faith and "in the sincerely held belief that such limitation is imposed in the interests of the adequate performance of the work involved with all reasonable dispatch, safety and economy"; *Ont. Human Rights Comm. v. Borough of Etobicoke*, [1982] 1 S.C.R. 202.

[11] *Ont. Human Rights Comm. v. Simpsons-Sears*, [1985] 2 S.C.R. 536.

of disability. It also highlights the effects that the broader social movement environment can have on opportunities to become involved in strategic litigation; *O'Malley* and *Bhinder* have no relevance to disability in light of the medical model. It is only through the lens of the social model that linkages between groups advocating for equality on the grounds of religious beliefs and disability rights groups can be understood.

One of the most significant early interpretations of Section 15 of the Charter was offered in *Andrews v. Law Society of British Columbia* in 1989.[12] In this case, the appellant successfully challenged the provision of a provincial statute that made only Canadian citizens eligible to be called to the bar in British Columbia. The Court stated that it should be recognized that not all differences in treatment will result in inequality and that identical treatment may result in inequality. This helped lay the foundation for substantive equality, building on *O'Malley*:

> ... discrimination may be described as a distinction, whether intentional or not but based on grounds relating to personal characteristics of the individual or group, which has the effect of imposing burdens, obligations, or disadvantages on such individual or group not imposed upon others, or which withholds or limits access to opportunities, benefits, and advantages available to other members of society. Distinctions based on personal characteristics attributed to an individual solely on the basis of association with a group will rarely escape the charge of discrimination, while those based on an individual's merits and capacities will rarely be so classed.[13]

The substantive approach obliges the Court to consider the place of its decisions in the broader social, political, and legal context and is meant to prevent dominant groups from undermining legislation and policy designed to improve the condition of the disadvantaged. The COPOH, in its legal intervention, flatly rejected a theory of formal equality:

---

[12] *Andrews v. Law Society of British Columbia*, [1989] 1 S.C.R. 143.
[13] Ibid.

"formal equality is furthered by the removal rather than the creation of distinctions by government. Thus it is hostile towards pluralism, and encourages homogeneity; its paradigm is the melting pot rather than the mosaic . . . "[14] Yvonne Peters writes that "the decision in *Andrews* was monumental, establishing a landmark precedent on which to build future equality rights jurisprudence."[15] And Orville Endicott states that "the Supreme Court used *Andrews* as the occasion on which to enunciate the fundamental remedial function of the section 15 equality rights provisions."[16]

Although not explicitly addressing disability issues, the conceptualization of equality that was advanced before the Court in these early cases was significant in terms of disability rights. The key organizations deliberately eschewed taking disability discrimination cases in the early years of the Charter's application, opting instead to gradually develop the underpinnings of a legal doctrine that was compatible with the social model of disability. This included 1) granting quasi-constitutional status to protection from adverse effect discrimination, so crucial to the barrier-removal approach advocated by disability rights advocates, in the *O'Malley* judgment; 2) establishing a strong foundation of judicial recognition of the concept of reasonable accommodation; and 3) the Court's espousal of the general concept of substantive equality and the requirement of considering historic disadvantage in *Andrews*.

DISABILITY RIGHTS CASES REACH THE COURT: *EVE* AND *RODRIGUEZ*

The foundation for substantive equality, laid in other equality realms, began to be tested in the area of disability equality. Significantly, in

---

[14] COPOH, "Factum of the Interveners," *Andrews v. Law Society of British Columbia*, [1989] 1 S.C.R. 143.
[15] Peters, "Twenty Years of Litigating," p. 18.
[16] Endicott, "Key Trends in Case Law."

1986, a crucial early disability rights case was decided not based on Charter protections, but with a substantive equality dimension nonetheless. The SCC unanimously ruled in *E. (Mrs.) v. Eve* that a mother did not have the authority to consent to a nontherapeutic sterilization procedure for her intellectually disabled daughter.[17] The judgment stated:

> The importance of maintaining the physical integrity of a human being ranks high in our scale of values, particularly as it affects the privilege of giving life. I cannot agree that a court can deprive a woman of that privilege for purely social or other non-therapeutic purposes without her consent. The fact that others may suffer inconvenience or hardship from failure to do so cannot be taken into account.[18]

Although the Charter was not explicitly instrumental in the Court's judgment (the equality provisions were not yet in effect when the case was argued – they came into effect in 1985), Section 15 rights were referred to by the respondent and interveners on both sides of the case, and the Court took some tentative steps toward a substantive understanding of equality in its decision. Justice La Forest, writing for the Court, highlighted the historic social and legal marginalization of disabled persons:

> There are other reasons for approaching an application for sterilization of a mentally incompetent person with the utmost caution. To begin with, the decision involves values in an area where our social history clouds our vision and encourages many to perceive the mentally handicapped as somewhat less than human. This attitude has been aided and abetted by now discredited eugenic theories whose influence was felt in this country as well as the United States.

---

[17] *E. (Mrs.) v. Eve*, [1986] 2 S.C.R. 388.
[18] Ibid.

118

Two provinces, Alberta and British Columbia, once had statutes providing for the sterilization of mental defectives.[19]

Another case where disability issues reached the SCC, in some instances before organizations had fully considered and articulated their policy positions on the issues, was *Rodriguez v. British Columbia (Attorney General).*[20] In the *Rodriguez* case, the Court and organizational interveners confronted the issue of physician-assisted suicide. Sue Rodriguez had been diagnosed with amyotrophic lateral sclerosis (more commonly known as Lou Gehrig's disease) and wanted to control the circumstances of her death. However, by the time she would reach a point of no longer being able to enjoy her life, she would not be able to end it without assistance. With her legal claim, she hoped to be able to allow a medical practitioner to set up a means to end her life at a time of her choosing. Although suicide is not prohibited by the relevant criminal statutes, providing assistance to commit suicide is.[21] The appellant sought a court order for the relevant section of the Criminal Code to be declared invalid on the ground that it violated her rights under the Charter, including Section 15. The logic underpinning the equality argument was that able-bodied persons would be able to control the manner of their deaths if they so chose and that she, who was disabled, could not benefit from the same option. One activist described the key issue in the following terms: "it was almost like accommodation theory taken to the nth degree. If, for reasons of disability, you were unable to end your own life, then you required assistance."[22] In the end, the SCC denied Sue Rodriguez's request by a 5-to-4 margin.

[19] Ibid. This case paved the way for a successful suit taken in 1995 by an Alberta woman, Leilani Muir, who had been sterilized under that province's Sterilization Act, without her knowledge or consent, when she had been placed at an Alberta facility for those with intellectual disabilities.

[20] *Rodriguez v. British Columbia (Attorney General),* [1993] 3 S.C.R. 519.

[21] *Canadian Criminal Code,* R.S., 1985, c. C-46, s. 241.

[22] Interview, January 22, 2008.

The issue of assisted-death has proved difficult for the disability rights movement: it has led to divisions among and within organizations and resulted in changes in policy positions over time of some of the key organizations. One human rights lawyer commented, "*Rodriguez* happened despite the best efforts of the disability community not to have that go to court."[23] The challenge was in the balancing of two conflicting issues, both of which can be understood to be compatible with a disability rights policy agenda. On one side is the issue of valuing disabled persons and overcoming prejudices regarding quality of life. COPOH's factum made this case:

> Both historically and to the present day the lives and freedoms of persons with disabilities have been threatened and, in some cases, eliminated by the insensitivity, ignorance and hostility of those who believe that the lives of disabled people are somehow of less value or quality than those of other people.[24]

On the other side were those advancing the argument put forth by the appellant that denial of the right to assisted suicide constitutes discrimination based on disability and denial of personal autonomy in making end-of-life decisions. In a magazine article published shortly after the case, the CCD leadership laid out their position on participating in *Rodriguez*:

> Frankly, we would have preferred to play only a supportive role with regard to this one, allowing our B.C. affiliate, British Columbia Council for People with Disabilities (BCCPD) to carry the flag. The BCCPD had been there from the beginning and had been exposed to a lot of heat for their stance from some fairly hardhitting quarters. But as last spring drew on and the calls for our involvement grew ever louder, it became clear that we would have to leave the bench,

---

[23] Interview, October 25, 2007.

[24] COPOH, "Factum of the Intervener," *Rodriguez v. British Columbia (Attorney General)*, [1993] 3 S.C.R. 519.

drop our gloves and take whatever lumps we had coming whether we liked it or not.[25]

CCD leaders felt compelled to intervene to ensure that the Charter of Rights and Freedom's equality provisions would not be undermined. As a compromise, CCD (then COPOH)'s intervention tried to strike the balance between the competing rights claims. In their intervention, CCD argued that an appropriate remedy would be a specific constitutional exemption for Sue Rodriguez, but that striking down the provision could place already-vulnerable people in a more precarious situation.

Both the *Eve* and *Rodriguez* cases had mixed implications. The former had important policy ramifications: the use of nontherapeutic sterilization on disabled persons without their consent had not been uncommon (in some jurisdictions, it had been standard practice), and the Court's decision made clear that this was completely unacceptable. Furthermore, *Eve's* social movement impact could be considered equally important (this is explored in detail in Chapter 2). The *Rodriguez* case dealt with vital questions of life, death, and freedom of choice and ignited public and social movement debate on the issues. But ultimately, the case had relatively little policy influence: the provisions in the Criminal Code, which were at the heart of the case, remained.

THE PROMISE AND PITFALLS OF PROACTIVE DISABILITY RIGHTS CASES: *EATON* AND *ELDRIDGE*

By the late 1990s, those involved with the disability rights movement felt that the time was ripe for policy issues to be pursued in a strategic

---

[25] COPOH, "*Rodriguez:* Autonomy and Vulnerability Must Both be Protected," *Abilities Magazine*, Fall 1993.

manner through the use of the courts.[26] The cases discussed below
can be distinguished from *Eve* and *Rodriguez* in the way that social
movement organizations approached them.

The CACL supported an early proactive test case on inclusive education, *Eaton v. Brant County Board of Education*,[27] believing "the time
was right for a Charter challenge... Section 15 [had been] in full force
since 1985, so it was time to go there."[28] Emily Eaton was a student
with a disability who was removed from her mainstream classroom
and placed in a special education class according to the provisions of
the Education Act, despite objections from her parents. The SCC was
asked in *Eaton* to determine whether the placement, absent parental
consent, infringed the child's Section 15 Charter equality rights. In the
Court of Appeal decision, Justice Louise Arbour upheld the principle of inclusive education relying on Section 15 of the Charter. She
found that the constitutional violation lay in the province's education
legislation, which had led to the placement in the segregated classroom
in the first place.[29] In contrast, Emily Eaton's parents argued that it
was the School Board's decision, not any flaw in the legislation, that
constituted the discriminatory act. One lawyer involved in the case
speculated that, by the time the issues reached the SCC, the Court was
more concerned with the relatively radical manner in which the Education Act was struck down than with issues of inclusive education.[30]
This speculation is further evidenced by the strong statement made by
the Court in the first paragraph of the judgment:

> In our constitutional democracy, it is the elected representatives
> of the people who enact legislation... To strike down by default a

[26] Interview, October 25, 2007.
[27] *Eaton v. Brant County Board of Education*, [1997] 1 S.C.R. 241.
[28] Interview, November 7, 2007.
[29] Justice Arbour was later appointed to the SCC and then subsequently named a UN Human Rights Commissioner.
[30] Interview, October 25, 2007.

law passed by and pursuant to an act of Parliament or the legislature would work a serious injustice not only to the elected representatives who enacted it but also to the people.[31]

A key facet of the *Eaton* decision was the Court's understanding of the "difference dilemma": the complexities involved in balancing human differences, on one hand, with the equal moral value of each individual, notwithstanding those differences, on the other. Justice Sopinka distinguished disability from the other Section 15 grounds, such as race or sex, because there is (arguably) no individual variation with respect to those characteristics, whereas disability means different things depending on the individual and the context. This raised what the Court called the "difference dilemma," whereby "segregation can be both protective of equality and violative of equality depending upon the person and the state of disability."[32]

Paradoxically, the Court used a substantive understanding of equality that disability rights campaigners (including CACL) had previously advocated to justify what the appellants and CACL saw as a discriminatory act. In doing so, the Court explicitly signaled its willingness to advocate a social model approach. The Court found that:

> Exclusion from the mainstream of society results from the construction of a society based solely on "mainstream" attributes to which disabled persons will never be able to gain access. Whether it is the impossibility of success at a written test for a blind person, or the need for ramp access to a library, the discrimination does not lie in the attribution of untrue characteristics to the disabled individual. The blind person cannot see and the person in a wheelchair needs a ramp. Rather, it is the failure to make reasonable accommodation, to fine-tune society so that its structures and assumptions do not result in the relegation and banishment of disabled persons from participation, which results in discrimination against them.

---

[31] *Eaton v. Brant County Board of Education*, [1997] 1 S.C.R. 241.
[32] Ibid.

The discrimination inquiry which uses "the attribution of stereotypical characteristics" reasoning as commonly understood is simply inappropriate here. It may be seen rather as a case of reverse
stereotyping which, by not allowing for the condition of a disabled
individual, ignores his or her disability and forces the individual to
sink or swim within the mainstream environment. It is recognition of
the actual characteristics, and reasonable accommodation of these
characteristics which is the central purpose of s. 15(1) in relation to
disability.[33]

In the *Eaton* case, the Court relied on a difference dilemma analysis
rather than an inclusion-based one to find that the separate educational
placement was constitutional.[34] The impact of the judgment is mixed:
On one hand, many disability rights activists consider it a significant
loss for the inclusive education agenda. On the other hand, it can
be considered a doctrinal victory, as it is the first case in which the
Court explicitly espouses a social model understanding of disability.[35]
Yvonne Peters feels that the *Eaton* case "represents a move towards
a social construction of disability. It advances the proposition that it
is no longer acceptable to expect persons with disabilities to fit into a
mainstream society premised on able-bodied norms."[36] The issue of

---

[33] Ibid.

[34] Legal analyses of the case have also suggested that the factual record in the *Eaton*
case may have played a significant role in the outcome. One interviewee speculated
that "maybe the *Eaton* case shouldn't have been the one they went forward with
because the evidence was not the best. There are so many variables to consider
when deciding to use a court room'" (Interview, October 30, 2007). Specifically,
the record did not provide any insight into the positive experiences of inclusion that
Emily Eaton had in a different school board's classroom, which she had attended
since the Special Education Tribunal handed down its decision three years before
the case appeared before the SCC. The only evidence before the Court, apart from
that of her parents, regarding her experience in an integrated classroom came from
witnesses of the appellant school board who were forced to keep her in the classroom
by the lower Court's injunction. Endicott, "Key Trends in Case Law."

[35] Armstrong, "Disability Advocacy in the Charter Era," p. 61.

[36] Peters, "Twenty Years of Litigating," p. 19.

inclusive education is one of the most controversial in the disability movement, and the Court's *Eaton* judgment mirrors this. The social model language adopted by the Court is seen as a victory, but many in the disability community are troubled by the Court's acceptance of segregation as a way of fulfilling the duty to accommodate. Peters argues that "segregation has been used to oppress and exclude persons with disabilities. Therefore any form of judicial sanctioning of the use of segregation clearly has the potential to ignite alarm bells within the disability community."[37] However, the issue of inclusive education is one that continues to be debated both within the community and in the field of disability studies. Ruth Colker writes,

> While integration is frequently the appropriate mechanism to overcome a history of discrimination and subordination against individuals with disabilities, this single-minded focus on integration has ignored or even silenced those who might want to argue for other options.[38]

Following the mixed results of the *Eaton* case, *Eldridge v. British Columbia (Attorney General)*,[39] the second proactive disability case, proved to be seminal. In *Eldridge*, a group of deaf people complained that they were wrongly denied the services of a sign language interpreter when they sought the care of a physician under British Columbia's health plan. Each of the appellants was born deaf, and their preferred means of communication is sign language. They felt that the absence of interpreters impaired their ability to communicate with their doctors and other health care providers, and thus increased the risk of misdiagnosis and ineffective treatment. They argued that this was a violation of their equality rights under Section 15, as it constituted a barrier that prevents the full participation and equality

---

[37] Ibid.

[38] Colker, *When is Separate Unequal?*, p. 14.

[39] *Eldridge v. British Columbia (Attorney General)*, [1997] 2 S.C.R. 624.

of deaf people on the basis of their different method of communication.

The SCC ruled unanimously in favor of the appellants, and in the judgment, Justice La Forest clarifies the essence of the remedial and substantive purpose of Section 15 protections for persons with disabilities:

> It is an unfortunate truth that the history of disabled persons in Canada is largely one of exclusion and marginalization. Persons with disabilities have too often been excluded from the labour force, denied access to opportunities for social interaction and advancement, subjected to invidious stereotyping and relegated to institutions. This historical disadvantage has to a great extent been shaped and perpetuated by the notion that disability is an abnormality or flaw. As a result, disabled persons have not generally been afforded the "equal concern, respect and consideration" that section 15(1) of the *Charter* demands. Instead, they have been subjected to paternalistic attitudes of pity and charity, and their entrance into the social mainstream has been conditional upon their emulation of able-bodied norms. One consequence of these attitudes is the persistent social and economic disadvantage faced by the disabled.[40]

A senior staff member at the Canadian Hearing Society noted the important movement and policy impact this case had:

> The *Eldridge* decision had a huge impact . . . The Canadian Association of the Deaf and the Canadian Hearing Society and the Council of Canadians with Disabilities all worked together to fight for the right to effective communication. That was a huge win for us: the duty to accommodate up to and including undue hardship.[41]

[40] Ibid.
[41] Interview, October 26, 2007.

The impact on the disability movement was two-fold. First, the enthusiasm with which the various cross-disability and impairment-specific organizations cooperated was important. The cooperation of the main deaf consumer organization, the service agency for deaf persons, and the main cross-disability organization in the *Eldridge* intervention highlights the opportunity that strategic litigation provides to bring organizations together to find a common agenda. Second, the *Eldridge* decision had an influence on levels of rights and legal consciousness. There is a high degree of awareness of the result and implications of the *Eldridge* decision among leaders within the disability rights movement. For example, sixteen of twenty-eight interviewees, in an unprompted manner, mentioned the *Eldridge* decision by name. Being the first active case to result in an unambiguous victory, *Eldridge* seems to have played an important role in heightening both awareness of the duty to accommodate across the community and increased recognition of the use of litigation in a strategic manner among the movement's leadership.

The initial wave of enthusiasm that the *Eldridge* decision sparked has since been replaced by a degree of disappointment. There is dissatisfaction with the slow and reactive manner in which provincial governments have implemented the *Eldridge* decision's requirement to provide access to sign language interpreters. Several activists expressed this sentiment:

> I think a lot of us are thinking . . . what impact is this having? For example the *Eldridge* case was a very significant victory. And I think probably there has been change, but it took a very long time for that decision to filter down. And the decision itself is more than just about deaf people. What the Court said is that if you're going to offer a benefit through a service or a program, then you have to do it in a way that doesn't discriminate. And I think if you look at the status of people with disabilities in Canada . . . I think, things are not getting better, in some ways it's getting worse. It doesn't feel to me like governments have sat down and said, "Well you know

the courts have made a pretty significant ruling here, maybe we better take notice of it and do some consistent and comprehensive disability-oriented policies."[42]

You would think that the government would look at the rulings and would say "ok how do we implement this? We better allocate money to train sign-language interpreters and get it going." You would think "ok here's a court order let's put it in place." But that's not the mindset.[43]

I think we become disappointed sometimes when we look at the remedies we obtain even in successful cases and how difficult it can be to enforce those across the board. The *Eldridge* case comes to mind . . . And particularly when you're talking about Charter cases and governments. How do you get governments to become proactive in addressing human rights issues, particularly if we're talking about access issues for people with disabilities? How do we get to the point where government is taking that responsibility seriously?[44]

Several interviewees criticized disability organizations for not doing more in the aftermath of the *Eldridge* decision to ensure more effective enforcement. One activist felt that "after *Eldridge* there was very little follow up. There would have been a great test case in each province six months after [the decision] saying 'where is your implementation plan?' That would have been really effective."[45] However, other interviewees pointed out that less costly and time-intensive methods of encouraging governments to implement the decision were used instead. For instance, six months after the decision, the CCD, noting the slow pace of change, undertook a letter-writing campaign to enquire as to the state of the implementation plans that the Court had mandated. One activist described this process:

We wrote to every Minister of Health in every province, saying "you must be aware of the *Eldridge* decision which required the BC

---

[42] Interview, October 5, 2007.
[43] Interview, November 9, 2007.
[44] Interview, November 2, 2007.
[45] Interview, November 6, 2007.

government to provide publicly-funded interpreters to deaf people. Because it is a Supreme Court decision it is precedent-setting and you should be developing your resource program." It was only after we wrote to them that they started doing it . . . We really didn't want to fight it through the courts again.[46]

Paradoxically, it was precisely the slow implementation of the *Eldridge* decision by provincial governments that bolstered other campaigns. For instance, an Ontario activist relied on Ontario's feet dragging on the *Eldridge* decision to lobby for provincial accessibility legislation: "I used the movement to say you know we won this case in 1997, its four years later and government hasn't spent a dime. This is why we need a strong disability act."[47]

In sum, the policy impact of the first strategic disability cases, from the disability movement's perspective, were mixed. In *Eaton*, the inclusive education agenda was dealt a blow by the SCC. However, inclusive education, although widely supported, has not achieved total consensus in the disability community in Canada. For example, the issue of integrated versus separate education has been dividing, and continues to divide, the deaf community.[48] Some advocates, basing their arguments on freedom of choice, feel that provision of separate education should be available for those who might want it.[49] However, disability rights advocates on both sides could find some hope in the judgment: the Court signaled an understanding of the social model of disability. In contrast to the mixed results of the *Eaton* case, the *Eldridge* decision was an unambiguous victory. The Court found that governments have a positive duty to promote equality for disabled persons. The case's impact on the community was largely positive: participating in the case brought organizations with a common agenda together. In

[46] Ibid.
[47] Ibid.
[48] Interview, October 26, 2007.
[49] Interview, November 5, 2007.

the longer term, however, it seems to have provoked questioning of the effectiveness of the use of litigation as a policy-influencing strategy. The tardiness of governments in considering the implementation implications of *Eldridge* and the follow-up work required on the part of activists to push governments to enforce the new policy led to disillusionment. Paradoxically, although this slow pace has provoked a degree of frustration among activists, it has also served as a useful political tool: the feet dragging by governments to implement the *Eldridge* decision has been used by activists to highlight the need for more effective legislation and enforcement mechanisms.

LATIMER AND *AUTON*: LOSING CONTROL
OF THE AGENDA

In the midst of the *Eaton* and *Eldridge* cases, in which the disability rights community pursued a litigation strategy to try to advance equality for disabled persons on the issue of inclusive education and the accommodation imperative and to encourage understanding of disability issues, a criminal case emerged that propelled contentious issues of importance to disabled persons into the public sphere.[50] The series of *R. v. Latimer* cases also had the effect of pulling organizational attention away from other issues.[51]

Robert Latimer was charged with the first-degree murder of Tracy, his twelve-year-old daughter, who had a severe form of cerebral palsy. He argued that he was driven to commit murder to spare his daughter continued pain and suffering. In two cases that reached the SCC that dealt with various factual, legal, and procedural issues, Latimer unsuccessfully argued a defense of necessity and was convicted of

[50] *Eaton v. Brant County Board of Education*, [1997] 1 S.C.R. 241; *Eldridge v. British Columbia (Attorney General)*, [1997] 2 S.C.R. 624.

[51] *R. v. Latimer*, [1997] 1 S.C.R. 217; *R. v. Latimer*, [2001] 1 S.C.R. 3.

second-degree murder. According to the Criminal Code of Canada, accused persons convicted of second-degree murder are required to serve a mandatory minimum ten-year sentence of imprisonment.[52] Mr. Latimer argued that this sentence amounted to cruel and unusual punishment and requested a constitutional exemption from the sentence. The technical and procedural legal complexities of the case are beyond the scope of this chapter; the discussion here focuses, instead, on the mercy-killing arguments the defendant put forward and the high-profile public debate surrounding the case.

The *Latimer* case thrust the issue of euthanasia onto the public agenda in an unprecedented way. The high-profile nature of the case and subsequent public debate took the disability rights community by surprise.[53] A CCD activist said:

> The public response to that murder, astounded our community. We could not believe the ways in which Tracey was portrayed, as less than human, as having no rights. And the public seemed to portray Robert Latimer as the victim in this case, not Tracy. It was a real shock to our community that we had come such a little way . . . the *Latimer* case consumed us for about five years. I never thought we would have to spend that kind of energy on a case like that. And it still comes back every once and a while.[54]

After years of concerted campaigning for the right to live, work, and participate equally in society, disability rights activists were taken aback by the "relentless, passionate, public-wide debate on the fundamental issue of whether it is legally and morally acceptable for a father to take the life of his severely disabled daughter."[55]

---

[52] Criminal Code, R.S.C. 1985, c. C-46.

[53] "Father's Killing of Canadian Girl: Mercy or Murder," *The New York Times*, December 1, 1997.

[54] Interview, January 22, 2008.

[55] Peters, "Twenty Years of Litigating," p. 22.

Disability rights activists, going against overwhelming public sympathy for Latimer's plight, intervened to encourage the Court to consider Latimer's actions and arguments in the light of the Charter's equality guarantees.[56] In addition to the interventions, disability rights organizations used other strategies to attempt to influence public opinion. The CCD, from 1996 to 2002, published an online newsletter called "Latimer Watch," in which the movement's perspective on issues arising in the case were presented. Interestingly, the Latimer case influenced CCD's position on the *Rodriguez* case discussed above. A long-time activist said:

> Half way through [the *Rodriguez* case] along came the murder of Tracy Latimer by Robert Latimer . . . and CCD reversed its position on Sue Rodriguez and basically said, people are so devalued and people are so vulnerable at certain points in their life that we cannot support assisted-suicide because we believe people will make choices for others in their life.[57]

The Court decision did not focus on the rights questions and, instead, strictly interpreted the defense-of-necessity provision to overturn Latimer's arguments. The Court found: "[t]he defence of necessity is narrow and of limited application in criminal law. In this case, there was no air of reality to that defence."[58] *Latimer* reinforced the law, and disability advocates lauded the SCC's treatment of Tracy Latimer's murder like any other murder case.[59] Although many see the *Latimer* case as a victory, ultimately, like the *Rodriguez* case discussed previously, it had few direct policy implications that advanced an equality agenda.

Another situation where disability advocacy organizations felt they were participating in litigation in a responsive fashion was with a series

---

[56] Ibid.

[57] Interview, January 22, 2008.

[58] *R. v. Latimer*, [1997] 1 S.C.R. 217.

[59] Armstrong, "Disability Advocacy in the Charter Era," p. 75.

of cases concerning autism and public funding of treatment. In the late 1990s, several parents of children with autism in British Columbia joined together to establish Families for Early Autism Treatment BC (FEAT BC). The organization lobbied the Ministries of Health, Education, and Children and Families to fund their children's participation in Applied Behavioural Analysis/Intensive Behavioural Intervention (ABA/IBI). The program costs were high at between $45,000 and $60,000 CAD per year per child; and, at the time, there were debates about the effectiveness of the treatment.[60] The intervention, however, is designed to be time-limited and could potentially avoid costly services in the long term. After an extensive lobbying effort, the organization turned to the courts, which they felt was their last-resort.[61] A FEAT BC activist highlighted the sentiment of desperation among parents:

> This is how unbelievably fed up people were...When I started organizing this lawsuit, people were practically throwing cheques at me. It was unbelievable. I wasn't convincing people like "oh c'mon let's go, throw your money in." I wasn't selling it. People were throwing money at me saying "thank you so much for organizing this." It was desperation.[62]

FEAT BC has sponsored a number of legal actions, including an unsuccessful application to be certified as a class for class-action proceedings and, more recently, a successful case against a school board in British Columbia (BC). However, the seminal autism case was *Auton (Guardian ad litem of) v. British Columbia (Attorney General)*, which

---

[60] Christopher P. Manfredi and Antonia Maioni, "Courts and Health Policy: Judicial Policy Making and Publicly Funded Health Care in Canada," *Journal of Health Politics, Policy and Law* 27(2), 2002, pp. 213–40.

[61] Interview, October 22, 2007.

[62] Ibid.

the SCC decided in 2004.[63] The *Auton* case considered whether the refusal by the BC government to provide funding for intensive behavioral therapy for preschool-aged children with autism violated their Section 15 equality rights. The province sought to justify the denial of funding for the treatment as a reasonable limit on the appellants' equality rights because of the high costs. The government argued that the courts should not interfere with the government's complex policy and resource-balancing decisions.

The BC Court of Appeal, relying extensively on the jurisprudence of earlier equality cases, such as *Eaton* and *Eldridge*, found that the denial of the treatment was a violation of Charter rights. Madam Justice Allan characterized the failure to provide the ABA/IBI treatment as the withholding of a component of essential medical services and claimed that, without the treatment, children with autism would be at a serious disadvantage compared with children who do not have autism when it comes to participating in societal life.[64] When the case reached the SCC, however, the Court overturned the judgment and found that there was no constitutional right to receive the treatment through provincially funded health care systems. The *Auton* case was considered a significant loss by FEAT BC, but many of the disability rights organizations that intervened in the case found the autism issue challenging. Several activists highlighted the various problems they found with the issues raised by the *Auton* case:

> I think the autism cases are very troubling ... We take a barrier-removal approach, and in the autism cases they are taking a different kind of ... health approach. So I think those are tricky cases. I think it's really raised some difficult issues within the disability movement. CCD intervened in the *Auton* case and I think we were very conflicted on the analysis and the argument ... I think we had

---

[63] *Auton (Guardian ad litem of) v. British Columbia (Attorney General)*, [2004] 3 S.C.R. 657, 2004 SCC 78.

[64] Endicott, "Key Trends in Case Law."

a difficult time saying whether that was a good decision or that was a bad decision because of the analysis.[65]

CCD will be very careful in any future interventions related to autism. The *Auton* case which we became involved in... the legal question, quite frankly, was simply too narrow. By the time we were sort of three-quarters of the way through, frankly there was internal questions of whether we should have been there at all. We should have just stayed out. It was not strategic. It was not test-case litigation.[66]

It was a challenging intervention because... what we were trying to do in that case is to characterize the medically necessary interventions that the claimants were going after as a disability support, and establish the principle that people had a right to the supports that they needed, without providing unqualified support for the ABA/IBI treatment that those particular claimants were going after because we have a lot of problems with it. So it was a very, very tricky manoeuvring. But I think we were able to articulate some really strong principles in our factum about access to disability supports. It's simply a political strategy... to try and get this articulated as a health need under the health act and we think that's a really problematic way to go. We spent a number of years trying to get disability-related support out from under a medicalized paradigm.[67]

Auton wasn't our case: it wasn't a disability movement designed case. Unlike *Via Rail* which was designed as a disability rights analysis from the beginning... [68]

The *Auton* case and other autism cases have proved challenging to disability rights organizations because, at times, the legal arguments and analysis conflict with the paradigm of disability as a social construction and, in some ways, represent a regression to a medicalized paradigm of disability. Some organizations explicitly attempted to

---

[65] Interview, October 5, 2007.
[66] Interview, January 22, 2008.
[67] Interview, November 12, 2007.
[68] Interview, November 9, 2007.

reframe part of the legal claim of FEAT BC to allow it to coexist with the broader disability movement's agenda. For example, the CACL and ARCH Disability Law Centre argued for a consideration of ABA/IBI treatment as a "disability support" instead of a "medical treatment," demonstrating the importance of framing processes to the disability movement. The impact of the case on the movement is mixed: it likely exacerbated existing tensions between parents supportive of the treatment, on one hand, who had reached a degree of desperation with the high financial costs and organizations, on the other hand, that were dubious of the treatment and the legal analysis put forward by the appellants.

RECAPTURING THE AGENDA: THE IMMIGRATION CASES AND *VIA RAIL*

Canada's exclusion of disabled persons via immigration policy was the subject of two cases argued before the Supreme Court. In *Hilewitz v. Canada (Minister of Citizenship and Immigration)* and *De Jong v. Canada (Minister of Citizenship and Immigration)*, two applicants applied for permanent residence for themselves and their families under categories of the Immigration Act that requires applicants have substantial financial resources to qualify.[69] They were denied admission solely on the basis that the Ministry felt that the intellectually disabled dependent children of the applicants "would cause or might reasonably be expected to cause excessive demands on . . . social services," despite the fact that both applicants had agreed to privately educate their children and cover other contingent costs.

The CACL and the Ethno-racial People with Disabilities Coalition of Ontario (ERDCO) intervened in the case, emphasizing a Charter

---

[69] *Hilewitz v. Canada (Minister of Citizenship and Immigration); De Jong v. Canada (Minister of Citizenship and Immigration)*, 2005 SCC 57, [2005] 2 S.C.R. 706.

rights and social model analysis. They argued first that immigration law must be interpreted in light of the Charter:

> The assessment of what constitutes excessive demands must be made in light of the objectives of immigration law, which in this case explicitly include the principles of equality and non-discrimination under s. 15(1) of the *Charter* and compliance with international human rights instruments. Section 3 of the *Immigration Act* outlines the objectives of Canadian immigration law and policy. In particular, s.3(f) expressly declares that an objective of the *Act* is " . . . to ensure that any person who seeks admission to Canada . . . is subject to standards of admission that do not discriminate in a manner inconsistent with the *Canadian Charter of Rights and Freedoms.*"[70]

They also argued that immigration policy should be guided by a social model understanding of disability, not a medical model:

> The provisions of both the former and current immigration legislation that require medical officers to predict whether a disabled applicant may reasonably be expected to cause excessive demands on Canadian health or social services is deeply entrenched in this antiquated medical model of disability. The excessive demands provisions operate on the assumption that disabling conditions are inherent defects rather than socially ascribed deficits, and that a suitable response to the condition is exclusion rather than accommodation and inclusion.[71]

Finally, an argument about the indirect discursive effects of an exclusionary immigration policy was made by the interveners:

> Canadians with disabilities are given the message that persons like them are not welcome in Canada. Canadians with disabilities see themselves identified by "impairments" and branded as a burden

---

[70] CACL and ERDCO, "Factum of the Intervener," *Hilewitz v. Canada (Minister of Citizenship and Immigration); De Jong v. Canada (Minister of Citizenship and Immigration)*, 2005 SCC 57, [2005] 2 S.C.R. 706.

[71] Ibid.

on the public purse, with no value attached to their role in society. The disparate and adverse impact experienced by prospective immigrants with disabilities also undermines the value placed on Canada as a diverse nation. By implication, the message given to *all* Canadians is that persons with disabilities are to be screened out as inferior, second class members of society.[72]

In a 7-to-2 judgment, the Court referred both applications back to the Minister of Citizenship and Immigration to be reconsidered in accordance with the reasons laid out in the decision. Although this was a victory for the applicants, the reasoning behind the decision was not based on the arguments made by the interveners regarding the Charter or notions of inclusion. Justice Abella, in writing the judgment, synthesized the issue to one of whether the financial resources that otherwise qualified the two families for admission to Canada could nonetheless be disregarded in assessing the impact of their children's disabilities on Canada's social services. However, there was mention of the importance of assessing individual characteristics rather than presumed group characteristics. Justice Abella writes,

> The issue is not whether Canada can design its immigration policy in a way that reduces its exposure to undue burdens caused by potential immigrants. Clearly it can. But here the legislation is being interpreted in a way that impedes entry for *all* persons who are intellectually disabled, regardless of family support or assistance, and regardless of whether they pose any reasonable likelihood of excessively burdening Canada's social services. Such an interpretation, disregarding a family's actual circumstances, replaces the provision's purpose with a cookie-cutter methodology. Interpreting the legislation in this way may be more efficient, but an efficiency argument is not a valid rebuttal to justify avoiding the requirements of the legislation. The Act calls for individual assessments. This

---

[72] Ibid.

means that the individual, not administrative convenience, is the interpretive focus.[73]

The result was a victory, but a limited one. One lawyer commented in interview: "there are some unfortunate comments [in the judgment] . . . which could lead a reasonable person to argue that the Court only intended to expand that rationale to this category of applicants and not to anybody else."[74] This led to a policy gap: it was unclear whether the principles articulated in the case applied to all categories of applicants or a limited group.

The policy gap established the need for further litigation or legislation to clarify the extent of the principle. In *Colaco et al. v. Canada (Minister of Citizenship and Immigration)* before the Federal Court of Appeal, the Minister's argument that the SCC's reasoning in *Hilewitz* and *De Jong* applies only to "business class" applicants was rejected by the Court.[75] The Court found that a skilled worker applicant – hence a different category of immigrant from that discussed above – with a disabled dependent should not have been rejected for an excessive demand on Canadian social services without assessing whether the family is willing and has the resources to pay for appropriate care and provide for employment. The visa officer and medical officer's decisions were overturned, as they did not complete an individual assessment of the information provided by the applicant.

The immigration cases demonstrate how strategic litigation can later pull organizations to the court. The first cases, *Hilewitz* and *De Jong*, were part of a selected priority-issue proactive campaign by CACL, ERDCO, and ARCH Disability Law Centre, who acted as legal counsel. *Colaco* was a follow-up case dealing with the same principles in a

---

[73] *Hilewitz v. Canada (Minister of Citizenship and Immigration); De Jong v. Canada (Minister of Citizenship and Immigration)*, 2005 SCC 57, [2005] 2 S.C.R. 706.

[74] Interview, October 30, 2007.

[75] *Colaco v. Canada (Minister of Citizenship and Immigration)*, [2008] 2 F.C.R.D-10.

slightly different situation. A staff member of ARCH noted the incremental nature of the strategy in these cases:

> We're sort of chipping away at it a little bit at a time . . . the next time there is a *Colaco* or *Hilewitz* type case ARCH is going to have be there because we have put our seal on it to begin with – it is one of our issues. And a case could come out of nowhere, somebody calls us today and says in two weeks this [type of case] is going to be moving forward, we are going to drop things and run to get involved in that.[76]

Another example of a litigation strategy whereby organizations felt compelled to become involved to ensure that previous victories were maintained was *Council of Canadians with Disabilities v. VIA Rail Canada Inc.*,[77] decided by the SCC in 2007. The organization became involved in the issues as a way to try and stop the regression of disability equality and the reasonable accommodation principle in transport policy. The CCD took the case from the administrative tribunal level up to the Supreme Court level over a period of more than six years.

In late 2000, VIA Rail, a crown corporation that is the national rail provider, received a significant discount on the purchase of 139 rail cars (known as "Renaissance cars") that were no longer required for overnight train service in England and continental Europe. None of the cars were accessible to persons who use wheelchairs. The CCD complained, in the first instance, in 2000 to the Canadian Transportation Agency (CTA), under s. 172 of the Canada Transportation Act, about the lack of accessibility of the Renaissance cars.[78] Over the next seven years, CCD remained embroiled in its legal dispute with the CTA through the Federal Court of Appeal. In April 2005, the organization decided to appeal the Federal Court's decision to the SCC.

---

[76] Interview, October 30, 2007.

[77] *Council of Canadians with Disabilities v. VIA Rail Canada Inc*, [2007] 1 S.C.R. 650.

[78] Canada Transportation Act, S.C. 1996, c. 10.

Ultimately, the SCC's decision was based on a combination of administrative law issues, rights considerations, and analyses of the concept of "undue hardship." Although the case was not technically based on Section 15(1), Justice Abella cast the key issue in terms of VIA Rail's duties to persons with disabilities under federal law. In the judgment, she lays out the accommodation duty first:

> The accommodation of personal wheelchairs enables persons with disabilities to access public services and facilities as independently and seamlessly as possible. Independent access to the same comfort, dignity, safety and security as those without physical limitations, is a fundamental human right for persons who use wheelchairs. This is the goal of the duty to accommodate: to render those services and facilities to which the public has access equally accessible to people with and without physical limitations.[79]

Abella also considered the issue of undue hardship in light of the *Eldridge* decision and found that it is a cornerstone of substantive equality to take positive action to remedy disadvantage. She concluded: "Undue hardship implies that there may necessarily be some hardship in accommodating someone's disability, but unless that hardship imposes an undue or unreasonable burden, it yields to the need to accommodate."[80]

A key issue that ultimately divided the Court (it was a 4-to-5 decision) was the "network defense": VIA Rail argued that because some of their routes are accessible, their accommodation requirements are met. As David Lepofsky correctly notes, "[t]o a passenger with a disability who needs to travel from Montreal to Toronto, it is immaterial whether VIA runs a fully accessible train from Calgary to Vancouver."[81] In

---

[79] Ibid.

[80] Ibid.

[81] David Lepofsky, "Federal Court of Appeal De-Rails Equality Rights for Persons With Disabilities – *Via Rail v. Canadian Transportation Agency* and the Important

the judgment, Justice Abella decisively rejected the network defense argument:

> The fact that there are accessible trains travelling along some routes does not justify inaccessible trains on others. It is the global network of rail services that should be accessible. The fact that accessibility is limited to isolated aspects of the global network – like VIA's alternative transportation policy or the suggestion that persons with disabilities can continue to ride the existing fleet for the time-being – does not satisfy Parliament's continuing goal of ensuring accessible transportation services.[82]

In policy terms, *VIA Rail* established the "duty to not create new barriers." Prior to *VIA Rail*, the CCD's legal mobilization activities to achieve their vision of a barrier-free society were primarily focused on the removal of barriers to enable the inclusion of persons with disabilities in all aspects of society. The CCD's case against VIA Rail was an active strategy to ensure the maintenance of legislative and regulatory victories that were won long before. There was concern that, if the CCD had not taken the case, the transport situation of disabled persons would have regressed enormously. A CCD leader framed it in the following terms:

> We would have seen a wholesale erosion of transportation. So the Board was adamant, and CCD actually laid off staff in order to have the resources to do this battle. And the Board said this is our priority and if we go down fighting over this one, we'll go down but we're going to fight it. The Board was fabulous. It was unanimous. There was no dissent . . . Transportation was the issue the organization formed around in the 1970s. People saw it as so fundamental: without transportation there won't be employment; there won't be mobility; there won't be participation in community life. And this action undertaken by Via in the year 2000 could unravel the last

Duty Not to Create New Barriers to Accessibility (2005–2006)," 18 *N.J.C.L.* 169, p. 188.

[82] Ibid.

25 years of good work. So the Board held really strong and said "no, we'll take the risk."[83]

There is consensus in the community that the *VIA Rail* decision is important and a major victory in terms of the investment CCD and others in the community made in the case: the organization would likely not have financially survived if the case had been lost.[84] However, the importance of the *VIA Rail* decision in policy terms is greater in respect to what was nearly lost rather than what was gained. Some in the community are cautiously optimistic about the impact of the decision:

> *Via Rail* is important to a lot of things . . . [but] on a careful read-ing doesn't really change the law much. But it does really give a wake-up call to big, big government corporations, like Via, that run our national rail system so it's absolutely clear that persons with dis-abilities are entitled to the same level of comfort and safety in their transportation as anyone else and that people with disabilities are the people of Canada.[85]

Another activist echoed how bittersweet the result of the case was for her. It was a feeling she had also experienced with the *Eldridge* decision:

> Hopefully, *Via Rail* will have an impact but again whether or not the government will take this seriously . . . I feel at this point quite skeptical. We've been talking about transportation for 30 years and it's very discouraging when you look around you and between 2000 and 2007 all kinds of things have happened that continue to create barriers.[86]

---

[83] Interview, January 22, 2008.
[84] Interview, November 6, 2007.
[85] Interview, October 30, 2007.
[86] Interview, October 5, 2007.

CONCLUSIONS

The case analyses here demonstrate that Supreme Court decisions have been important in defining understandings of equality in relation to a wide variety of policies affecting the rights and lives of persons with disabilities. Whereas some cases have resulted in important policy victories, others are seen as major setbacks, and some victories have been bittersweet due to the slow implementation of the decision.

The evolution of a substantive approach to equality for persons with disabilities is one of ebbs and flows. By building an important foundation in early, nondisability-specific cases, such as *Andrews* and *O'Malley*, concepts important to the social model of disability, such as adverse effect discrimination and reasonable accommodation, were constitutionally recognized. In later disability-specific cases, such as *Eaton* and *Eldridge*, the very definitions of disability, discrimination, and accommodation were expanded and refined. In addition, recent cases, such as *VIA Rail*, articulated new obligations, such as the duty not to create new barriers. In many ways, this latter principle seems so fundamental to a civil rights understanding of disability that its articulation is somewhat absurd. Although there have been many policy gains, the principles used to achieve them have not been applied without limits. The decisions in the *Eaton* and *Auton* cases demonstrated that governments remain free to choose the policies they wish to fund and that the duty to accommodate can be curbed by cost and/or safety justifications. The cases dealing with life and death issues, such as *Rodriguez* and *Latimer*, had less policy impact. Although both of these cases sparked wide public debate, the resulting judgments left the relevant Criminal Code provisions in place and maintained the policy status quo in terms of euthanasia and mercy killing. In sum, judicial understandings of disability equality have been defined through both court decisions that have transformed policy and those that have not.

Balancing Structure and Agency

The account here highlights how changing legal frames shaped the litigation terrain faced by disability advocacy organizations. It also focuses on their agency: the way they approach the opportunity to litigate. However, the terms "opportunity" and "agency" may mask what are, in fact, more complicated social movement motivations behind participation in legal cases. Certainly on some issues the organizations discussed here did not simply wait for cases representing common grievances to arise; they actively worked to find cases. For example, *Hilewitz*, *De Jong*, and *Eaton* were cases planned to try and advance the equality agenda in the areas of immigration policy and inclusive education. However, another clear finding is that sometimes opportunities for legal mobilization are not welcomed by social movement actors. The *Rodriguez* case, and to a certain degree the *Auton* case, raised difficult issues, ones that divided the disability community. Being forced to articulate positions on contentious issues can have negative social movement effects. In the *Latimer* case, the disability community was united but found themselves at odds with large parts of the Canadian public. It demonstrated to the community the extent to which public understandings of disability remained rooted in the medical model. Although these cases nonetheless provided prospects to advance policy through the Court, they were opportunities that the social movement actors would have liked to forego. In other cases, the use of strategic litigation encourages organizations to cooperate and articulate joint agendas where they might not have otherwise done so. This can create a shared agenda to carry into the future and also encourages organizations to manage the boundaries between them. Chapter 4 explores similar issues but shifts attention to the politics of the disability movement in the UK. Although the fundamental premise of the disability rights claims made by the movement are similar to those in Canada, the terrain of the organizational environment and the shape of legal mobilization have been very different.

4

Disability Organizations and the Diffusion of Rights in the United Kingdom

INTRODUCTION

This chapter paints a picture of the disability community in the United Kingdom and explains how disability organizations have approached the opportunity to undertake legal mobilization as part of their strategies to influence public policy. I provide a brief overview of the history of three main types of organizations that have operated in the sphere of disability policy from the 1970s to 2005: the grassroots organizations of disabled persons; the traditional disability charities; and a quasi-nongovernmental organization, the Disability Rights Commission (DRC). I explore the evolving attitudes within and across organizations toward social model understandings of disability and also their attitudes toward, and (where relevant) their usage of, strategic litigation as a policy-influencing tool. The analysis in this chapter demonstrates that there is significant variation, both among and within, the three types of organizations in the disability sector in the UK regarding the use of (and organizational values on the use of) strategic litigation. This is in contrast to Canada, where the majority of the main disability organizations have turned to the courts. Included in the sample of organizations chosen there are cases of important disability organizations that have not adopted the use of litigation. This allows for the exploration of some "negative cases": groups that have not used (or in some cases, even considered using) legal action to pursue policy goals.

146

Presented in this chapter is the argument that, in order to account for the cross-organization and temporal variation in the adoption and attitudes toward the use of strategic litigation, there is a need to consider social movement identity politics. I trace the emergence and diffusion of dominant social-movement meaning frames and discuss how this has influenced relations among organizations, and correlate this diffusion with the turn to the courts by some organizations but not others.

The remainder of the chapter is divided into four sections. Section one explores the emergence of the grassroots disability rights movement. Section two argues that contention over meaning frames helped to establish legal mobilization as an appropriate strategy in the pursuit of policy goals, even though these groups themselves have not used this tactic. Section three looks to a second category of organizations active in the disability sector: the disability charities. It describes which of the main disability charities have turned to strategic litigation and which have not, and then explores in greater detail the case of two specific organizations in order to trace the processes leading to the use or nonuse of this strategy. Section four explores the unique situation of the DRC as a policy actor and key proponent of the use of strategic litigation to enforce and expand disability rights.

THE EMERGENCE OF A DISABILITY RIGHTS CONSCIOUSNESS

In the 1960s, early signs of the consciousness that led to the emergence of a new movement of people with disabilities asserting the right to self-determination, independent living, and nondiscrimination were being seen. There were forerunners of this movement going back to the nineteenth century, such as organizations controlled by people with disabilities within class and trade union campaigning movements, as well as organizations such as the National League of the Blind and Disabled (NLBD), whose focus was on establishing sheltered employment. Yet it was only in the 1970s that the leaders of the movement began articulating the political principles that would come to be known as the social model of disability. As a result, overtly political organizations controlled by disabled persons began to emerge.

A driving factor in the emergence of the disabled people's movement in the UK was the visceral response by some activists in the 1970s to the conditions they experienced in institutions owned and run by the traditional charities (discussed below), or to the service-provision ethos that dominated social policy. As in Canada, early leaders in the movement can trace the evolution of a disability political consciousness, on individual and collective levels. For some, this included overcoming perceptions, and particularly self-perceptions, of disability as "illness" or "personal tragedy":

> I think disability was very much illness-based for me. I was ill. I was perceived to be ill by everybody including the professional people and other people that visited me. I think I perceived myself as being ill, though in retrospect I certainly wasn't most of the time. I was ill at times but I wouldn't have said that was the predominant feature. The predominant feature throughout my institutional life was the fact that I was left in bed a lot of the time when I could have been up . . . I was very much kept where they wanted me to be kept.[1]

Other activists point to the lack of a political consciousness in relation to their disability at the time:

> As a disabled person growing up at that time, there was nothing to identify yourself with. You couldn't identify with a group or anything like that but I don't think I thought in those terms anyway. I think what we were desperately doing, what I was doing and probably all of us were doing, was normalizing like mad, and reflecting what was

---

[1] Ann McFarlane cited in Jane Campbell and Mike Oliver, *Disability Politics: Understanding Our Past, Changing Our Future* (London: Routledge, 1996), p. 36.

going on around us . . . Certainly disability consciousness or politics weren't on our agenda at that time.[2]

I think we were just very disempowered . . . I don't think we felt empowered to answer back, to even begin to talk about rights. That just wasn't there as far as I remember. It was supposed to be a great thing when services gradually came in so that you could get the equipment. You could get some of your needs met, but the greater needs of the right to actual education, transport, employment and so on – that just wasn't mentioned as far as I remember. It just wasn't within our kind of scenario.[3]

Another activist discussed her implicit rights-based understanding of disability, of the type that began to lay the foundation for the development of a social model understanding of disability.

I was in an institution at Stoke Mandeville [the National Spinal Injuries Centre] after my accident and I knew something was desperately wrong. I knew that I didn't have the rights that other people had; i.e. able-bodied people, but I could not figure out quite what it was all about. And I couldn't see why. I mean, being able-bodied before, I couldn't see why I just couldn't go back into society and have a flat and have somebody to help me and get a job. I actually presumed that this is what I would be able to do and I must admit I had a very rude awakening when there was nowhere to go, nobody would take me back in the job I had before, and there just wasn't any help in the community.[4]

Campbell and Oliver, disability studies scholars and activists within the movement, sum up the roots of discontent that was the catalyst for an emerging rights consciousness:

By the 1960s, as far as disabled people were concerned, we were faced with the choice of a range of dependency-creating services or nothing at all, and a plethora of disability organizations which spoke

---

[2] Anne Rae cited in Campbell and Oliver, *Disability Politics*, p. 38.

[3] Elsa Beckett cited in Campbell and Oliver, *Disability Politics*, p. 39.

[4] Maggie Davis cited in Campbell and Oliver, *Disability Politics*, p. 34.

in our name but neither represented us accurately nor met our needs. It is scarcely surprising, therefore, that most of us were isolated, disempowered, impaired individuals. But . . . a political consciousness concerning disability issues was beginning to emerge among some disabled individuals.[5]

This political consciousness began to develop largely as the result of a cyclical organizational process, whereby people with disabilities came together and formed grassroots organizations or coopted those established by some of the disability charities and their institutions. It was within these organizations that people with disabilities began to discuss and rethink the concept of disability and developed the fundamental principles of the social model that became the unique hallmark of the disability movement's struggle.[6] One of the junctures in the emergence of the movement, highlighted throughout the secondary literature, was the publication in *The Guardian* newspaper, on September 20, 1972, of a letter written by Paul Hunt, a key figure in the early movement. He stated that "severely physically handicapped people find themselves isolated in unsuitable institutions where their views are ignored and they are subject to authoritarian and often cruel regimes."[7] Hunt proposed the formation of a consumer group to put forward nationally the views of actual and potential residents of the institutions. Hunt's letter resulted in the swift establishment of one of the early, politically radical organizations of disabled persons, the Union of the Physically Impaired Against Segregation (UPIAS), which is regularly identified as developing the intellectual foundation upon which the disability rights movement was based. One activist and leading academic in the movement describes how the concrete experience of disability and institutionalization began to be articulated in a theoretical way, through engagement with other disabled persons:

[5] Campbell and Oliver, *Disability Politics*, p. 45.
[6] Jane Campbell, "Joined Up Thinking," *The Guardian*, April 30, 2008.
[7] Cited in Campbell and Oliver, *Disability Politics*.

I started attending various meetings and set up a meeting with Paul Hunt, who lived in Cheshire Homes at the time. I knew about the Cheshire Homes but Paul introduced me to the real criticisms about them, about the institution approach. It seemed to me that the clearest perception of what was wrong with disability was in relation to these homes. It was around the issue of controlling your life and the ability to get out of the homes and to get into the community . . . The position that UPIAS then took was that if you understood what was happening with the homes you actually understood a lot about disability. Basically it goes back – and I'm using the words that I have now – to the fact that disabled people are socially dead so you don't need a home. We didn't use those terms but that's what it was about.[8]

As in Canada, some female activists cited an implicit sexism within the emerging movement as an exclusionary element. One female activist stated,

Well, it [UPIAS] can be criticized from all kinds of points of view. From the female perspective, I'm sure that there was more than a hint of a hard, not necessarily macho, style in terms of the political and analytical debate; in terms of the dialectic and the rigour by which people were expected to defend their positions and stand or fall by them in a process of self, personal development within the collective ethos. In some sense that has got a very typical masculine political feel to it, and I think that it has to live with that kind of criticism. Later on, when we [the women involved] looked back at the circulars, we saw that fairly clearly. Although we still agreed that it was the right direction that we took.[9]

These tensions led to the emergence in the mid-1970s of a short-lived organization, the Liberation Network of Disabled People (LNDP), a loosely organized leftist network. In contrast with the more consensual, emotional, and co-counseling approach taken by LNDP, UPIAS was

[8] Vic Finkelstein cited in Campbell and Oliver, *Disability Politics*, p. 54
[9] Maggie Davis cited in Campbell and Oliver, *Disability Politics*, p. 67.

perceived by some as being exclusive, adversarial, and analytical.[10] One of the founders of the LNDP highlights the differing organizational model and ethos of the group:

> LNDP was a woman-led organization, and it embodied female values, although it included men right from the beginning. Through the support group, and later through the magazine *In from the Cold*, we began to challenge the traditional view of disability as an individual health problem. We challenged the effects of "internalised oppression," recognized by all marginalised groups as the major "tool" of the oppressive society; we challenged the conditioned hatred of ourselves and each other as disabled people; we challenged the desire to assimilate; we challenged the denial of "hidden" disabilities; we challenged the fierce competition between us; we challenged the inability to champion, appreciate and support each other's achievements or thinking (especially when it challenges our own); we challenged the lack of information and understanding about the issues of other oppressed peoples.[11]

Despite these ideological and organizational tensions, a strong consensus about the importance of the language of rights and the social model emerged. The meaning frames of the social model are now hegemonic across the movement and have spread so that now government policy, and even the traditional disability organizations, speak "the same language," focusing on rights and self-determination. Although some disability academics have argued for a tweaking of the social model, critiquing it from feminist or Marxist perspectives, the basic premise remains the same.[12] The social model's meaning frames gave disability

---

[10] Allan Sutherland, "The Other Tradition: From Personal Politics to Disability Arts," http://www.leeds.ac.uk/disability-studies/archiveuk/Sutherland/The%20Other%20Tradition.pdf (accessed June 11, 2008).

[11] Micheline Mason cited in Campbell and Oliver, *Disability Politics*, p. 69.

[12] Tom Shakespeare, ed., *The Disability Reader* (New York: Continuum, 1998); Susan Wendell, "Toward a Feminist Theory of Disability," in Lenard J. Davis, ed., *The Disability Studies Reader* (New York: Routledge, 2006), pp. 260–78.

activists a framework to distinguish between organizations, policies, laws, and ideas that they began to see as emancipatory, and those that were increasingly viewed, at least by a radical minority, as oppressive and/or inadequate.[13] Furthermore, I argue that the overarching ideational frames contribute to laying the foundation for the use of legal mobilization as a legitimate strategy. As hypothesized in Chapter 1, when the creation and enforcement of rights is established as the pre-eminent goal of a movement, the use of strategic litigation gains credibility as an effective tactic to achieve those goals.

UPIAS invited the few national groups managed by disabled people that existed at the time to come together to form a council. This became the British Council of Organizations of Disabled People (BCODP), which remains the main umbrella organization today, now known as the UK Disabled People's Council (UKDPC).[14] As in Canada, international developments also encouraged organization: 1981 was declared International Year of Disabled People by the United Nations, and there was a move to form Disabled Peoples' International (DPI). Vic Finkelstein, Chair of BCODP and a UPIAS activist, attended the inaugural conference in Singapore and pushed the idea of the social definition of disability to the DPI, where it was accepted over the World Health Organization's medical definitions.

In addition to the groups discussed above, other types of organizations – including single-impairment groups, groups organizing within care homes, and locally organized campaigns for independent living – were emerging in different parts of the country. As mentioned previously, for leaders of the movement, the need for a coordinating

---

[13] Speech by Jane Campbell, "Valuing Diversity – The Disability Agenda. We've Only Just Begun," Bristol University, November 2001, available at http://83.137.212.42/sitearchive/DRC/library/drc_speeches/jane_campbell_-_bristol_univer.html (accessed August 8, 2008).

[14] After several name changes, the organization is now called the UK Disabled People's Council (UKDPC), but for simplicity's sake, I will refer to it as the BCODP throughout this chapter.

body was becoming clear by the late 1970s. A combination of skills that had been acquired in previous years, the theoretical base that UPIAS had established, and an external stimulus in the form of a request for a British representative to the newly established DPI led to the founding of BCODP in 1981/1982. The BCODP inherited the intellectual tradition of the earlier movement, and Campbell and Oliver write that the organization "quickly adopted the social model as the basis for organizing its own activities, which gave it credibility among other disability organizations and assisted in their development."[15] UPIAS, after establishing the ideational and stylistic foundation for the movement, disbanded in 1990 due to low membership numbers and relative confidence that the BCODP would sustain the social model. Today, BCODP (now UKDPC) remains the main, overarching, disability-led organization in the UK, advocating for the promotion of full equality and participation of disabled people. The organization represents approximately 65 groups – each of which must be run by at least 75 percent disabled people – accounting for around 350,000 disabled people, which represents approximately 5 percent of all disabled persons in the UK.

Since the early to mid-2000s, the organized grassroots movement has been experiencing a nadir. However, at its height, BCODP represented up to 140 different organizations, many of which have now disappeared. Two disability academics and activists stopped just short of proclaiming the death of the movement. They write:

> Since the turn of the millennium we have witnessed the growing professionalization of disability rights and the wilful decimation of organisations controlled and run by disabled people at the local and national level by successive government policies despite rhetoric to the contrary. As a result we no longer have a strong and powerful disabled people's movement... the BCODP, historically, one of

---

[15] Campbell and Oliver, *Disability Politics*, p. 89.

the leading organisations in the disabled people's movement, has experienced considerable political isolation in the last few years.[16]

Some activists attribute this weakening of the movement to a government agenda of funding the voluntary sector for the provision of services as opposed to campaigning. Some asserted that the government did not want to fund groups who would oppose them; some attributed it to the existence of the DRC and argued that this resulted in perceptions among policy makers of a lessened need for the voice of disabled people's organizations in the policy sphere, and diminished levels of available resources for civil society actors advancing a comparable disability rights agenda.[17]

A major constraint faced by the BCODP throughout its existence has been the organization's chronic lack of resources. Whereas in the early years some funding was made available to the BCODP from the Department of Health, this was significantly diminished in the mid-1990s. Similarly, local councils have also reduced their funding for grassroots organizations, leading in some cases to the dissolution of BCODP's member organizations.[18] This has had a significant impact on the movement: for example, according to available annual reports, BCODP had to lay off a significant proportion of staff in the 2000s. Table 4.1 further highlights the rapidly diminishing resource base through the 2000s. One of the reasons put forth by activists for this constant resource shortfall is the fact that BCODP must compete with the traditional disability charities for financial support.[19]

---

[16] Mike Oliver and Colin Barnes, "Disability Politics and the Disability Movement in Britain: Where Did It All Go Wrong?," http://www.leeds.ac.uk/disability-studies/archiveuk (accessed August 8, 2008).

[17] Interviews August 8, 2007 and December 10, 2007.

[18] Interviews July 11, 2007 and August 3, 2007.

[19] For example, Section 64 of the Health Services and Public Health Act 1968 creates the provision of funding to assist voluntary organizations in the health and social services field in promoting or providing similar services to the statutory authorities. Campbell and Oliver, *Disability Politics*, p. 104.

Table 4.1. *BCODP Financial Resources, 2000–2007*

Financial year	Gross income	Total expenditure
2000–2001	£758,000	£807,000
2001–2002	£655,000	£703,000
2002–2003	£764,000	£810,000
2003–2004	£337,000	£478,000
2004–2005	£300,000	£292,000
2005–2006	£228,000	£224,000
2006–2007	£227,000	£224,000

Source: The Charity Commission Web site, http://www.charity-commission
.gov.uk/ (accessed June 25, 2008).

ORGANIZATIONS *OF* PERSONS WITH DISABILITIES VERSUS ORGANIZATIONS *FOR* PERSONS WITH DISABILITIES: THE SOCIAL MODEL AND LEGAL MOBILIZATION

These antagonistic relationships with the disability establishment have been one of the defining features of the disability rights movement, and particularly of BCODP. The early radical organizations were often the progeny of residents of institutions run by the disability charities. For these activists, the disability charities embodied all of the worst characteristics of traditional, paternalistic approaches to the issues of disability. Oliver and Campbell write, "The new movement was built in the teeth of opposition from the traditional voluntary organizations which . . . had been in control of disability."[20] Andy Rickell, former chief executive of BCODP, published an opinion piece in *The Guardian* in 2003, in which he argued:

> [T]he disabled people's movement has some animosity to disability charities, particularly the "Big Seven" – Scope, the RNIB, the RNID, Radar, Mind, Mencap and Leonard Cheshire. The primary

[20] Campbell and Oliver, *Disability Politics*, p. 20.

reason (apart from the fact that they suck up to the government) is the way these organizations treat disabled people. They are slow to insist on disabled trustees, and the number of disabled staff is pitiful, particularly at senior levels. They use negative imagery and language in fundraising activity, and continue to run care and educational facilities rooted in segregation. They are an institutional reminder of the attitude that disabled people are charity cases, rather than citizens with equal rights.[21]

Similarly, Mike Oliver, a disability studies scholar and key proponent of the social model, argues:

One of the things I've written about quite extensively is that organisations like these, the Royal National Institutes, SCOPE and RADAR, are not just irrelevant to the lives of disabled people: they are actually downright dangerous. Why are they dangerous? For two reasons, one because they give the impression that society cares and is doing something useful, but second because they take money and resources away from the BCODP and organisations controlled by disabled people.[22]

The antipathy between the BCODP and traditional disability organizations has persisted for more than twenty years, but relations between the two groups of organizations are beginning to change. Although the BCODP organized separately from, and often in opposition to, the traditional charity organizations throughout the 1980s, in the early 1990s, the two groups of organizations came together under a benefits consortium. Furthermore, the BCODP collaborated with the large organizations for disabled people; and, in 1995, organizations *of* and *for* disabled people came together to campaign for civil rights under the banner of the Rights Now Campaign, which led to the passage of the Disability Discrimination Act (DDA).[23] This suggests that, as in

[21] Andy Rickell, "Our Disability is Political," *The Guardian*, October 1, 2003.
[22] Campbell and Oliver, *Disability Politics*, p. 194.
[23] Ibid., p. 57.

the Canadian case, a more pragmatic approach by BCODP was necessary, and that at least some of the traditional organizations were beginning to recognize the BCODP as a legitimate policy actor with important influence over the agenda. Despite this period of cooperation, and the subsequent legislative victory, the BCODP maintains a degree of opposition to the charities. This was manifested by an unwillingness to accept funding from disability charities until very recently, a significant policy considering the serious funding difficulties faced by the organization. In a BCODP newsletter, the leadership asserted: "BCODP National policy is not to work with organizations which oppress disabled people. The social model, rights-based society we want will have no place for charities, as people will be able to get their needs met as of right."[24]

Although some activists and academics insist that the traditional charities, despite name changes or rebranding, have not abandoned their paternalistic, medical model-based approaches, others perceive a change in relations between the two types of organizations. These changes have been driven by a combination of three factors that are not mutually exclusive and are, to a certain extent, constitutive and generative. The first, at the micro-level, is the increasing pragmatism of some activists and their belief that working within or closer to traditional organizations they opposed may be the more effective route to change. Whereas blind and vision-impaired activists have pursued this strategy since the early 1970s (discussed below), there are a number of more recent examples of leaders of the disabled people's movement moving into positions in the disability establishment. For example, Jane Campbell, a leader of the disabled persons' movement, was appointed Commissioner to the DRC and is now Chair of the Statutory Disability Committee of the Equality and Human Rights Commission (EHRC). Former chief executive of the BCODP, Andy Rickell,

---

[24] BCODP Newsletter 55, April 2005, http://www.bcodp.org.uk/activate/Activate%20Issue%2055%20-%20April%202005.txt (accessed May 20, 2008).

created a stir within the community when he was recruited to a senior management position within Scope, the cerebral palsy charity, and an organization he had heavily criticized in his previous role. In a radio interview, Rickell highlighted his reasons for the move:

> Rickell: We have to start from where we are, and it's inevitable that the world is not ideal and therefore if we're going to make a change to where we want to be, we're going to have to start somewhere where we don't want to be. But we have to start there, if we just say that we don't like the way things are, how are they ever going to change if the people that want to make those changes are unclear about how to do that. Ideally I'm the right sort of person who understands the sort of changes we want to see to actually assist the organisation in doing that...

> Robinson (Interviewer): The group that you used to work in – The British Council of Disabled People – is run with very limited resources and now you're moving to Scope, which is a multimillion pound charity. Do you think that some of the money that Scope and these other big disability charities have ought to be given to campaigning groups so that it can be controlled by disabled people?

> Rickell: Undoubtedly I think the sort of money that Scope has should be much more under the control of disabled people, whether it's within Scope or in other organisations. That's the crucial issue – it's the extent to which the money is directed for what disabled people want to see and for their rights.[25]

A second driving force leading to the change in relations has been the urgent need for funding by BCODP and their grassroots groups. A former BCODP leader noted that many small organizations of disabled people have folded within the last four years because of a lack of funding. As a result, BCODP began to collaborate in the mid-2000s with Scope (and eight other organizations) in applying for lottery funding

---

[25] "You and Yours," *BBC Radio 4 Broadcast*, April 22, 2004, transcript at http://www.bbc.co.uk/radio4/youandyours/yy_20040422.shtml (accessed March 17, 2008).

because they believe they are more likely to get money bidding with them, as opposed to in competition with them. However, one BCODP activist noted that this was done in spite of the consternation of some of their members who maintain a hard-line against working with charities like Scope. This hard-line stems from the latter's role in the establishment and maintenance of residential homes and special education programs that are in conflict with the disability movement's emphasis on independent or integrated living and education. A third factor in changing relations may be an implicit recognition within the grassroots organizations that at least some disability charities are transforming their governance structures and representations of disabled persons, and that their critiques may no longer be as relevant as they used to be.[26]

Organizations *of* Disabled Persons and Strategy Choice

In deconstructing the ways in which the ideational meaning frames of the social model of disability and the adversarial, analytical style of engagement came to dominate the movement, we would expect organizations of disabled persons to be broadly supportive of the use of strategic litigation. Indeed, several interviewees argued that it was disability rights activists who first identified the need for enforceable and enforced antidiscrimination legislation.[27] Activists interviewed in the early 1990s acknowledged strong support for effective enforcement mechanisms for the antidiscrimination legislation they were lobbying for:

> I think this single-minded approach to it [the establishment of anti-discrimination legislation] is absolutely necessary and it will win the day . . . It is going to happen, and once it's happened then the disability movement has got to make sure that, having achieved the

---

[26] Tom Shakespeare, *Disability Rights and Wrongs* (London: Routledge, 2006), p. 160.
[27] Interviews July 11, 2007; August 3, 2007; and March 17, 2008.

legislation, it works and people do have these rights, because it's still going to take a hell of an effort to get equal rights – to get them actually implemented, not just on the statute book.[28]

Two scholars highlight the contemporary calls that organizations of disabled people had to be at the heart of enforcement mechanisms:

> Although we used slightly different language we argued that what has now come to be known as the rights based approach to disability would be counter-productive if pursued as an end in itself rather than as a means to an end. Having legal rights does not mean that they will be enforced and even if they are, that enforcement will achieve the desired aims . . . we further suggested that organizations of disabled people were needed to ensure that such an [legalistic] approach remained accountable to disabled people who, after all, had produced the idea in the first place.[29]

Some interviewees expressed concerns that not enough has been done by grassroots organizations to cultivate political and rights conscious-ness more widely in the community. One activist argued,

> Having rights in law . . . is very important to people who don't have them. But I think there is less understanding of how tenuous those rights are unless they are backed up by litigation because I think people go "isn't this fantastic, I've now got the right to do this." And on a personal level there is a time lag with understanding that just because you have the paper right to do something, doesn't mean you have anything.[30]

Importantly, support for the use of strategic litigation by these organi-zations has, generally, remained in the realm of principle, not practice. As discussed above, the grassroots movement began a period of decline just as the hard-fought-for DDA was implemented. As a result, the grassroots groups discussed in this section, particularly BCODP – while playing a pivotal role in establishing the social model and

---

[28] Joe Hennessey cited in Campbell and Oliver, *Disability Politics*, p. 140.

[29] Oliver and Barnes, "Disability Politics."

[30] Interview, July 11, 2007.

associated rights discourse as the dominant meaning frames among the grassroots movement and the adversarial approach as the norm in terms of engagement style – have generally not opted to undertake strategic legal action, focusing instead on direct action and parliamentary lobbying. Examples of grassroots groups using test case litigation are very far and few between: one notable exception is that of the Norfolk Coalition of Disabled People (NCODP), as well as local campaigners from the Thetford Access group, who originally launched the legal action in the *Roads v. Central Trains* case discussed in Chapter 5.[31]

The overwhelming reason cited by interviewees for lack of use of strategic litigation by organizations of disabled people was limited funding. Most interviewees felt that, although litigation was a legitimate strategy and its use was important for the effective enforcement of the DDA, a lack of resources meant that the use of the courts as policy-influencing venues was generally not an option. Knowledge of less expensive forms of legal action, such as intervening before courts, was not demonstrated. Indeed, even these relatively cost-effective forms still have a minimum resource threshold that many of these organizations would not have been able to afford. Based on this analysis, it becomes clear that the resource mobilization explanation becomes the most convincing approach in accounting for the lack of participation in legal venues by organizations of disabled persons.

DISABILITY CHARITIES, THE DIFFUSION OF MEANING FRAMES, AND LEGAL ACTION

The animosity the grassroots movement has felt toward the traditional disability charities has led some disabled activists and academics to lump charitable organizations into one group – organizations *for* disabled persons – to assert their very existence as inconsistent with the

---

[31] *Roads v. Central Trains*, [2004] EWCA Civ 1541.

social model and to write them off as illegitimate actors in the sphere of disability issues. For some disability scholars, this took the form of refusing to explore the role of the disability charities in their studies, even though this neglects the power these organizations wield with the government and the public (including many people with disabilities).[32] For others, this has meant a wholesale, unwavering suspicion of these organizations. For example, Oliver and Barnes write,

> Our history has taught us that in the recent past these organisations played a leading role in keeping us oppressed and out of society. Name changes, tidying up their language and employing token disabled people cannot disguise the underlying reality that these agencies are interested primarily in self preservation and that they will say and do anything that is politically expedient in order to retain their influence in Government circles.[33]

In contrast, representatives of all of the major disability charities, when interviewed, said that rights were now at the core of organizational identity. Interestingly, some interviewees chose to classify their organizations in the *of* or *for* camps, whereas others refuted the validity of this categorization. Activists' critiques have often failed to take into account the real steps some of these organizations have taken to respond to the criticisms made by people with disabilities both within and from outside the organizations. There is even contention over who launched the drive for antidiscrimination legislation. One interviewee, who has worked in the disability sector for more than twenty years, argued that some of the disability charities, even the most criticized, in fact helped lead the rights agenda:

> One of the big myths about the disability lobby is that somehow the big organizations were dragged along to supporting the rights agenda late. When I arrived at Spastics Society [now Scope] in 1985,

---

[32] See Campbell and Oliver, *Disability Politics*.
[33] Oliver and Barnes, "Disability Politics."

there had been in existence for four years already . . . the voluntary organizations disabilities group that was all about lobbying for anti-discrimination legislation . . . it was only after about a year that I joined that Rights Now was actually founded and the administration and the driving force moved towards the radical lobby.[34]

The interviewee qualified this assertion by arguing that there was large variation in a rights-based ethos within the organizations:

Certainly, it would be true that the campaign bits of the organization were years ahead of the rest, so it's certainly true that in 1985 services were very old fashioned . . . The rights agenda was also driving change within the organization that were having to catch up. In that sense – on the care side, concepts of independent living, moving out of an institutionalized model of social care – it was true that the big organizations were behind the pace but those kinds of rights concepts were being picked up by the campaigners within the organization who were driving the campaigning, public face of the organization. [They were] frankly years ahead of where the bulk of the organization was. In that sense, the disability rights movement would be right if they talked about the service philosophies – I think that would be absolutely right – but in terms of being politically dragged along, I honestly believe it's a bit of a myth.[35]

In some cases, these changes may be more rhetorical than real, and it becomes apparent that assessing whether a disability charity conforms to the social model, or can be classified as an organization *of* (versus *for*) disabled people, is anything but a straightforward exercise. What is needed is a more nuanced approach to categorizing these organizations according to whether they have moved toward adopting a social model framework or not, and identifying the attempts some of these organizations have taken toward implementing a social model approach in their work, particularly in their policy and campaigning

---

[34] Interview, December 4, 2007.
[35] Ibid.

work. This section focuses specifically on the Big Seven disability charities – the best-known and among the best-resourced in the country.
Although some of these organizations have existed for more than a
hundred years, most emerged in the immediate post-war period, but
all have relatively long histories compared with the grassroots groups
discussed above. By focusing on the Big Seven, we can then begin to
make some propositions about what is happening in the sector as a
whole in terms of changing meaning frames, rights discourse, and the
use of strategic litigation.

Although a detailed analysis of all seven organizations and the extent
to which they conform to the social model is beyond the scope of this
book, a high-level analysis for the period 1995–2005 provides a picture
of which organizations have begun to move toward the social model
framework and rights talk in the way they work, and which were slower
to take this up.[36] From this we can draw a tentative picture of the
correlation between a social model ideational framework and the use
of legal mobilization among these organizations. To do this, the Big
Seven organizations were categorized in a binary manner as either
moving toward a social model framework or displaying evidence of the
resilience of a charity model framework. This was done first based on
data collated on the percentage of disabled staff among the charities
in 2002–2003 (shown in Table 4.2). This is the single year that these
comparative data were available, and so it provides only a snapshot
of the attitudes these organizations have toward the importance of
disabled persons in their staffing. It can nonetheless serve as a useful
indicator for the categorization exercise: having a larger proportion
of disabled persons on staff would lead, it is expected, to cultural
changes in the organization, which would diminish the use of negative

---

[36] It is important to note, however, that all of these organizations have now to varying degrees adopted rights-language and some campaigning priorities focused on
equality. Some came to this very recently; however, this overview picture focuses on
the period 1995–2005.

Table 4.2. *Overview of the Big Seven Disability Charities, 2002–2003*

Disability charity	Income	Total national staff	Percentage of disabled staff
Mencap	£120.4m	5500	2.8
Leonard Cheshire	£115.1m	7500	2.0
Scope	£93.8m	3900	3.5
RNIB	£84.2m	3000	7.7
RNID	£44.6m	1200	17.0
Mind	£15.2m	130	4.6
RADAR	£0.96m	16	44.0

Sources: The Charity Commission Web site, http://www.charity-commission.gov.uk/ (accessed June 25, 2008); Disability Now's 2003 Disability Charities Employment Survey and BBC Ouch Web site, http://www.bbc.co.uk/ouch/news/btn/bigseven/ (accessed July 2, 2008).

representations and paternalistic service philosophies. The year 2002–2003 is useful for our categorization, as it provides a relevant point at which to measure whether the organizations had begun to implement social model understandings in the make-up of their workforces.

According to these data, three organizations – RADAR, RNID, and RNIB – had relatively higher proportions of people with disabilities working for them, suggesting a heightened commitment to inclusivity.[37] This information was compared with findings from the secondary literature on the disability rights movement's perceptions of the disability sector and then tested through interviews with independent experts (generally lawyers in the field). Impressions of the degree to which the Big Seven organizations had adopted social model understandings of disability generally conformed to those shown through the staff statistics. Mind – the National Association for Mental Health – was more difficult for interviewees to classify because of its slightly different focus and remit on mental health as opposed to disability. It

[37] The figure for RADAR should be read with caution because of the small number of employees in the organization.

was placed in the "moving toward a social model framework" category after analysis of its consultation and governance mechanisms, which have long placed users of mental health services at the heart of the organization.

Heads of policy, chief executives, and other members of senior management of the Big Seven organizations were then interviewed to determine whether the organizations had used, or even considered using, strategic litigation in pursuing their campaign goals. If they had supported applicants, taken judicial reviews, or participated as inter-veners in a strategic manner to support campaign objectives at any time from 1995 to 2005, they were classified as having participated in legal mobilization. As discussed in Chapter 1, the passive use of litigation by organizations for noncampaigning purposes would not qualify them for the "legal mobilization" category. For example, Leonard Cheshire was the subject of test case litigation by a group of residents in one of their care homes regarding the application of the Human Rights Act to independent organizations providing services contracted out by government: this would not qualify as the use of legal action to pursue policy goals.[38] Determining the number of cases where organizations supported applicants or used interventions is difficult because of the relatively ad hoc nature of this activity within some of these organiza-tions and/or the lack of knowledge of most interviewees of the history of this type of activity (as far as it had existed) because of the relatively high rate of turnover in senior management within these organizations. Thus, what is focused on here is the general use of, and attitudes toward, legal mobilization as a campaigning tool.

Of the Big Seven disability charities, four used strategic litigation to varying degrees in the period between the drafting of the DDA in 1995 and 2005: RNIB, RNID, RADAR, and Mind.[39] Three of the Big

---

[38] *Heather, Ward and Callin v. Leonard Cheshire*, [2002] EWCA Civ 366.

[39] Mind has relied largely on mental health legislation, which has existed since the early 1980s, and less on the DDA.

Seven have not used stratetic litigation: Leonard Cheshire Disability, a cross-disability organization; Scope, the disability organization whose focus is people with cerebral palsy; and Mencap, the charity for people with learning disabilities and their families.

Unlike in Canada, where the use of intervention as an interested party in cases has been the predominant method of legal mobilization by organizational actors, none of the Big Seven charities had used this as a method. One reason for this may be the relative novelty of interventions as a way of participating in legal action in the UK; they had only begun to be used in 1994, and so there was a lack of consciousness among organizations about this method.[40] This explanation was tested through the interviewing process: interview questions explicitly did not refer to the use of various methods of undertaking legal mobilization, which made it possible to wait for the interviewee's invocation of an understanding of the use of intervention (or its absence). A senior staff member at RNIB was the only interviewee from a Big Seven organization to allude to this method of legal mobilization.[41] Further, one disability lawyer commented, "One of the things I've been talking to RNIB about is intervening... it's cheaper, it's much easier because you're not tied to either claimant or defendant. It has its disadvantages but it's a very useful method and it's profile-raising as well."[42]

A particularly striking finding about the organizational use of strategic litigation is that the three organizations that have not used litigation are also the wealthiest of the Big Seven. Their annual income for 2002–2003 ranged from £94m for Scope to £120m for Mencap (see Table 4.2).[43] Paradoxically, it was a senior staff member at Mencap, the

---

[40] The Public Law Project, *Third Party Interventions in Judicial Review: An Action Research Study* (London: Public Law Project, 2001).

[41] Interview, December 7, 2007.

[42] Interview, December 10, 2007.

[43] The period 2002–2003 again is chosen as a proxy year because data were available and it again fit into the time period. This can be justified because the relative rankings of organizational income did not significantly vary over the period examined. The

wealthiest of the Big Seven charities, who highlighted the cost argument as one of the primary reasons the organization has eschewed litigation as a campaigning tactic. He argued, "It's that practical constraint. And we as a charity haven't really got the resources to say 'we will go to court and have our day in court regardless.'"[44] Similarly, a senior member of the campaign team at another Big Seven organization that has not used litigation highlighted resources and capacity constraints for the lack of use of litigation: "[Our organization] doesn't take cases on. We don't pursue cases through the courts and we don't pick up individual cases at this stage, but that's mainly a resource and capacity thing rather than a policy decision and I wouldn't rule us out in the future."[45] Interestingly, it appears that the use of strategic litigation was not actively considered a tactic in the period examined: I found no evidence of considerations within the organization regarding the use of litigation, whereas at Mencap, the head of policy confirmed that the organization had on several occasions considered taking cases, and then opted against it, citing the reason that the use of legal action was a "blunt instrument" in terms of campaigning. In contrast with the lack of litigation activity by Scope, Mencap, and Leonard Cheshire, the four less wealthy organizations among the Big Seven all participated in strategic litigation at some point between 1995 and 2005.[46] While also having substantial incomes relative to the grassroots groups, ranging

one exception may be that some of these organizations, e.g., RNIB and RADAR, suspended their strategic litigation activity in the early 2000s. Although, in the case of RADAR this may have been due to financial difficulties, in the case of RNIB it was more the loss of a key staff person to the DRC. In any case, it demonstrates the weakness of resource mobilization explanations when used on their own to explain variation in litigation activity. Another potential weakness of this argument is that this is total organizational income, not the budget spent on campaigning (data that are not easily available for past years).

[44] Interview, August 6, 2007.
[45] Interview, December 13, 2007.
[46] This is not to suggest they were all using litigation throughout this entire period. I am looking here at whether they had used strategic litigation at all.

from £1m to £84m, this contrast between organizations that have used litigation and those who have not, when correlated with their incomes, suggests that resource mobilization explanations fail when accounting for variation in the use of litigation.

Instead, relying on a sociological–institutionalist perspective, we can begin to account for why some organizations might be more willing to commit resources to ensure the effective enforcement of rights through an understanding of the organizational adoption of social model meaning frames. A detailed discussion of the degree to which the social model and its associated rights talk has influenced all Big Seven organizations is beyond the scope of this analysis. Instead, two organizations, one that has adopted the use of strategic litigation and one that has not, will serve as the focus. These cases were chosen for being relatively similar in terms of income and size (see Table 4.2). The next section assesses the changes (or lack thereof) that these organizations underwent over time in their frames and organizational identity, as well as data on attitudes within these organizations toward the use of strategic litigation as a campaigning tool. It traces the correlation between those that have adopted a social model approach and the use – or potential use – of strategic litigation.

From Royal National Institute *for* the Blind to Royal National Institute *of* Blind People: RNIB and Strategic Litigation

RNIB was founded in 1868 and developed in the context of the emerging nineteenth-century charity ethic. It is a national registered charity that offers information, support, and advice to more than 2 million people with sight loss. RNIB has become one of the best-known and wealthiest charities in the country. In many ways, the RNIB represented a classic *for* disabled persons organization, well-resourced and guided by the charity (or medical) model of disability rejected by the disability rights movement. However, the organization has undergone a number of changes in the last twenty-five years: changes that have led to some controversy amongst grassroots activists over how it should be classified. The critiques made by grassroots activists about the Big Seven charities neglect the ideational transformation of organizations like RNIB that has resulted in the implementation of accountability mechanisms and changes in campaigning priorities.

This transformation began when grassroots organizations of blind people, from the early 1970s onward, took up a strategy of infiltrating and taking over the organizations for the blind. They particularly targeted the high-profile RNIB. Colin Low, an activist, argued that,

> [t]he organizations of blind people have accepted that power, resources and expertise resided in the traditional voluntary organizations. They recognized that this was not something which was going to be turned around overnight and that it was necessary to work with this situation and direct it to their own ends. This has inclined them towards a more coalition style of politics which recognized that disabled people need allies, and that it was necessary for them to work with able-bodied people and with existing institutions if they were to get anywhere.[47]

The outcomes of this strategy began to be realized in the early 1980s. A change in organizational leadership with the appointment of a new chief executive wanting to modernize the organization, and a push among several key players on the organizational board to become an *of* organization, resulted in the organizational identity beginning to shift.[48] A senior staff member at RNIB notes, "the Chief Executive realized that the days of the 'for' charity – that model – is outmoded, outdated. Also, within the ranks of RNIB and on the board were [blind] people who were saying 'this is our organization and we should be running it.'"[49] Perhaps predictably, part of this shift also resulted in

---

[47] Campbell and Oliver, *Disability Politics*, p. 99.
[48] Interview, December 7, 2007.
[49] Ibid.

a changing dynamic between the traditional charity and the population of grassroots organizations. From the early 1980s, the RNIB supported the growth of organizations of blind persons and the policies and campaign objectives those organizations prioritized.[50] By the mid-1990s, there was some recognition by a minority within grassroots organizations that there was an emerging commitment to a social model framework within RNIB.[51] Further changes since that time have included reforms of governance structures: the majority of trustees are now blind or partially sighted persons, and RNIB established a membership scheme to enable an even greater proportion to get involved and have input into how services are delivered. It was also part of an attempt to have a stronger voice when negotiating with the Government and other organizations on behalf of people with sight loss.[52]

Finally, the organization's name changes over the last six years represent a symbolic shift in identity. In 2002, the organization changed its name from Royal National Institute *for* the Blind to Royal National Institute *of* the Blind; and in 2007, the name changed again to Royal National Institute of Blind People, which they felt emphasized their role as a campaigning organization and the voice of people with sight loss. A representative of RNIB asserted, "I think we're much more comfortable with ourselves now. RNIB is run by blind people. That's how things should be . . . the feel of the organization has changed."[53]

RNIB represents an example of a traditional charity that has undergone changes in organizational identity, governance structures and leadership, and representations of disabled persons in marketing material over the last twenty-five years. The case of RNIB is also illustrative of a method of diffusion of ideational frames, whereby activists began to infiltrate the organization to embed the social model in organizational

---

[50] Colin Low cited in Campbell and Oliver, *Disability Politics*, p. 99.

[51] Stephen Bradshaw cited in Campbell and Oliver, *Disability Politics*, p. 172.

[52] RNIB Web site, "About Us," http://www.rnib.org.uk (accessed May 20, 2008).

[53] Interview, December 7, 2007.

practices.[54] Low argues that the strategy of infiltrating and working within the traditional organizations, adopted in the 1970s by organizations of blind people, has been more successful than that by the movement as a whole: "The BCODP has adopted a more straightforwardly oppositional stance which, I would argue, has not only secured fewer gains, but has also meant that the disability movement has been divided in its approach."[55]

RNIB and Strategic Litigation

RNIB has been among the most active disability charities in terms of the use of strategic litigation. The organization developed a position for in-house legal counsel shortly after the implementation of the DDA in 1995 to develop and support a litigation strategy to test the scope of the new legislation and its provisions for blind and partially sighted people. In addition to litigation work, the organization undertook an outreach program in the late 1990s, working with local associations of blind people to make individuals aware of their rights. In the early 2000s, the position of in-house legal adviser to the campaigns team was left empty, partly because the DRC was pursuing its litigation strategy, and an unspoken division of labor emerged. More recently, in late 2007 and early 2008, the organization reassessed what the job description of the position should entail and, due largely to encouragement from trustees, the campaigns team hired a new lawyer, signaling a renewed commitment to the use of strategic litigation. As one RNIB interviewee points out:

> It had become a routine service and we had rather forgotten about the importance of test cases I think. Plus our trustees – we're an "of"

---

[54] Colin Low cited in Campbell and Oliver, *Disability Politics*, p. 99.
[55] Campbell and Oliver, *Disability Politics*, p. 99.

organization – so 90 percent of our trustees are blind or partially sighted, and they were encouraging us to do more legal work in a variety of areas, so we've taken the opportunity to rethink [the position]. So the new lawyer will be active across more areas.[56]

A lawyer connected to RNIB explained how the organization had tried to balance being strategic in its approach, on one hand, and dealing with the volume of cases on the other.

We didn't take bog-standard cases, we had taken quite a few, "guide-dog refused entry to restaurant" types of cases so instead of taking those we provided people with a set of pleadings that they could use in court. We provided them with information and support but we wouldn't actually run the case ourselves. It was too resource-intensive and there were other things we needed to be doing.[57]

The organization established case selection criteria, the most important being that the case tied in with campaign priorities: for example, issues of recruitment, access to health care, and access to information. The case had to have a decent prospect of success (unless the case was taken to show a particular gap in the law). There also had to be no other potential source of support for the litigant. For example, if the person who was blind or partially sighted was a trade union member, RNIB would encourage the person to pursue that avenue first. RNIB would also want the client to agree to publicity in order to generate media interest.[58] The threat or initiation of legal action has resulted in some important wins, representing significant benefits for blind individuals backed by the RNIB. To name just a few, this has included funding cases against employers for discrimination in employment or recruitment, against goods and service providers for discrimination,

---

[56] Interview, December 10, 2007.
[57] Ibid.
[58] Ibid.

and against primary care trusts for operating blanket bans on the provision of sight-saving treatments.

Despite evidence of a commitment on the part of RNIB to the use of strategic litigation, this strategy has not been unquestioned. The constraints identified in the case of RNIB are exemplary of the limits experienced by many of the Big Seven disability charities. What this case study reveals is that RNIB has overcome them. First, although resource mobilization theorists would argue that, as a charity with plenty of resources, funding should not be a constraint, this negates the source of funding and donors' attitudes regarding the appropriateness of strategic litigation, which may be a constraining condition. One lawyer argued,

> I think if you've got organizations that are dependent on donations, spending money on the law is more difficult to sell to people [funders]. Particularly if you are talking about strategic litigation and not just helping blind people generally. That's my personal view. I don't think people want to fund lawyers. It's different if you're able to say "we're able to help every blind person who comes through the door by providing advice on employment rights" than saying "we're going to cherry-pick these particular cases."[59]

A second constraining factor may be tensions or incompatibilities in the goals, strategies, or values of various parts of the organization. Several pertinent situations illustrating this have arisen at RNIB. First, the libraries services team works very closely with librarians to enhance the rights to access information for blind and partially sighted people, and has taken time to develop that close collaboration. However, at one point, the campaigns team debated taking a legal case against a local authority under the Libraries Act, potentially jeopardizing the goodwill established by the libraries services team.[60] Another example was an implicit conflict between RNIB's corporate fundraisers, who

[59] Ibid.
[60] Interview, December 7, 2007.

were seeking to be the charity of the year as chosen by a major retailer, and the campaigns team, which was threatening legal action against the same retailer because their online store's Web site was not accessible. Finally, a third constraining factor is fear of an intraorganizational backlash against (what some might perceive as) the zealous use of legal action. Although trustees have encouraged the use of legal resources for campaigning purposes, there is also an awareness of the potential negative effects of using strategic litigation. A senior staff member deduced that,

> There is definitely a feeling among trustees that we shouldn't be overly litigious. We shouldn't be constantly taking cases. We got incredible media coverage for our case against a primary care trust, and all of that is always good for the visibility of the organization, but I think the trustees did feel a little uncomfortable. They wouldn't want to see a whole stream of cases.[61]

In sum, although there are considerable constraints on the use of strategic litigation, RNIB has nonetheless subscribed to its use as a policy-influencing tool. Furthermore, its use will potentially become even more significant in the future with RNIB's institutional commitment to litigation as a campaign strategy, as signaled by the hiring of in-house counsel and explorations of the role the organization could play as an intervener in the courts. Although the availability of financial resources is certainly an important condition influencing RNIB's use of strategic litigation, the role of the meaning frames associated with the social model has also played a significant, and potentially even more important, role than resources, especially considering the fact that sometimes the policy team and counsel have to convince donors of the utility of legal mobilization. The meaning frames imported into the organization by grassroots activists shifted the identity of the organization to one where rights and equality became key campaign priorities, which

---

[61] Ibid.

subsequently led to a commitment to effective enforcement of those rights, in part through the use of strategic litigation.

From Spastics Society to Scope

Scope (formerly known as the Spastics Society), focusing on people with cerebral palsy and more recently with those with complex needs, was formed in 1952 as an incorporated charity and drew together middle-class parents' groups that had previously been organizing on a local level. In the period examined here and that preceding it, the organization had not used strategic litigation or legal action to pursue policy goals, enforce legislation, or test the law. As a "negative case," this section aims to explore a range of possible explanations for the eschewing of this strategy. I argue that it was the organization's resistance to collective action frames embracing the social model, and its status quo orientation, that led to a culture whereby strategic litigation is not within the realm of "appropriate strategies." One author argues that:

> Throughout its history Scope has not been known for being particularly radical. It is an irony that, although it came into existence precisely because parents could not accept the status quo in terms of provision for people with cerebral palsy, it has still been resistant to change and prefers to maintain its own status quo.[62]

Although the organization has since undergone changes, in the early days, the types of changes were criticized from those both within and outside the organization for being symbolic and rhetorical as opposed to real and embedded.

---

[62] Chris Davies, *Changing Society: A Personal History of Scope*, at http://www.scope.org .uk/sites/default/files/pdfs/History/Scope_changing_society.pdf, p. 89 (accessed May 20, 2008).

Throughout the 1970s, the Spastics Society epitomized, for grass-roots activists, the paternalistic approach with which the traditional charities treated disabled persons. This included negative representations of disabled persons in their fundraising appeals, institutionalization as their main policy for housing severely disabled persons, and education service provision and governance structures that focused almost exclusively on parents and caregivers. In the 1980s, and under a new chief executive, the organization took some tentative steps toward a more inclusive model of the organization's governance structures by expanding the role of disabled persons in consultation processes and attempting to increase the number of disabled staff within the organization.

> We also made a more deliberate attempt to appoint people with disabilities to key jobs within the organization. I have to say I was quite surprised when I started working for the organization at how relatively few of the senior management positions were held by people with disabilities . . . I think that those were aims that were in my mind. I daresay that we didn't fulfil them as much as we should have done, but at least they were there in my mind.[63]

The chief executive of that period, however, pointed out that changes he envisioned were slowed or stalled by the continued involvement of parents, who dominated the organization. He argues the following:

> I think it was at a transitional stage in terms of the influence of the parents, the parental generation that had founded the organization. It was ready to be handed over to allow disabled people themselves to play a much bigger role in the management of the organization, both as volunteers and as staff . . . I was lucky that I was able to recruit quite a lot of the staff whilst I was there: a lot of the senior jobs became vacant, and so we had, I think, for a time a very enthusiastic group of staff, many of whom had quite radical ideas about what

---

[63] Ibid., p. 92.

they wanted to do, and there was no resistance from them at all. I think they were very supportive of the changes, but there was, I have to say, some resistance – I don't want to stigmatize the Executive Council because they are volunteers and a lot of them have been extraordinarily dedicated in what they've done, and Scope wouldn't exist if it hadn't been for them over the years, but nevertheless, I feel that they were resistant to change in a way which many staff members were not resistant to change.[64]

Intraorganizational tensions about the direction and identity of the organization with regards to governance structures and accountability mechanisms stalled embryonic processes of organizational change through the 1980s and early 1990s. This tension culminated with a major organizational endeavor that resulted in the changing of the organization's name in 1994 from the Spastics Society to Scope. The organization's own account of the drivers of change include people with cerebral palsy, particularly younger adults living more independently in the community, affirming their disquiet over the use of the word "spastic," which had come to be seen as a term of abuse, as well as the significance of a number of younger parents who had not chosen to seek the services of the organization to avoid their children being associated with the stigmatizing label. One member of the organization's management at the time particularly emphasized this latter concern:

> It was nice to do it for all sorts of other reasons that may or may not be seen as politically correct, but actually there was a very strong business driver which is that we weren't representing the younger parents anymore. There was a big debate about whether we should invest in de-stigmatising the term spastic rather than change it to something else altogether and, in fact, a lot of groups – including parents' groups – the membership were in favour of doing that, but our PR advisers said it would cost us four times as much to change

[64] Tim Yeo cited in Davies, *Changing Society*, p. 93.

everyone's perception of "spastic" as it would be to just change the name. So the analogy was gay pride so what the gay movement had done is re-invest a positive meaning into the term "gay" to something to be proud of, so the idea was to re-invest pride in the term "spastic" and take away the medical connotation. But it would have cost a lot of money to do that.[65]

The case of Scope's name change adds complexity to our understanding of how to measure whether an organization is guided by principles of the social model of disability. Although on the surface this example may seem similar to RNIB's name changes over the last several years, there are two crucial differences: these include the drivers of the change, which in the case of Scope did not coalesce with the social model, and the difference between organizational rhetoric and reality as experienced by those within the organization. At RNIB, where the main trigger of the name change had been growing demands by the majority of trustees, at Scope it was business concerns and worries that parents (and, to a lesser extent, disabled persons) were not joining the organization that drove change. Significantly, research conducted by the organization at the time of the name change highlighted a number of fundamental issues that affected the organization's image. This included a clear need for greater involvement of people with cerebral palsy in the organization and its day-to-day work and the need to establish a mechanism for active involvement of far more individuals with cerebral palsy in the constitutional framework and governance of the organization.[66] Despite recognition that these were fundamental issues, the organization chose instead to focus its attention and resources on the rebranding, with comparatively little action taken to change the organization's own culture.

[65] Interview, March 11, 2008.
[66] SCOPE Web site, "The Spastics Society to Scope: The Story of the Name Change and Relaunch," November 1994, http://www.scope.org.uk/publications/aboutscope.shtml (accessed May 20, 2008).

The name change, on one level, clearly signals a shift within the organization toward a more inclusive, less stigmatizing identity. Yet the drivers and "options not pursued" are also important indicators of the organization's "logics of appropriateness." Additional evidence suggests that Scope was still, as an organization, firmly rooted in the status quo charity and medical model of disability. The legacy of the parents' role in the organization remained in the 1990s and, arguably, even into the 2000s. Several members of the organization commented that the staffing and governance structures remain a pivotal issue:

> I don't know how many cerebral palsied people are working for it. I find attitudes still in Scope, like everywhere I suppose, how we know what's good for you – and they dish it out accordingly . . . Scope and their conferences are full of able-bodied people. Where are these cerebral palsied people? In my opinion Scope is not fulfilling its full duty.[67]

> I think they're making progress. They're getting more people with cerebral palsy interested in the running of Scope. But, at the end of the day, I still worry how far they're going to allow people with cerebral palsy to have the power: whether they'll just go so far, and that's it.[68]

In celebration of the organization's fiftieth anniversary in 2002, a personal retrospective of Scope, based on interviews with seventeen key figures in the organization's development, was published. A review in *The Guardian* newspaper on the publication of the personal history describes this as an indication of the organization's willingness to transform: "It is a measure of the transformation undergone by Scope that Davies should have been commissioned to put together the book to mark the charity's 50th anniversary. And although it is described as a 'personal history,' what is striking about the book is the licence that Davies has been allowed." Some of the opinions expressed in this seem

---

[67] Hilda Davies cited in Davies, *Changing Society*, p. 133.
[68] Pat Entwhistle cited in Davies, *Changing Society*, p. 133.

to echo, from those on the inside (members of the executive council, staff, or consultants who have worked with the organization), the major critiques put forth by the grassroots activists.[69] These include the role of disabled persons in the organization's staff and governance, its service provision ethos, and the continued dominance by parents:

> I think Scope at the moment is in transition. I think it's looking for a future. It's still tied up a lot in the past. It's still got a lot of services, which it didn't know how to get rid of, because people are still using them, and a lot of people don't know any other alternative, and Scope feels that it owes those people something – which it does. But I'm not sure that the answer is to carry on in the way that they were.[70]

> As far I'm concerned, Scope are still very disabling, they don't practise what they preach as far as inclusion and rights, and it's not about inclusion and rights. Staff are still very much working from the medical perception of what this disability is; they aren't aware that it is now a social issue rather than a medical issue . . . I also think they've also got a problem because they are a charity, they need to raise money, if they seem to be too rights-orientated they won't raise enough dosh.[71]

> There are some changes. There are more disabled people in it. Scope has also been doing a lot more campaigning on disability rights, but the thing is, they still have non-disabled people in the powerful positions. I feel they're more like government lackeys. I think they work more with the government than they do with the grass roots disabled people. It needs to be more democratic. It's not.[72]

In the late 1990s and early 2000s, the organization underwent a number of changes and repositioned itself in relation to the grassroots disabled

---

[69] David Brindle, "A Very Telling Tale," *The Guardian*, May 22, 2002.

[70] Glynn Vernon cited in Davies, *Changing Society*, p. 135.

[71] Allison John cited in Davies, *Changing Society*, p. 148.

[72] Angela Smith cited in Davies, *Changing Society*, p. 149.

people's movement.[73] In 1998, Scope's executive council consisted for the first time of a majority of people with disabilities, and the organization announced its new aim that disabled people achieve equality. In the early 2000s, changes in leadership and recruitment also resulted in some shifts within the organization; these included a new chief executive and the recruitment of former grassroots activists and BCODP chief executive, Andy Rickell, to the senior management team in 2004. Rickell saw his recruitment as a radical move by the organization to counter the notion that Scope "was just using words like 'equality' without really seeking to embed it."[74] His role was to change the culture of the organization, focusing specifically on employment. Upon his arrival, less than four percent of staff were disabled; Scope expressed a desire to change that and, more broadly, to change perceptions within the organization. They set a target of having twenty percent disabled staff by the end of December 2007, which, according to Rickell, was achieved in April 2007, resulting in a "radical change in the culture in terms of employment."[75] Recent changes in the service provision ethos of the organization also seem to be taking place with a focus on closing segregated institutions and educational facilities and providing support for disabled persons to live in the community instead. In 2005, *The Guardian* reported that:

> The politics of disability moved forward this week with a significant change of tack by charity Scope. It has taken on board many of the criticisms levelled by disabled activists against segregated accommodation. Chief executive Tony Manwaring says he intends to change the focus of the organisation to concentrate its £100m-a-year budget on helping people with a disability to live in the community, instead of housing them in separate institutions and schools.[76]

---

[73] Interview, December 14, 2009.

[74] Interview, March 17, 2008.

[75] Ibid.

[76] John Carvel, "Scope for Improvement," *The Guardian*, March 2, 2005, at http://www.guardian.co.uk/society/2005/mar/02/charitymanagement.socialcare (accessed May 22, 2008).

Finally, Scope has also shown recent changes in how it relates to organizations of grassroots activists, most notably BCODP (now UKDPC). Indeed, according to the BCODP, Scope twice requested to work with the grassroots organization. In response to rumors that they were working with Scope, the leadership of BCODP made it clear in their 2005 newsletter that they were not accepting funding.

> To put the record straight and reassure our members, it is worth stating in the clearest possible terms that at no time has BCODP ever accepted money from Scope. (A quick glance at our annual audited accounts will reassure any doubters.) Over the last few months, the BCODP National Council has twice voted overwhelmingly to reject requests from Scope to work together on two projects. One was a request to support Scope in developing its own Disability Equality Training programme, which we rejected in favour of promoting our own in-house training programme. At least our programme is based on the social model of disability and only uses disabled trainers who have been accredited through our training and support services . . . The long standing commitment of BCODP to promote and support the independent disabled peoples movement is still solidly in place.[77]

However, since then, BCODP worked with Scope to successfully bid for funding. This could be explained by the grassroots organization's dire financial situation, but a senior staff member at Scope identified a second motivating factor: Scope is taking proactive steps to change and may become "an organization that radical organizations could do business with."[78] More recently, Scope has focused on building capacity within disabled people's organizations; supporting the local campaigns of grassroots organizations; facilitating dialogue between parents, other caregivers, and service users; and encouraging the coproduction of strategy and policy between these different stakeholders.[79]

---

[77] BCODP Newsletter 55.
[78] Interview, March 17, 2008.
[79] Interview, December 14, 2009.

This case was chosen as an example of an organization that has not used strategic litigation. In the period examined, no evidence was found of Scope being involved in cases, supporting applicants, or even providing general legal advice, and interviews with senior staff confirmed that the organization had not used legal mobilization as a campaigning strategy.[80] The very detailed 2002 organizational history makes no mention of discussions within the organization about rights enforcement or the use of legal mobilization of any type. Although it would be difficult to make the argument based on the available data that the organization has been hostile to the use of strategic litigation, it is clear that, at least until very recently, this tactic did not seem to be on the radar of key decision makers within the organization. This can be correlated with the relatively slow diffusion of meaning frames that define disabled persons first and foremost as rights-bearing citizens rather than objects of charity.

Several recent developments, in internal staffing, relationships with grassroots organizations, and shifts in campaign priorities, signal that this it is changing, potentially explaining the very recent consideration within the organization of the use of strategic litigation and the policy of empowering local groups to use legal action.[81] In 2007, the organization began to turn toward the use of law. According to one senior staff member, "discussions are happening now, previously the organization wouldn't have done that [taken legal cases]. We're prepared to be in the public spotlight... to be confident."[82] This is evidenced in part by discussions that representatives of Scope have had with legal counsel about pro bono work. Although it is too early to trace the impact of the changes discussed above, it would confirm the theoretical argument put forward that shifts in the organization's identity and collective action frames are important determinants of the range of appropriate policy-influencing strategies.

[80] Interviews, March 17, 2008 and December 14, 2009.
[81] Interview, December 14, 2009.
[82] Interview, March 17, 2008.

THE UNIQUE ROLE OF THE DISABILITY
RIGHTS COMMISSION

A third type of organization has played a unique and significant role in the enforcement of disability rights legislation in the UK. The DRC was established as a nondepartmental public body (NDPB) under the DRC Act 1999. With the establishment of the EHRC, the DRC closed its doors on September 30, 2007, and its responsibilities and functions have been subsumed by the new commission (this is discussed further below). The DRC was mandated to work toward the elimination of discrimination against people with disabilities, promote equal opportunities, and encourage good practice in the treatment of disabled people. The DRC operated in England, Scotland, and Wales, and its main activities included provision of advice, information, and publications on rights and good practice to disabled people, employers, and service providers; provision of support to disabled people in achieving their rights under the 1995 DDA; reviewing the legislation and producing statutory codes of practice; supporting legal cases to test the scope and boundaries of the law; organizing campaigns to change policy, practice, and awareness; and producing policy statements and research on disability issues. DRC leadership consisted of fifteen nonexecutive commissioners (a majority of whom are disabled). Funded by the Department for Work and Pensions (DWP), the DRC workforce consisted of approximately 180 employees, of whom roughly 35 percent were disabled. As an indication of its funding levels, in the last year of its operations, the DRC was granted £21.2m by DWP.

The DRC is not a social movement organization per se but a publicly funded body with a mandate to work toward the elimination of discrimination against disabled people and promote equality. In some ways, the DRC could be considered part of the political and legal opportunity structure, but there is also a case to be made for treating the DRC as a key movement policy actor in the realm of disability rights in the UK. First, during its existence, the DRC had considerable impact in policy areas of relevance to disabled persons, often in a manner contrary to government interests: it valued its role as an independent actor. Second, an independent evaluation of the DRC's consultation mechanisms was generally positive and particularly highlighted the variety of processes relied on to involve people with disabilities in its work, including formal consultation exercises relating to specific strategic plans, research, reports, and other documents as well as action groups and forums.[83] Third, several interviewees (from both inside and outside the DRC) pointed out that many key policy entrepreneurs in disability organizations became commissioners or were employed in key positions within the DRC during its existence. One chief executive of a disability organization noted that "when the DRC was formed, in a way, some of the energy in the voluntary sector around some of that work [legal cases in particular] moved into the Commission."[84] Another interviewee commented on the reliance the disability sector developed toward the DRC: "I think people thought, 'well the DRC is there, they'll do it' and their knowledge wore down as well so it made it much more difficult to get involved. I do think they became dependent on the DRC to a certain extent . . . because the DRC was quite a good resource."[85] In this way, the organization corralled expertise, resources, and a diversity of perspectives from the sector.[86] On both a macro- and a micro-level, the DRC can be considered one of the key organizational actors advancing a disability rights and social model agenda during its existence.

---

[83] Disability Rights Commission, *Evaluating the Impact of the Disability Rights Commission: Final Report* (Manchester: Disability Rights Commission, 2007).

[84] Interview, December 10, 2007.

[85] Ibid.

[86] It was, however, susceptible to criticism for not representing the ethnic diversity of disabled persons.

The DRC and Strategic Litigation

Framing the mandate and mission of the organization primarily in terms of rights, laid the foundation for the relatively uncontroversial use of strategic litigation by the Commission. Yet despite this general consensus, there were tensions over the notion of who it would be used against, to what extent it would be used, and how many disabled persons might benefit from the results. Like the other equality commissions in the UK, the DRC was organizationally well suited to deploy legal tactics in combating discrimination.[87] It developed a team of lawyers experienced in employment and disability law and designed intake processes, both to identify systemic barriers to the full inclusion of disabled persons in society and to filter potential legal cases for test case litigation. Yet the DRC's Legal Services department was not solely focused on test case litigation. In fact, the Legal Director often publicly expressed skepticism regarding the use of litigation to achieve social change compared with the effect of its other statutory powers. These included the provision of conciliation services and the power to conduct formal investigations into any area relevant to the participation of disabled people in society concerning, for example, employment, education, or the provision of services.[88] Reflecting back on the range of work undertaken by the legal department, Bert Massie, the Chair of the DRC, wrote in the report on the legal achievements of the Commission:

> In April 2000, I said that the policy of the DRC would be to use the force of argument, but if people failed to listen we would use the argument of force. That is what we have done. Our helpline (which has won national awards) has advised hundreds of thousands of disabled people on how to assert their rights in the face of discrimination. Our Conciliation Service has helped people to resolve issues

[87] Alter and Vargas, "Explaining Variation," pp. 452–82; Interview, August 8, 2007.

[88] Interviews, February 15, 2005 and August 8, 2007.

Table 4.3. *Number of Complaints of Discrimination Made to the DRC Helpline, 2004–2007*

Year	Employment	Access to goods, facilities, and services	Education	Premises	Total
2004–2005	7,546	5,242	1,864	822	15,474
2005–2006	8,590	7,198	2,111	890	18,789
2006–2007	15,710	10,441	3,284	1,745	31,180
Total	31,846	22,881	7,259	3,457	65,443

Sources: Disability Rights Commission. 2007. *DRC Legal Achievements 2000–2007.* Manchester: DRC.

without recourse to the courts. Through our Codes of Practice, our website, and our work with the public and private sectors, we have sought to ensure that ignorance of the law should never be a valid excuse for discriminating.

But none of this work would have been effective if the DRC had not had a clear legal strategy to enforce the law. We have used the nation's highest courts to test the law. We have shown that human rights principles can inform and strengthen equality law. We have proven that the DDA is not a paper tiger but has sharp teeth and strong jaws. But although the DRC is to end, the struggle must not. There is still a long road to travel. The Disability Equality Duty remains untested. Others must take the reins and set the future direction. If they do so in the style of the DRC, disabled people will have the ability to use the DDA to free themselves from the curse of discrimination.[89]

Intake processes to identify legal cases for potential support by the DRC evolved over time, becoming more efficient and targeted. The DRC helpline was the first point of contact with the Commission for disabled people, and this was one channel through which legal cases to be supported by the DRC would be picked up. Table 4.3 highlights records of alleged cases of disability discrimination made

[89] Disability Rights Commission, *DRC Legal Achievements 2000–2007.*

via the helpline.[90] Discrimination complaints almost doubled within this three-year period, likely signifying increasing awareness among disabled persons of their rights and a growing recognition of the role of the DRC as a source of information and advice when those rights had been violated. The early approach to screening cases was not very targeted, and one interviewee noted: "There wasn't much strategic litigation going on to be honest. If the case hadn't settled by the time it got to Legal [Services] then they would fund it."[91] However, as the number of complaints grew, this became unsustainable. One former member of the legal team noted: "In terms of the number of calls the Commission received, it just grew and grew. And it became clear that we couldn't support all the cases and we needed some sort of filter... And at that point [around 2003/2004] you began to have some sort of structure... over time, the strategic litigation developed."[92] Along with the switch to a more strategic approach to case selection, there was a shift to a more proactive form of intake procedures. The helpline was not completely abandoned as a source of cases, but the director of Legal Services noted that it was not a particularly productive source.[93] Instead, the Legal Services department began to proactively reach out to key law firms specializing in discrimination and disability to encourage solicitors to try to identify, and bring to the Commission's attention, cases that had reached the appellate level.

> The cases that we run now are very often brought to us by solicitors who are acting in an appeal already and therefore know that the

---

[90] These figures represent the number of issues for which records were created, rather than the number of contacts to the DRC helpline. This distinction is important because the same person could have had a number of different issues to discuss with the DRC or may have contacted the DRC on a number of occasions about the same issue. Figures prior to April 2004 are not available in comparative breakdown format. Figures for the period from April 2007 to the end of the DRC's functioning in September 2007 were not available.

[91] Interview, March 11, 2008.

[92] Ibid.

[93] Interview, August 8, 2007.

Table 4.4. *Number of Legal Cases Supported by the DRC, 2000–2007*

Year	Employment	Services	Education	Judicial review/ intervention	Total
2001–2002	41	23	0	1	65
2002–2003	34	20	2	2	58
2003–2004	23	6	19	2	50
2004–2005	12	12	22	4	50
2005–2006	21	17	13	4	55
2006–2007	14	20	12	4	50
April 1, 2007–June 29, 2007	3	4	1	2	10
Total	148	102	69	19	338

Sources: Disability Rights Commission. 2007. *DRC Legal Achievements 2000–2007.* Manchester: DRC.

issues have crystallized and they might be of interest to us. We might fund them to continue the case or we might take it in-house because sometimes funding might be an issue for them.[94]

Over its seven years of existence, the DRC supported 338 cases and participated in a number of different ways in legal actions (see Tables 4.4 and 4.5). Employment cases represented the most common type of case supported by the DRC (about 44 percent of all cases). The number of education cases increased in 2003–2004 as part of the DRC's commitment to test the education provisions that came into force in 2002. The shift between 2003–2004 and 2004–2005, with a drop in employment cases and an increase in services cases and judicial reviews/interventions, reflects the explicit priorities of the case-selection strategy adopted by the Legal Services department at that time.

When the DRC began its work, the available research suggested that, whereas approximately 1,700 cases had reached a hearing under the DDA's employment provisions, just 53 cases had been commenced

[94] Ibid.

Table 4.5. *Examples of Involvement of the DRC in Key Cases, 2002–2008*

Case name	Year	Court	DRC involvement
Cruickshank v. VAW Motorcast Ltd	2002	Court of Appeal	Supported the appellant
McNicol v. Balfour Beatty Rail Maintenance Ltd	2002	Court of Appeal	Intervened in this case as an interested party
Ford-Shubrook v. St Dominics Sixth Form College	2003	Manchester County Court	Supported the appellant
The Queen (On the Application of A,B) v. East Sussex County Council	2003	High Court	Intervened as an interested party
Archibald v. Fife	2004	House of Lords	Supported the appellant
Roads v. Central Trains	2004	Court of Appeal	Supported the appellant
Ross v. Ryanair Ltd and Stansted Airport Ltd	2004	Court of Appeal	Supported the appellant
Essa v. Laing Ltd	2004	Court of Appeal	Joint intervention of three statutory commissions (CRE, EOC, and DRC)
R (on the application of Burke) v. General Medical Council	2005	Court of Appeal	Intervened as an interested party
Igen Ltd v. Wong and two other cases	2005	Court of Appeal	Joint intervention of three statutory commissions (CRE, EOC, and DRC)
Smith v. Churchills Stairlifts Plc	2006	Court of Appeal	Supported the appellant
YL (by her litigation friend the Official Solicitor) v. Birmingham City Council and others	2007	House of Lords	Intervened as an interested party
London Borough of Lewisham v. Malcolm	2007	Court of Appeal	Intervened as an interested party
Coleman v. Attridge Law	2008	European Court of Justice	Supported the appellant

Sources: Disability Rights Commission. 2007. *DRC Legal Achievements 2000–2007.* Manchester: DRC.

under the legislation protecting against discrimination in the provision of goods and services. The early years of the DRC's work continued with the focus on employment, but this changed with the adoption of the first litigation strategy. The DRC recognized that focusing on a strategic number of key cases at appellate level that would lead to binding precedents would have far more impact in the longer term on the rights of disabled people than running or supporting hundreds of cases in the employment tribunal.

The DRC's litigation strategy aimed at prioritizing those cases that would clarify or test the law, and so extend in impact beyond the specific circumstances of the particular case. It also targeted those areas of the law that were not being enforced by individual disabled persons in the courts. Originally, the strategy prioritized two issues: first, areas where the Commission wanted to test the law, to understand the boundaries and highlight areas where the legislation was incomplete, inconsistent, or functioning in perverse ways; and second, issues of access to justice.[95] This strategy was overhauled several years later, signaling a shift in emphasis toward testing the legislative provisions that had recently come into force. In practice, the intraorganizational working relationships that developed within the Commission functioned to put the litigation strategy in practice and then to highlight the policy implications of cases that were won or lost in the courts. Several interviewees highlighted the dynamic that developed:

> So you begin to get legal policy people saying "this is a problem," us [the legal team] taking cases, the legislation people saying "this is where the law needs to change" and then us picking up more cases. It was a really really good time. You began to get us losing or winning cases on the boundary of the law, them [the legislation team] arguing that it needed to be clarified, and then the policy people saying this is how we need to change for the future and it just worked really well.[96]

---

[95] Interview, March 11, 2008.
[96] Ibid.

> When we litigated at DRC we had a very multi-disciplinary approach to it. We would have a discussion about where we thought the law needed to go, how it was being interpreted and how to argue it. And then we would go and have a conference with counsel and tell them that's what we thought.[97]

In terms of case selection, all cases passed through the legal committee to be approved for funding. One point closely considered was whether a loss in the courts would be of greater cost, in terms of policy loss, than a benefit in case of victory.

> I know many times the Disability Rights Commission legal committee has wavered on whether or not to fund something because the question had been posed, "What happens if we lose – won't it make it worse?" It would make it worse to have a bad decision from the House of Lords or Court of Appeal rather than settle for a bad one at the EAT [Employment Appeal Tribunal] or lower-rung down.[98]

Another consideration was the selection of opponents where, like in the case of RNIB discussed above, the needs and requests of certain parts of the Commission had to be balanced with the aims of the litigation.

> There are political issues on selection of opponents. Certainly in the early days there was a bit of a temptation to want to find big name opponents and our press people wanted cases against big names, and of course there was a fear that doing that would create a backlash because people would be saying "you're only suing us because we're [a major supermarket chain], or whatever, if we were a small supermarket you wouldn't care." And there might be some merit in that because the argument would be a) well, if we're thinking about the public interest, more people use [the large chains] and b) if you're the field leader you should be setting the standards and it's a legitimate strategy to target you. But you can create a sense of resentment if you do that too crassly.[99]

---

[97] Interview, December 10, 2008.
[98] Interview, August 8, 2007.
[99] Ibid.

This played out in the goods and services cases discussed in Chapter 5. "Ideal opponents" emerged in those situations that allowed the DRC to avoid the danger of diminishing goodwill through the targeting of businesses who might simply be ignorant of the law. Those cases allowed the DRC to target high-profile companies that generated media coverage.

Despite a list of case-selection criteria, several interviewees also highlighted the importance of what could be described as a more "gut feel" approach. One said,

> You know those [cases] because when you see it you straight away have sympathy with the client, you don't have to try and construct a factual scenario that makes the court come to your side. We would have lots to choose from . . . and most people in the legal team felt that they knew exactly what the DDA says and you could predict whether an act was unlawful or not.[100]

This contrasts with points made by other interviewees who emphasized the difficulty in sometimes recognizing a strategic case.

> The difficulty is often knowing a strategic case when it comes in the door. Because it's often impossible to know. What can look like a really ordinary case, suddenly takes on a different character because the defendant says "actually I'm using this particular defence here, or this is what I'm saying." It becomes a strategic case but you don't necessarily see that, it develops. By that point it may be too late because you've turned it away.[101]

> You have to pick your cases fairly carefully. You can't predict reliability. You can certainly rule out the ones that look like horror stories from the start either from the facts or because the arguments are weak . . . By and large we haven't lost many cases and that's probably because we've been pretty choosy about the ones we have

---

[100] Interview, March 11, 2008.
[101] Interview, December 10, 2007.

taken and we've been very careful and settled those that have gone wrong.[102]

You can have the best strategic case in the world, and in some ways if it's too good it won't go anywhere because the other side will realise and settle it. There's a sort of optimum type of case which is quite difficult to find, and you can never be quite sure when you've got it, it needs to be just good enough.[103]

One of the most significant constraints on the DRC's use of strategic litigation was its inability, because of the group's defined mandate, to touch many of the issues of gravest concern to disabled people, namely, issues that are more easily seen as human rights breaches than as discriminatory acts. Almost half of the calls taken by the DRC's helpline from disabled people concerned matters such as welfare benefits and community and social care issues, which lay beyond the discrimination, rather than human rights or social care, remit of the DRC. However, the Commission developed a strategy whereby they expanded their ability to weigh in on some of these issues through the use of interventions and judicial reviews. The use of interventions also had indirect benefits within the organization for the Legal Services team in that it broadened opportunities to engage with the Commissioners and involve them in legal policy issues. One interviewee highlighted the advantages of the use of interventions and the mechanisms the Commission generally relied on to get involved.

Intervention is an appealing method, it's relatively quick, it's relatively cheap, you don't have to worry about the facts of the case so much, you can get in and make a policy intervention without having to worry about the case so much, it's a good way of engaging people across the organization, it's a good way of engaging the commissioners who very often gave evidence from their own experience about particular policy issues that were being considered.[104]

---

[102] Interview, August 8, 2007.

[103] Ibid.

[104] Ibid.

Michael Rubenstein, writing in the report assessing the legal achievements of the DRC, highlighted the importance of the power to intervene and its influence on the development of the powers of the new single commission:

> A key component of this part of the DRC's legal strategy was its pioneering approach of seeking leave from the court to intervene in some of the most important test cases, on grounds that it was an organisation having an interest in the outcome of the proceedings. Until this role was accepted, the only way a statutory commission could have its voice heard was by taking on the claimant's case. The new approach allows the Commission to set out its opinion, as the expert body, on how the law should be interpreted without having to take a view on the detailed facts of an individual case. This important role has now been formalised by the Equality Act 2006, which gives the CEHR [Commission for Equality and Human Rights] the statutory right to intervene in judicial proceedings. It is to be hoped that they will regard this power as a core part of their legal strategy.[105]

The role of the DRC in the disability rights sector is unique. With its specific, publicly mandated role, relatively ample resources, and corralling of legal and policy expertise, it was better suited than either grassroots organizations or the traditional disability establishment to pursue a coherent litigation strategy. The DRC was created well after a consensus over the social model understanding of disability had been reached among grassroots activists and an increasing number of traditional charities were subscribing to rights-based norms, at least in their policy and campaigning work. This ideational starting point and demands from the radical component of the movement, first that the DRC should be created and later that the DRC should be more aggressive in its legal enforcement, meant that the use of strategic litigation had a great degree of legitimacy as an "appropriate" strategy. However,

---

[105] Disability Rights Commission, *DRC Legal Achievements*, p. 12.

although post hoc assessments of the DRC's work – particularly its legal work – have been largely positive, there have also been suggestions that the DRC, through its very existence, has led to the disintegration of the grassroots disability movement. This has also left a space for traditional disability charities, some of which are now vying to cover the rights-based ground that was left by the disappearance of the DRC.[106]

In September 2007, the DRC and the other domestic equality commissions – the Equal Opportunities Commission (EOC) and the Commission for Racial Equality (CRE) – were replaced by a single body: the Equality and Human Rights Commission (EHRC). The EHRC covers the three strands under the mandate of the previous organizations in addition to advocating against discrimination based on three further grounds: age, religion, and sexual orientation. It also has enhanced powers, for example, the ability to intervene in cases (the DRC did this but required special permission), which may allow for increased variation on the types of legal action that can be undertaken. In defining their own role, on their Web site, they place significant emphasis on the strategic enforcement side:

> The Equality and Human Rights Commission has extensive legal powers and a dedicated directorate of expert lawyers who are specialists in equality law. This means that the commission is well equipped to take legal action on behalf of individuals, especially where there are strategic opportunities to push the boundaries of the law. Where there are chances to create legal precedents or to clarify and improve the law, the commission will seek to do so.[107]

However, according to some interviewees (most of whom requested anonymity when asked to comment on their predictions of the activity or efficacy of the new Commission), the practice in terms of the use of strategic litigation to enforce or expand disability equality may end up

---

[106] Interview, August 8, 2007.

[107] EHRC Web site, http://www.equalityhumanrights.com/en/aboutus/whatwedo/pages/whatwedo.aspx (accessed July 3, 2008).

being very different from the principles advertised in their public communications. Among the more pessimistic interviewees, the impression that the EHRC would not efficiently use its powers was based on various perceptions. Some cited the apparent aversion Trevor Phillips, the Chair, has in using strategic litigation in pursuit of equality goals;[108] others felt that disability would fall to the bottom of priorities or felt that disability issues, because of their complexity (e.g., in terms of reasonable adjustments), would not be properly addressed. Even among the more optimistic interviewees, there was consensus that, like any new organization, it would simply take some time for the organization to gather steam in terms of strategic litigation.

CONCLUSIONS

The use of legal mobilization by disability organizations in the UK has taken a different form than in Canada, where it was largely led by grassroots organizations. I argued here that the emergence of grassroots organizations *of* disabled persons, their subsequent contestation over meaning frames, and diffusion of the social mode and its associated rights discourse among the movement laid an important normative foundation where rights legislation and its enforcement became the primary goal of addressing the issues of disabled persons. Although these organizations, by and large, have not gone to the courts (due mainly to their financial limitations), they have nonetheless played an important role in both diffusing the social model through, at least some, more resource-rich organizations that have turned to the courts and encouraging the DRC in its use of litigation. The contrast with Canadian grassroots organizations' use of legal mobilization is interesting

---

[108] The CRE, under the leadership of Trevor Phillips, supported only a single case in its final year. Many of the lawyers interviewed mentioned this point when discussing the EHRC and strategic litigation.

and is likely due to a combination of three factors: greater resources of the Canadian movement; the use by Canadian organizations of less expensive forms of legal mobilization, such as interventions; and the absence in Canada of a dedicated quango advocating a disability rights agenda and taking on much of the litigation work.

Over their relatively long histories, the traditional disability establishment, made up of the disability charities, has been relatively slow, when compared with the women's movement or environmental advocacy organizations, to acknowledge the potential use of strategic litigation as a campaigning tactic. A prominent disability discrimination lawyer noted: "there are a lot of voluntary-sector organizations who have been very slow to appreciate the benefit that legal staff can bring to their campaigning work."[109] The traditional disability establishment in the UK has been much more resistant to change than in Canada, where charities (with few exceptions) either adopted a social model understanding of disability relatively early on or moderated their claims of speaking on behalf of disabled persons. The Big Seven UK charities varied in their adoption of a social model understanding of disability, and this, at first glance, correlates with their use of strategic litigation. This correlation allows us to make some claims regarding the influence of meaning frames in circumscribing "appropriate" strategies. The case studies of RNIB and Scope demonstrate how these meaning frames can diffuse through organizations or be met with resistance and how they begin to shape governance structures, representations of disabled persons, the service-provision ethos, and policy priorities, which in turn influence campaign strategy choice. They also showed how intraorganizational tensions may constrain the use of a particular strategy, even when other enabling conditions, such as adequate resources, are in place.

The DRC has played a unique role in the disability sector in the UK. As an independent organization, which was able to garner policy

---

[109] Interview, December 10, 2007.

entrepreneurs, legal expertise, legitimacy, and resources from across both grassroots organizations and the traditional establishment, it has been the most active organization in promoting a disability rights agenda in the courts. Although other factors, such as funding and legal expertise, are certainly important in explaining the use of strategic litigation, the fact that the social model of disability was at the core of its work from its inception is also a significant explanatory variable. Grassroots activists lobbied hard for the creation of the DRC, and then, once it was established, pushed it to become more litigious. Paradoxically, although it is still too early to draw firm conclusions about the impact of the DRC on the grassroots movement, there have been some suggestions that it may have played a role in the movement's weakening. This is even more important in light of the fact that the DRC has now wrapped up its work and has been replaced by the EHRC, which many activists have expressed disquiet over.

What light does this shed on theoretical understandings of the turn to strategic litigation? The case of legal mobilization by the disability rights movement in the UK illustrates the importance of complementing existing explanations for the adoption of strategic litigation with an understanding of social movement theory, specifically the influence of meaning frames and their diffusion within and across organizational settings. This is particularly highlighted when contrasting the goals and strategies in a cross–social movement manner. Existing research documenting the adoption of strategic litigation by the women's movement and the environmental movement in the 1980s and early 1990s in the UK has pointed to a Conservative government hostile to their goals as an explanatory factor in the adoption of a legal strategy, and particularly a European legal strategy.[110] However, these political and legal opportunity approaches cannot explain the adoption of disability rights legislation nor the subsequent support for litigation by sections

---

[110] Alter and Vargas, "Explaining Variation"; Hilson, "New Social Movements," pp. 238–55.

of the disability movement during a similar period. It was the same Conservative government that proved receptive to lobby and protest pressure to adopt what has been described by some as the most progressive disability equality legislation in Europe.[111]

I argued that, whereas resource mobilization understandings are clearly important in explaining why grassroots organizations have not turned to the courts, they cannot explain why the well-resourced Big Seven charities did not eagerly embrace strategic litigation. This suggests that these explanations are incomplete and provide simplistic understandings of causality in explaining the turn to litigation by collective actors. Instead, by acknowledging that resource mobilization is but one component of the use of strategic litigation and that ideational factors matter, we can begin to move toward a more systematic, synthetic analytical framework to understand strategy choice in civil society organizations. A sociological–institutionalist approach analyzing the spread of the rights model and broad-based support within the grassroots movement of strategic litigation can help to explain both why traditional disability charities adopting the social model have begun to use legal mobilization to pursue policy goals and also why grassroots organizations have been broadly supportive of strategic litigation and regularly encouraged the DRC to use it more vigorously than it did. In Chapter 5, I continue my exploration of the adoption of a rights understanding of disability issues in UK court decisions by examining the DRC's use of strategic litigation.

---

[111] However, the disability movement was highly critical of certain aspects of the legislation.

5

Framing Disability Equality in the UK Courts

INTRODUCTION

In a country that has been traditionally averse to the concept of enumerated rights, there has been a remarkable shift over the last fifteen
years toward a rights-based framework in disability law and policy
in Great Britain.[1] Since 1995, four related acts providing legal protections against discrimination based on disability have been adopted
by the UK parliament; one of these implements supranational European Union (EU) legislation. In addition, the European Convention on
Human Rights (ECHR), signed by the UK in 1951, was incorporated
into domestic law with the passing of the Human Rights Act (HRA)
1998, also offering protection to persons with disabilities. These pieces
of legislation have, as this chapter demonstrates, served as the basis for
an expanding role of the courts in defining, clarifying, and expanding
on policy relevant to persons with disabilities. As in Canada, disability
activists have turned to the courts to advance their own conceptions

---

[1] The legal jurisdictions of the UK are complex. The UK includes Great Britain and
Northern Ireland. Great Britain includes England, Wales, and Scotland. Within the
UK, there are three distinct court systems: England and Wales share one, and Scotland and Northern Ireland each have their own. However, the Appellate Committee
of the House of Lords (now known as the Supreme Court) is the court of final
appeal for each of the court systems. Although my discussion of the political context
includes some matters having implications for the UK as a whole, I have focused
most of my attention on England and Wales.

of disability equality and human rights. In contrast to the Canadian case where many organizations have become involved in strategic litigation efforts, in the UK it was one institution – the publicly funded Disability Rights Commission (DRC) – that (until it closed its doors in 2007) was the key organizational driver of legal mobilization on disability issues. This chapter argues that, due largely to the prompting by the DRC through its proactive litigation strategy, the UK courts have played a seminal role in the way the rights of persons with disabilities are interpreted and implemented.

The remainder of the chapter is structured as follows. The next section briefly surveys existing legislation that lays the foundation for legal mobilization of disability rights in the UK; it focuses on a variety of legislative mechanisms – domestic, supranational, and international – that create enforceable rights for persons with disabilities in the UK. The following section surveys key decisions that have influenced policy relevant to persons with disabilities. I also discuss how the DRC generally approached the issues raised in the cases and some of the unintended consequences of taking legal action. Where relevant, I embed this analysis within the sociolegal context of landmark court decisions – both in terms of input and output. This dimension is important for creating a more complete picture of the forces at work in the construction of disability policy.

HUMAN RIGHTS AND DISABILITY EQUALITY IN BRITISH LAW

In contrast with Canada, where a general constitutional equality guarantee has shaped the development of jurisprudence on disability rights, British law contains no general equality guarantee for persons with disabilities. Rather, it contains a set of specific statutes, augmented by relatively recent EU law and the ECHR, partially incorporated by the HRA 1998 (see Table 5.1).

Table 5.1. *Equality Protections for Disabled Persons in British and European Law*

Legal protection	Provisions
Disability Discrimination Act 1995	It is unlawful to discriminate against people in respect of their disabilities in relation to employment, the provision of goods and services, education, and transport.
Disability Rights Commission Act 1999	Established the DRC as a nondepartmental public body to adminster and enforce the DDA.
Special Educational Needs and Disability Act 2001	Inserted new provisions in Part 4 of the DDA 1995 in connection with disability discrimination in schools and other educational establishments.
Disability Discrimination Act 1995 (Amendment) Regulations 2003	Amended the DDA in line with the EU Framework Directive.
Disability Discrimination Act 2005	Established the public sector equality duty and extended duties of transport providers.
Equality Act 2006	Transferred the role of the DRC to the EHRC. The EHRC took on this role from October 1, 2007 and has powers to issue guidance on and enforce all the equality enactments (covering race, sex, disability, religion and belief, sexual orientation, and age).
Human Rights Act 1998	Gives further effect in UK law to the rights contained in the ECHR. Makes it unlawful for any public body to act in a way which is incompatible with the Convention. The Act makes available in UK courts a remedy for breach of a Convention right.
European Union Equal Treatment Framework Directive 2000	Implements the principle of equal treatment in the area of employment, covering disability, religion or belief, sexual orientation, and age.

Domestic Antidiscrimination Legislation

After fourteen previously unsuccessful attempts at lobbying for effective legal protection throughout the 1980s and early 1990s, the Disability Discrimination Act (DDA) became law in 1995 under John

Major's conservative government.[2] Success was achieved after a coalition of more radical disability-run organizations joined forces with some of the traditional charities to form the Rights Now Group in 1992. The campaign promoted and publicized the need for antidiscrimination legislation protecting persons with disabilities. The DDA makes it unlawful to discriminate against disabled people in the field of employment; provision of goods, facilities, and services; education; and buying or renting land or property.[3] The Act's framework roughly paralleled the statutes outlawing discrimination on grounds of race and sex but was much weaker. In the early years of the DDA, it was heavily criticized by both the disability community and some prominent members of the bar for several reasons. These included the following: concerns regarding the scope of the law to tackle individual instances of discrimination, its basis on a medical model of disability as opposed to a social model, its complex and restrictive definition of disability, and the perverse results that sometimes were the consequence of the implementation of the legislation. The community was sharply divided over whether the legislation should be repealed. Among activists there was a strong belief about the DDA's inadequacy in light of the hard-fought campaign they undertook to establish the legislation in the first place.[4] This controversy and calls for the repeal of the legislation died down over time, partially due to the broadening of the legislation and correction of the fundamental weaknesses by the UK courts.

The DDA was particularly strengthened by the establishment in 2000 of the DRC, which had a mandate to work toward the elimination of discrimination against disabled people. The role of the DRC

---

[2] Barnes, "Disability, Policy and Politics," p. 315.

[3] According to the DDA, a person has a disability if he/she has a physical or mental impairment that has a substantial and long-term adverse effect on his/her ability to carry out normal day-to-day activities.

[4] Interview, December 10, 2007.

is discussed in detail in Chapter 4. The Government's DDA 1995 (Amendment) Regulations in 2003 introduced significant modifications, from October 2004, in order to bring the DDA in line with the EU Framework Directive.[5]

The Human Rights Act 1998

The HRA 1998 partially incorporated the ECHR, which the UK had signed in 1951, into domestic law. Under the HRA, the courts have the power to declare primary legislation incompatible with Convention rights, and the courts may strike down secondary legislation, the use of discretionary powers, and other types of executive action.[6] More broadly, the UK government said that its intention with the introduction of the HRA was to create a "human rights culture" among public authorities and the public at large. At the time, this sparked optimism among the disability community: "disabled people had special reason to welcome it. They have much to gain from its philosophy of the equal dignity of each individual, each person's right to fulfil his/her potential and respect for the diversity of life experience."[7]

A number of articles provide protections that are potentially useful to persons with disabilities in the UK. Article 14 protects against discrimination but still falls short of a comprehensive equality guarantee:

---

[5] The Regulations make a number of significant changes to the employment provisions of the DDA, including ending the exemption of small employers from the scope of the DDA and ending a number of occupational exclusions (e.g., the police, prison officers, and barristers in chambers). They outlaw harassment of disabled people and ensure that discrimination motivated by prejudice can never be justified.

[6] It is important here to note the distinction with the Canadian situation where the Supreme Court can overturn primary legislation: in the UK, it remains up to parliament to relegislate after the courts have made a declaration of incompatibility.

[7] Caroline Gooding, DRC paper, "The Application of the ECHR in British Courts in Relation to Disability Issues," http://archive.cabinetoffice.gov.uk/equalitiesreview/review_panel/hre.html (accessed May 17, 2008).

it is a derivative equality provision. The Article states that "the enjoyment of the rights and freedoms set forth in this Convention shall be secured without discrimination." In practice this means that no claims of unequal treatment can be made, except in conjunction with one of the specified rights.[8] Furthermore, the nature of the HRA sets the equality protections contained in Article 14 apart from other domestic antidiscrimination legislation in that the primary target of the human rights legislation is the State. According to the HRA, it is only public authorities whose actions must be compatible with Convention rights. In addition to the antidiscrimination provision, two further protections have been relied on for test cases: Article 3, conferring the right to freedom from inhuman and degrading treatment; and Article 8, protecting the right to private and family life. These provisions have proven to be highly relevant to disabled people, particularly in their relations with health and social services.

European Community Law

It is impossible to examine British discrimination law in isolation from developments at the European level: there is an active dialogue between activists in Britain and those in Brussels.[9] Within the EU, it was British disability activists who were among the first to raise nondiscrimination issues in the early 1990s.[10] However, a major barrier to establishing a Europe-wide antidiscrimination policy was the lack of EU legal

---

[8] This limitation has been somewhat mitigated by the fact that it has been held not to be necessary to show an actual breach of one of the substantive rights.

[9] Gooding, "The Application of the ECHR in British Courts"; Interview, February 15, 2005.

[10] Thomas F. Burke, "The European Union and the Diffusion of Disability Rights," in Martin A. Levin and Martin Shapiro, eds., *Transatlantic Policy-Making in an Age of Austerity: Diversity and Drift* (Washington DC: Georgetown University Press, 2004), p. 160.

competence in this area: the European Treaties simply did not grant the EU power in this realm. At the time, disability issues were firmly placed within the context of redistributive social policy, specifically welfare and rehabilitation – areas in which the EU was supposed to play only a minor role.[11]

Nevertheless, broader changes in the understanding of the concept of "disability" combined with a series of EU action programs, which funded information sharing on disability-related issues, allowed advocates to move forward. It was funding from one of these action programs, Helios II (1993–1996), that underwrote the creation of the European Disability Forum (EDF), an association of member–state disability groups dedicated to the social model of disability.[12] The EDF played a crucial role in lobbying both the European Commission and Parliament. As Burke points out, "with the arrival of EDF at the EU, disability began to be seen as a matter fit for non-discrimination policies, a mechanism that the EU had before only considered in the context of race and gender."[13]

With growing support from within the European Commission, disability rights advocates lobbied to expand EU competence to cover antidiscrimination measures during the Treaty amendment in Amsterdam in 1997. Disability rights advocates "rode in the slipstream" of growing concern across Europe about racism and discrimination based on ethnicity.[14] In its Communication setting out a new Community Disability Strategy, the Commission endorsed the move toward a rights-based approach in the disability policy field. It stated:

> [t]his new approach is based on the notion of right rather than charity and an accommodation for difference rather than a

[11] Burke, "The European Union and the Diffusion of Disability Rights," p. 160.
[12] Lisa Waddington, "The European Community's Response to Disability," in Melinda Jones and Lee Ann Basser Marks, eds., *Disability, Divers-ability and Legal Change* (The Hague: Martinus Nijhoff Publishers), p. 142.
[13] Burke, "The European Union and the Diffusion of Disability Rights," p. 161.
[14] Interview, February 15, 2005.

compulsory adjustment to an artificial norm. It therefore advocates a full notion of citizenship and inclusion rather than segregation and exclusion.[15]

The result of this campaign was Article 13 of the Amsterdam Treaty, which granted the EU competence to take action on discrimination across a range of grounds, including disability. It states:

> Without prejudice to the other provisions of this Treaty and within the limits of the powers conferred by it upon the Community, the Council, acting unanimously on a proposal from the Commission and after consulting the European Parliament, may take appropriate action to combat discrimination based on sex, racial or ethnic origin, religion or belief, disability, age or sexual orientation.[16]

The general principles of Article 13 themselves are not legally binding. To give effect to Article 13, the Council of Ministers approved two directives proposing minimum standards of legal protection against discrimination throughout the EU. In 2000, the Racial Equality Directive established the principle of "equal treatment between persons, irrespective of racial or ethnic origin,"[17] and the Equal Treatment Framework Directive[18] was enacted to protect individuals against discrimination based on religion, belief, disability, age, or sexual orientation.

The next section, through an analysis of landmark equality and human rights case law relevant to disability issues, outlines

---

[15] Commission of the European Union, Directorate-General V, *Mainstreaming Disability within EU Employment and Social Policy* (Brussels: DG V Services Working Paper, 1996), p. 3.

[16] Article 13 of the EC Treaty (as amended by the Treaty of Amsterdam, 1997).

[17] Racial Equality Directive 2000/43/EC, Official Journal L180, 19/07/2000 P, 0022-0026.

[18] Equal Treatment Framework Directive 2000/78/EC, Official Journal L303, 02/12/2000 P, 0016-0022.

Table 5.2. *Key Disability Rights Cases before UK and European Courts, 1998–2008*

Case name	Year	Court	Disability rights issue
Botta v. Italy	1998	ECtHR	Positive obligations imposed on the state to facilitate disabled people's access to essential economic and social activities and to an appropriate range of recreational and cultural activities.
Price v. UK	2001	ECtHR	Duty of the state to ensure protection against inhuman and degrading treatment, even if that requires differential treatment.
McNicol v. Balfour Beatty Rail Maintenance Ltd	2002	Court of Appeal	It is the effect of a person's impairment, rather than its cause, that is important for the purposes of meeting the definition of disability.
Pretty v. UK	2002	ECtHR	Terminally ill patient denied assistance to commit suicide.
Ford-Shubrook v. St Dominics Sixth Form College	2003	Manchester County Court	Discrimination and reasonable accommodation in education; the second case in which the Court provided injunctive relief under the DDA and the first time in education.
The Queen (On the Application of A,B) v. East Sussex County Council	2003	High Court	In terms of social care, a lifting policy is most unlikely to be lawful which, either on its face or in its application, imposes a blanket ban on manual lifting of disabled persons.
Archibald v. Fife	2004	House of Lords	A broadened interpretation of the duty of employers to provide a reasonable adjustment.
Roads v. Central Trains	2004	Court of Appeal	A service should, wherever possible, be provided to a disabled person in the same way as for a nondisabled person.
Ross v. Ryanair Ltd and Stansted Airport Ltd	2004	Court of Appeal	Where more than one service provider has duties to provide reasonable adjustments in the same situation, it is important to agree how those duties are met.
R. (on the application of Burke) v. General Medical Council	2005	Court of Appeal	Right of a patient to require life-prolonging treatment.
Coleman v. Attridge Law	2008	ECJ	Whether discrimination by association with a disabled person constitutes discrimination on grounds of disability.

court-influenced developments in disability policy over the last ten years. Table 5.2 summarizes the issues addressed in these cases.

EARLY CASES: CLARIFYING THE MEANING OF DISABILITY AND DISCRIMINATION

One of the early critiques of the DDA was that, in practice, the tribunals adopted a particularly narrow approach to defining disability.[19] To claim protection under the DDA, claimants had to establish that they were "disabled" by demonstrating a physical or mental impairment that had a substantial and long-term adverse effect on their abilities to carry out normal day-to-day activities. An early case shifted the balance to a broader and arguably more social model-consistent understanding of disability by the courts.

In *McNicol v. Balfour Beatty Rail Maintenance Ltd*, the DRC intervened as an interested party and established the principle that it is the effect of a person's impairment, rather than its cause, that is important for the purposes of meeting the definition of disability: this takes the focus away from the medical problem associated with the individual to one which implicitly focuses on the concept of reasonable adjustment.[20] In *McNicol* and other early cases, the higher courts began to lay the groundwork for a purposive interpretation of the DDA by shifting the focus away from an individual's impairment to her ability to perform certain tasks.[21]

Discrimination claims brought in the field of employment have been the most numerous type of claim, and understandings of disability equality have been advanced by the courts. This survey focuses

---

[19] Caroline Gooding, "Disability Discrimination Act: From Statute to Practice," *Critical Social Policy* 20(4), 2000, pp. 533–49.

[20] *McNicol v. Balfour Beatty Rail Maintenance Ltd*, [2002] ICR 1498.

[21] Gooding, "Disability Discrimination Act: From Statute to Practice."

on the case of *Archibald v. Fife*, which has been described as "the jewel in the DRC legal team's crown" because of its significance in encouraging courts to develop a broad understanding of the concept of accommodation.[22] Robin Allen QC writes:

> Mrs. Archibald's case presented dream facts for strategic litigation. Her plight could not fail to engage sympathy; once known, the facts of her determination and feistiness in the face of her disability could not fail to engage profound admiration. Moreover, the Employment Tribunal seemed to have made a fair mess of the issues and the appellate litigation produced more heat than light.[23]

Mrs. Archibald was a street sweeper for Fife Council, but she was unable to continue with that line of work when she became disabled. She successfully retrained in information technology and then applied for more than 100 jobs in the Council. But, though interviewed, she was never successful. Mrs. Archibald argued that a reasonable adjustment should be made to enable her to transfer within the Council without a competitive interview. The Council, as part of their equal opportunities policy, required all appointment decisions to be made by competitive interview, and eventually she was dismissed. Mrs. Archibald's case eventually reached the Employment Appeal Tribunal (EAT), where her appeal was dismissed on the basis that there was nothing in the interview processes that placed her at a substantial disadvantage because the policy applied to everyone.

With the support of the DRC, Mrs. Archibald's appeal reached the House of Lords – it was the first disability discrimination case to reach the Law Lords. There, her argument was principally concerned with whether or not it was a possible reasonable adjustment for a Council to be asked, in a case such as this, to suspend its equal opportunities

---

[22] *Archibald v. Fife*, [2004] IRLR 651; Interview, December 10, 2007.

[23] Disability Rights Commission, *DRC Legal Achievements*, p. 21.

policy. Underlying the decision was a fundamental philosophical disagreement between Fife Council, on one hand, and Mrs. Archibald and the DRC, on the other, about the acceptable limits of positive discrimination that the duty to accommodate inevitably entails. Interestingly, both sides relied on principles in the EU's Equal Treatment Framework Directive to make their arguments. Baroness Hale considered these points and concluded by arguing that:

> [n]one of this helps us much in defining the limits of what should be done to safeguard or promote the integration of disabled people in the working environment. But that is clearly an important overall aim which justifies making a reasonable accommodation in what the employer would otherwise do in order to cater for the needs of a specific disabled person.[24]

The Lords upheld the appeal but also acknowledged that the crux of the issue was based on principle, not the specificities of the case before them. Baroness Hale expressed this by pointing out that "the tribunal will have quite a difficult exercise to undertake and it is not for this House to predict the ultimate outcome. This was a test case on a point of principle which the Commission wished to have resolved whatever the outcome of the individual case."[25]

The case had an important impact in three ways. First, much has been made by legal scholars of the important points of law clarified in this case. Without going into legal technicalities in detail, it is worth pointing out that the justification provisions (the reasons employers can legitimately discriminate) in the original text of the 1995 DDA, as they applied to discrimination in failing to make a reasonable adjustment, were removed as a result of the case. This means that the dominant issue for any litigant in an employment case is whether or not there was a failure to make a reasonable adjustment. The obligation to make

---

[24] *Archibald v. Fife*, [2004] IRLR 651.
[25] Ibid.

the reasonable adjustment is not qualified and cannot be stalled by a justification argument.[26] The policy status quo changed to one where the burden is on the employer to think proactively about reasonable accommodation instead of waiting for an applicant to demand it. A second reason why *Archibald* is important is the way in which the Lords referenced the DRC's arguments: they provided high-level affirmation of the role and expertise of the Commission. This bolstered the legitimacy of the organization and its litigation strategy. Third, the case made clear that the responsibility to make reasonable adjustments is much greater than the lower courts believed, and employers have an obligation to consider carefully what positive measures they can take to remove the disadvantages that disabled employees or prospective employees may face. This purposive approach to the accommodation duty affirmed that positive action provisions were not only lawful, but also the most effective method to ensure equality: what was previously framed as "preferential treatment" is now understood as "equal treatment." The Court essentially adopted what Ruth Colker has coined an "antisubordination approach" in its reasoning.[27] Lord Hope, in his opinion stated: "it is not simply a duty to make adjustments. The making of adjustments is not an end in itself. The end is reached when the disabled person is no longer at a substantial disadvantage, in comparison with persons who are not disabled."[28]

In contrast with the Canadian case, in which the legal frames of the concept of reasonable accommodation were developed in the sphere of religion in the *O'Malley* and *Bhinder* cases, in the UK the concept of accommodation was first developed in case law on disability and later applied to other grounds, such as discrimination based on pregnancy.[29] Litigants began to advance arguments based on the

---

[26] Disability Rights Commission, *DRC Legal Achievements*, p. 22.

[27] Colker, *When is Separate Unequal?*

[28] *Archibald v. Fife*, [2004] IRLR 651.

[29] Fredman, *Discrimination Law*, p. 100.

social model of disability and the importance of "positive action" in the form of reasonable adjustment to convince the courts that disability discrimination is different from discrimination on other grounds. A member of the legal team at the DRC emphasized the specificity of disability discrimination:

> In particular because the Disability Discrimination Act is not like the Sex Discrimination Act or the Race Discrimination Act... One of the big battles that we've had with the courts is persuading them to see that it's not meant to work in the same way. It's actually meant to work differently, and the reasonable adjustment provisions particularly are nothing like you get in any other discrimination legislation. And the way that they work it is really very interesting because in a sense they're the heart of what makes the DDA work: it's all about how do you promote inclusivity; you do it by enabling participation. How do you enable participation? You make adjustments to enable participation and it kind of works that way. But actually, saying that to a court, saying it's not about do you dislike me because I use a wheelchair, that's not what disability discrimination is about at all, I mean that's one aspect of it, but not the main aspect.[30]

To compare, the two national movements had broadly similar paradigms that they were trying to advance in the courts, but they chose differing emphases in the early cases. In Canada, the focus was on similarities of the experiences of other marginalized groups to advance a substantive understanding of the actual experience of inequality across all grounds; in the UK, the emphasis was on convincing the courts that the antidiscrimination legislation concerning disability was meant to be interpreted differently from that on other grounds.[31]

---

[30] Interview, February 9, 2005.

[31] This changed over time, and the DRC intervened in a number of key cases with the other equality commissions to present shared understandings of how the legislation was meant to function.

Another point of contrast in the development of early case law was the difference in the respective national courts' own perceptions of their role in influencing equality policy and disability. In Canada, in the period immediately following the implementation of the Charter, the Supreme Court was a relatively willing and proactive participant in identifying the principles of equality and reasonable adjustment. In the UK, however, the courts in this area regularly signaled their reluctance to be seen as "activist." For example, the arguments put forth by the DRC in the *McNicol* case are illustrative of attempts to expand the legal opportunity structure for taking disability discrimination cases. In its intervention, the Commission submitted that tribunals should adopt "an inquisitorial and more pro-active role in disability discrimination cases, as they can be complex and involve applicants, whose impairment leads them to minimize or to offer inaccurate diagnoses of their conditions and of the effects of their impairment."[32] By encouraging tribunals to become more applicant-friendly, they were attempting to expand access to justice, particularly in the early days of the legislation. This was, however, rejected by the Employment Appeal Tribunal:

> I do not think that it would be helpful to describe the role [of] the Employment Tribunal as "inquisitorial" or as "pro-active." Its role is to adjudicate on disputes between the parties on issues of fact and law . . . It is not, however, the duty of the tribunal to obtain evidence or to ensure that adequate medical evidence is obtained by the parties. That is a matter for the parties and their advisers.[33]

Despite attempts by the DRC to influence a major policy issue for persons with disabilities – access to justice – the Tribunal conceived of its role in remedying this situation in a limited way.

[32] *McNicol v. Balfour Beatty Rail Maintenance Ltd*, [2002] ICR 1498.
[33] Ibid.

Discrimination in Education

Employment cases make up the large majority of all disability discrimination claims. In 2002, the DRC, as part of its litigation strategy, began to focus on discrimination in education.[34] The Special Education Needs and Disability Act (SENDA) 2001 had just come into force.[35] The intersection of disability law and education is extremely complex, and for that reason, a full survey of the education provisions and the impact of court decisions on education policy is beyond the scope of this study. One education case, however, mentioned by several interviewees, is worth examining because it significantly advanced a social model understanding of disability in education policy, but also because of the relatively innovative use of the law in the form of an emergency injunction.[36] In *Ford-Shubrook v. St Dominics Sixth Form College*, the claimant, supported by the DRC, alleged discrimination on the basis that the College refused to admit him because it believed that certain classes could not be made safely accessible to him because he used a wheelchair.[37] Interestingly, the claimant was not seeking changes to the building, but rather he was ready to absorb the significant costs of a stair-climbing wheelchair to be able to attend the College. The College, without conducting an individual assessment, decided that his potential use of the stair-climbing wheelchair might be a threat to the health and safety of other students. The claimant sought

[34] Interview, March 11, 2008.
[35] Prior to that, disability discrimination in education was only outlawed where it fell within the "service provider" provisions of the DDA. There have been several failed attempts by parents to use the European Convention right to education to obtain either mainstream or special school placements for their children. The ECtHR has generally argued that governments have a large measure of discretion on how to make best possible use of the resources available to them in the interests of disabled children.
[36] Interviews, July 26, 2007; December 10, 2007; March 11, 2008.
[37] *Ford-Shubrook v. St Dominics College*, [2003] MA315699, Manchester County Court.

an injunction to be allowed to enroll and begin classes while waiting for the hearing to begin; this was only the second injunction granted under the DDA and the first in the area of education.[38] The Court was especially concerned that, given the balance of available evidence and the likely outcome of the substantive hearing, the interim denial of admission would cause disproportionate disadvantage to the claimant. The case settled prior to the full hearing, and the claimant was able to continue his studies at the college of his choice.

The awarding of the mandatory injunction likely had an important influence on the decision to settle in a number of ways. First, the injunction shifted the policy status quo from one of exclusion to one of inclusion. This had the effect of shifting the evidentiary burden as well: if the case had gone to a full hearing, the school would have been forced to justify its reasons for exclusion as opposed to the claimant having to justify reasons for inclusion. Second, by beginning classes at the College, the underlying idea was that the applicant would have been able to counter the head teacher's assumptions regarding his ability to integrate into the educational setting. There would have been a "soft" process of learning by the school's staff and students that challenged their prejudged opinions of his abilities. Third, the DRC used the awarding of the injunction as a peg on which to hang a wider publicity campaign regarding the relatively novel education provisions contained within the DDA.[39] For example, the Director of Policy at the time, Liz Sayce, was cited in news coverage on the issue and interviewed on the radio:

> I think what's so important about this injunction is it's the first time that a college has been told, through law, that it has to accept a disabled student, and that's a result of the Disability Discrimination

---

[38] Interview, December 10, 2008.

[39] "Wheelchair User Wins Right to Start College," *The Guardian*, September 1, 2003, http://education.guardian.co.uk/further/story/0,,1033409,00.html (accessed May 12, 2008); "Disabled Student Wins College Fight," *BBC News Website* http://news.bbc.co.uk/2/hi/uk_news/england/london /3201927.stm (accessed May 12, 2008).

Act coming into force in colleges and schools just a year ago, and it means that he like any other young person is, at least for the moment, at the college that he wants to be at that offers the A Level courses that he wants to do, and it's just what every young person wants, and it should be available to young disabled people just like to any other young person.[40]

Even though the case had yet to be decided on substantive issues, the DRC exploited the opportunity presented by the awarding of the injunction by subtly framing it in the mainstream media as a *fait accompli.*

Discrimination in Service Provision

The UK legislation on service provision is relatively advanced, particularly when compared with recent case law in Canada in the *VIA Rail* decision. Under the DDA, a service provider's duty to make reasonable adjustments is owed to disabled people at large and not just one that is triggered in relation to each individual disabled person when they decide to access a service. The duty has thus been described as an anticipatory one and "a major driver in encouraging service providers to think in advance about removing barriers experienced by disabled customers – or would-be customers."[41]

In 2004, the Court of Appeal heard two cases within the space of a few days that brought the section of the DDA on access to goods, facilities, services, and premises to center stage: *Roads v. Central Trains* and *Ross v. Ryanair Ltd and Stansted Airport Ltd.*[42] Both cases concerned the

---

[40] Transcript of BBC Radio 4 Programme *You and Yours*, Interview with Liz Sayce, Director of Policy, http://www.bbc.co.uk/radio4/youandyours/yy_20030904.shtml (accessed March 15, 2008).

[41] Interview, December 14, 2007.

[42] *Roads v. Central Trains*, [2004] EWCA Civ 1541; *Ross v. Ryanair Ltd and Stansted Airport Ltd*, [2004] EWCA Civ. 1751.

duty of service providers to make reasonable adjustments for disabled people – including the provision of a reasonable alternative method of service where a physical barrier prevents persons with disabilities from using a service. In *Roads v. Central Trains*, the claimant was unable to access the train platform for his desired destination. He claimed that Central Trains, with sufficient notice, should have provided an accessible taxi to take him to the platform. Central Trains suggested that Mr. Roads should travel in the opposite direction to the next accessible station, change platforms there, and travel back and on to his destination – this would have added considerably to his journey. Mr. Roads was a member of the Norfolk Coalition of Disabled People – a human rights group controlled by disabled people. On the organization's behalf, he wrote to Central Trains in February 2002 about the lack of disabled access at the station, proposing a foot-crossing and an accessible toilet and offering to work with Central Trains on the problem. In April 2002, joined by a group of disabled people, Mr. Roads met with Central Trains, but nothing came of the meeting and Mr. Roads put himself forward as a test case. His claim for unlawful discrimination was dismissed by the County Court and Mr. Roads, supported by the DRC, appealed.

In a landmark judgment, the Court of Appeal held that the underlying purpose of the DDA requires that a service should, wherever possible, be provided to a disabled person in the same way as for a nondisabled person. Lord Sedley, in the decision, wrote:

> The policy of the Act, as I would accept, is . . . to provide access to a service as close as it is reasonably possible to get to the standard normally offered to the public at large . . . The policy of the [1995 Act] is not a minimalist policy of simply ensuring that some access is available to the disabled: it is so far as reasonably practicable, to approximate the access enjoyed by disabled persons to that enjoyed by the rest of the public.[43]

---

[43] *Roads v. Central Trains*, [2004] EWCA Civ 1541.

Further, the Court of Appeal accepted that the reasonable adjustment provisions are anticipatory in nature and the duty is not triggered by a single disabled person expressing their needs but rather the concept is more abstract and proactive than that. Lord Justice Sedley's comments were cited and applied in *Ross v. Ryanair Ltd and Stansted Airport Ltd*, which was decided shortly thereafter.

In *Ross v. Ryanair*, the claimant had cerebral palsy and was unable to walk long distances. He was charged £18 by Ryanair for the hire of a wheelchair at Stansted Airport because of his inability to walk from the check-in counter to the gate. Although both Ryanair and Stansted conceded that Mr. Ross should not have been charged, they disputed who was liable. Ryanair aggressively refuted the charge of discrimination. In response to a letter the DRC had written regarding the issues at hand, Ryanair's Customer Standards Manager wrote:

> If RA [Ryanair] is guilty of discrimination (which we deny) it is discrimination in favour of wheelchair bound passengers. This is because we personally absorb third party charges levied by totally separate handling companies at Stansted, Gatwick, Dublin, Leeds, Bradford, Manchester and Shannon Airports, despite the fact that in many cases these charges are greater than the total airfare paid us. In the case of such wheelchair bound passengers, we actually spend more money to carry them to/from our aircraft than they pay us for the entire fare. While given the substantial numbers involved, we will not extend the subsidy to non wheelchair bound passengers because if these passengers are not wheelchair bound, they are clearly capable of walking to/from the airport check-in areas, and it is not unreasonable to ask them to walk to the aircraft.[44]

The County Court found against Ryanair, who then appealed. The Court of Appeal decided that Ryanair and Stansted Airport Ltd were jointly liable for discriminating against Mr. Ross, by charging him for the use of a wheelchair. The Court of Appeal accepted that the size of

---

[44] *Ross v. Ryanair Ltd and Stansted Airport Ltd*, [2004] EWCA Civ. 1751.

the airport gave rise to a reasonable adjustment duty for Mr. Ross, and that the cost of meeting that legal responsibility should not have been passed on to him. The *Ross* decision established that, where more than one service provider has duties in the same situation, it is important to agree how those duties are met. The Court's concern was to ensure that the duty is discharged one way or another.

There was an interesting twist to these cases that is worth mentioning. Both Mr. Roads and Mr. Ross had problems getting to the Court to hear the appeals because of physical accessibility issues. When Mr. Ross's difficulties were mentioned, the Court of Appeal requested a report from the DRC.[45] This has resulted in some improvements in accessing the Royal Courts of Justice, though physical access to justice continues to be an issue for many disabled persons.[46] This illustrates the potential for unintended consequences of legal action that can have a much broader impact on the legal opportunity structure for legal mobilization.

It is also worth noting that taking a strategic approach in selecting cases for support in the area of goods and service provision is a particularly difficult task for organizations using strategic litigation under the DDA. Employment cases are heard in venues with specialist jurisdiction, whereas goods and services cases are heard in regular county courts, where judges may or may not possess a very close understanding of the complex legislation in this area; related to this, they may lack insight into gray areas or boundaries of the law. Therefore, it is generally considered more difficult for claimants to identify opportunities for appeal to the higher courts because of a relative lack of predictability on what the judge may decide.[47]

---

[45] "Wheelchair Search Delays Court Case," *The Guardian*, November 8, 2004, http://www.guardian.co.uk/society/2004/nov/08/disability.equality (accessed June 7, 2008).

[46] Disability Rights Commission, *DRC Legal Achievements*, p. 30.

[47] Ibid.

The DRC had made it a priority within their litigation strategy to pursue goods and services cases to highlight the protections and duties within the legislation to both persons with disabilities and service providers. This entailed strategic teamwork across the Commission's legal team and the policy section. Jenny White, a former DRC Commissioner, describes the process:

> The policy lawyers worked alongside their colleagues in the legal department, and several discussions took place with Counsel to tease out the key issues and ensure that the arguments reflected the policy intent. We were fortunate to have Counsel who were open to this kind of dialogue.[48]

Further, there was an emphasis on effectively communicating to the appropriate audiences the key messages coming out of the judgments to ensure that they would have a wider effect. Following the judgments, the legal department, policy advisors, and publicity team agreed what points needed to be conveyed to whom and how best to achieve that: through the DRC Web site and briefing of helpline staff, articles in the legal press, and changes to the code of practice.

DISABILITY AND THE EUROPEAN COURT OF HUMAN RIGHTS

Appellants in early employment cases faced the hurdle of convincing British tribunals and courts of the importance of a broadened understanding of how disability discrimination operates and the importance of the accommodation imperative. Judicial governance by supranational legal regimes means that decisions of courts, such as the European Court of Human Rights (ECtHR) and the European Court of Justice (ECJ), influence court-defined disability rights. This also means

[48] Ibid., p. 29.

that disability rights activists have encouraged these courts to adopt a social model understanding of disability. However, legal cases invoking the HRA have been relatively rare.[49] This section discusses those cases, both before the ECtHR and in the UK, which are considered seminal to understandings of disability equality.

For disabled people, the case of *Botta v. Italy* is a landmark decision. The case itself was ultimately unsuccessful, but it was among the first significant cases taken by a disabled person to the ECtHR (and hence had effect in the UK).[50] The claim was brought by a physically disabled man who was on an Italian seaside holiday but was unable to access a private beach and the sea because they were not equipped with disabled facilities. The applicant complained of infringement of his right to private life and the development of his personality as a result of the state's failure to take appropriate measures to remedy the inaccessibility of the private bathing establishments (created by a lack of accessible toilets and ramps providing access to the sea). Mr. Botta relied on Article 8 to assert that the Italian government failed to adopt measures and to monitor compliance with domestic provisions relating to private beaches. The conceptualization that the issue was not the government's interference, but rather its failure to undertake positive policy action, is one that had developed in national disability discrimination law but was not enunciated in the Convention. The claimant lost the case, largely because Mr. Botta was claiming the right to gain access to the beach on a holiday, as opposed, for example, to access an important service at his normal place of residence. The Court found that there was nothing to indicate that the applicant's life was so circumscribed and isolated that the occasional inconveniences and

---

[49] The exception being the field of mental health law, which has proved to be one of the most fertile areas of challenge under the Act, both before the Strasbourg Court and in UK courts since the introduction of the HRA. The breadth and depth of mental health case law is so extensive that it cannot be covered here.

[50] *Botta v. Italy*, [1998] 26 EHRR 241.

troubles he suffered violated his right to develop social relations with others.

Despite the loss on the facts of the case, the Court's decision reveals a sophisticated understanding of the depth and breadth of social exclusion that disabled people experience and the types of mechanisms that are required to remedy this. The most important outcome of the decision was the Court's ruling that Article 8, the right to private and family life, imposes positive obligations on states to facilitate disabled people's access to essential economic and social activities as well as to a suitable range of recreational and cultural activities.[51] A concurring opinion laid this out:

> Although the object of Article 8 is essentially that of protecting the individual against arbitrary interference by the public authorities ... this provision may nonetheless, in certain cases, impose on those States positive obligations inherent in an effective respect for private life. These positive obligations may involve the adoption of measures designed to secure respect for private life even in the sphere of the relations of individuals between themselves.[52]

The *Botta* judgment, in effect, signaled a dual expansion of the role of the state in ensuring that persons with disabilities are able to effectively enjoy their right to participate in social life. First, the Court found that Article 8 can impose on governments positive obligations in ensuring the right to a real private life. The "freedom from interference" conceptualization, which was the standard one, assumes that all persons are able to enjoy access to social life as long as the state does not bar their path. It takes a neutral and formal approach to equality in that it regards as invidious any distinction between persons based on different grounds.[53] The *Botta* decision reinterprets this duty and acknowledges that Article 8 should be conceptualized in terms of actual disadvantage:

---

[51] Gooding, "The Application of the ECHR in British Courts."

[52] *Botta v. Italy*, [1998] 26 EHRR 241.

[53] Fredman, *Discrimination Law*.

a substantive vision of equality. Through explicitly acknowledging that states may have a role to play in proactively ensuring access to community life, the Court implicitly promoted the social model of disability. Second, the existence of this positive duty can mean that the state has a responsibility to delve into the sphere of relations between individuals to ensure that the right is not infringed. This puts a burden on governments not only to implement legal protections where necessary but also to ensure reasonable levels of enforcement of those protections when and where they do exist.

Another seminal ECtHR case for persons with disabilities, *Price v. UK*, was a landmark decision in relation to Article 3, which protects against inhuman and degrading treatment.[54] Ms. Price has all four limbs foreshortened as a result of thalidomide, which led to numerous accompanying health problems. During civil proceedings, she was sentenced to three days in prison for contempt of court. While in prison, she was denied use of her battery charger for her wheelchair and was provided with sleeping conditions that were unsuitable for her. As a result, she had to endure pain and cold – to the extent that, eventually, a doctor had to be called. The Court found that this treatment breached Article 3. It ruled:

> There is no evidence in this case of any positive intention to humiliate or debase the applicant. However, the Court considers that to detain a severely disabled person in conditions where she is dangerously cold, risks developing sores because her bed is too hard or unreachable, and is unable to go to the toilet or keep clean without the greatest of difficulty constitutes degrading treatment.[55]

The concurring opinion of Judge Greve has been identified as particularly important by human rights and disability discrimination lawyers

---

[54] *Price v. UK*, [2001] 34 EHRR 1285.
[55] Ibid.

in the UK for its explicit assertion that different situations merit different treatment.[56] It states:

> In a civilized country like the United Kingdom, society considers it not only appropriate but a basic humane concern to try to ameliorate and compensate for the disabilities faced by a person in the applicant's situation. In my opinion, these compensatory measures come to form part of the disabled person's bodily integrity... The applicant's disabilities are not hidden or easily overlooked. It requires no special qualification, only a minimum of ordinary human empathy, to appreciate her situation and to understand that to avoid unnecessary hardship – that is, hardship not implicit in the imprisonment of an able-bodied person – she has to be treated differently from other people because her situation is significantly different.[57]

Although this case, as well as many of the other early ECtHR cases, concerned a disabled prisoner, the decision's underlying logic has been applied to institutions other than prisons.[58] It acknowledges a central concept in the practical implementation of the social model, that of the appropriateness and even necessity of different treatment for differently situated persons. In a subsequent decision, *A and B v. East Sussex County Council*, the *Price* decision was cited as recognizing the

> enhanced degree of protection which may be called for when the human dignity at stake is that of someone... who is so disabled as to be critically dependent on the help of others for even the simplest and most basic tasks of day to day living. In order to avoid discriminating against the disabled one may need to treat the disabled differently precisely because their situation is significantly different from that of the able-bodied.[59]

---

[56] See Gooding, "The Application of the ECHR in British Courts."

[57] *Price v. UK*, [2001] 34 EHRR 1285.

[58] Gooding, "The Application of the ECHR in British Courts."

[59] *The Queen (On the Application of A,B) v. East Sussex County Council*, [2001] CO/4843/2001.

DISABILITY AND DIGNITY

As we saw in Chapter 3, "right to die" and "right to life" cases tend to garner a great deal of publicity and provoke widespread public debate. The same is found in the UK. One chief executive of a disability organization made this point:

> Those life and death and extreme ethical cases seem to get quite a bit of attention. Sometimes I think they aren't as significant as a person not being able to move from one area of the country to the other because you can't get your social care package moved . . . I guess that's a bit of a practical thing to say. They are critical in terms of how disabled people are viewed, value-based and ethics. But there are ethical issues in how we allocate resources.[60]

The case of *A and B v. East Sussex County Council* addressed an issue that, on the surface, dealt with relatively technical concerns in the realm of social care regarding policies on lifting persons and the scope of responsibilities of local authorities in their provision of care services.[61] At its heart, however, the case was one of the most significant human rights cases decided by the UK courts thus far: it delved into important issues of dignity, autonomy, and self-determination of persons with disabilities across the UK.

The claimants, two sisters (A and B), both with profound physical and learning disabilities, had always lived in the family home and been cared for on a full-time basis. Both sisters have impaired mobility, and in order to carry out many of their daily activities – for example, getting out of bed or into the bath – it was necessary for them to be moved and lifted by their caregivers. A long-running dispute with the local authority, East Sussex County Council (ESCC), stemmed from the fundamental difference of view as to whether this moving and lifting should be done manually – as the parents preferred – or, as ESCC

---

[60] Interview, December 10, 2008.
[61] *Price v. UK*, [2001] 34 EHRR 1285.

would have it, using hoisting/lifting equipment. The issue decided by
the Court concerned the legality of the local authority's blanket policy
of not permitting care staff to lift A and B manually.[62]

Although dealing with the specific issues of A, B, and their parents,
the case took on a much broader significance. The DRC intervened
in the case to comment on the fact that a number of local authorities
had developed and applied blanket "no lifting" policies that they felt
were highly prejudicial toward, and affected the quality of life of, large
numbers of disabled people. The DRC argued that an across-the-
board ban on manual lifting failed to take into account the individual
needs of the disabled people involved. It argued that, although the local
authority had a legitimate concern for the safety of its staff, this had not
been balanced against recognition of the impact that such a policy had
on the quality of disabled people's lives.[63] They argued that the bans
would result in loss of dignity and autonomy for the disabled person
and sometimes compel the disabled person to go into residential care,
resulting in their loss of independence.

The Court ruled in favor of the applicants. The judgment drew on
the implications of the *Botta* and *Price* decisions discussed previously.
The judge took a novel approach in acknowledging both the univer-
sality of the concept of dignity and the very individualized actions the
concept dictates when put into practice.

> The positive obligation of the State to take reasonable and appro-
> priate measures to secure the rights of the disabled under Article 8
> of the Convention calls for human empathy and human concern as
> society seeks to try and ameliorate and compensate for the disabilities
> faced by persons in A and B's situation . . . This brings out the en-
> hanced degree of protection which may be called for when the
> human dignity at stake is that of someone who is, as A and B are
> in the present case, so disabled as to be critically dependent on the

---

[62] Gooding, "The Application of the ECHR in British Courts."
[63] Ibid.

help of others for even the simplest and most basic tasks of day to day living.[64]

The judgment stretches the concept of accommodation of difference, developed in more practical cases, particularly employment law to questions of dignity. That is, in order to avoid violating someone's dignity, one may need to treat disabled people differently, precisely because their situation is significantly different from individuals who are not disabled. In practice, this means that any social care policy that does not at least consider individual needs or preferences may be in danger of violating the rights of persons with disabilities. In this case, the claimants and the DRC argued that the preference was for allowing, or even encouraging, manual lifting in some situations. The judgment, however, does warn against a dogmatic approach:

> One must guard against jumping too readily to the conclusion that manual handling is necessarily more dignified than the use of equipment. A disabled person or invalid may prefer manual handling by a relative or friend to the use of a hoist but at the same time prefer a hoist to manual handling by a stranger or a paid carer. The independently minded but physically disabled person might prefer to hoist himself up from his bath or chair rather than to be assisted even by his devoted wife.[65]

During the course of the hearing, the DRC and the parties were able to reach agreement on the wording of a model manual-handling policy that was approved by the Court. The DRC has since carried out promotional work to ensure that local authorities (and others) develop and operate policies that ensure a proper balance is struck between meeting the needs and rights of disabled people on the one hand, and ensuring a safe environment for staff working with disabled people

---

[64] *The Queen (On the Application of A,B) v. East Sussex County Council,* [2001] CO/4843/2001.

[65] Ibid.

on the other. Although the case of *A and B v. ESCC* did not establish a precedent because it was effectively an administrative decision, there is some evidence that it was among the most significant disability human rights cases decided thus far. First, the case was widely reported in the health and social work press, and one commentator has pointed to this publicity of having "helped change attitudes throughout those professions."[66] Second, the DRC was contacted by many disabled people through their call-in lines wanting copies of the judgment to help them in their own situations with their local authorities.[67]

THE RIGHT TO LIFE AS A RIGHT TO DIE?

Much like in Canada, in the UK, just when the social model began gaining legitimacy in the courts and there was room for some optimism among activists that the use of litigation could lead to some systemic change in the barriers disabled people face, a series of high-profile cases on the right to die and right to life arose and posed a serious challenge to the attempts to reframe the concept of disability in the public sphere. The "right to die" argument asserted by Diane Pretty received among the most publicity of any disability rights agenda thus far.[68]

Diane Pretty's case, asserting the right to die, attracted considerable public sympathy.[69] Ms. Pretty had motor neurone disease, a progressive condition that had left her unable to do most things unaided.

---

[66] Disability Rights Commission, *DRC Legal Achievements.*
[67] Gooding, "The Application of the ECHR in British Courts."
[68] Ibid.; *Ms. B. v. An NHS Hospital Trust* [2002] EWHC 429 (Fam).
[69] *Pretty v. UK, Application no.2346/02,* [1998] 27 EHRR 163; "Diane Pretty Makes Final 'Death with Dignity' Plea," *The Guardian,* March 20, 2002, http://www. guardian.co.uk/society/2002/mar/20/health.uknews (accessed March 20, 2002).

Knowing that, in the final stages of the condition, she would be unable to do anything for herself but would remain intellectually able, she wanted to be assisted in dying at a time of her own choice and wanted this assistance to be provided by her husband rather than by a doctor. Backed by the human rights group Liberty, she took her case to the High Court after the director of public prosecutions refused to rule out prosecuting Mr. Pretty for aiding and abetting a suicide, which is a criminal offense, if he helped his wife to die. Her lawyers argued that, under the European Convention, which guarantees the right to respect for private life and bans inhuman and degrading treatment, she should be allowed to die with dignity, rather than face the distressing final stages of the disease. In this way, they attempted to frame the right to life safeguarded by the convention as the right to die. They asserted that she would suffer discrimination because her physical condition would deny her the right an able-bodied person would have to end her own life. She argued that the imposition of a blanket ban on assisted suicide was disproportionate because it was unable to take account of individual circumstances. This reframing paralleled the arguments made in the *Rodriguez* case in Canada.

The Court did not accept Ms. Pretty's arguments. They rejected that Article 2 could be read as a right to die or that there was a positive obligation to permit assistance in dying, even if it were accepted that the progression of a condition could amount to inhuman or degrading treatment. The Court also accepted that the Secretary of State was justified on the grounds of the existing law to enforce its application to the case at hand. The Court expressed concern that reform in the law might encourage others to opt for a premature end to life, potentially for the wrong reasons.

Disability rights campaigners fought to impede victory in her case. Following the judgment, the Director of Disability Awareness in Action said it would be "very wrong for justice to say in certain circumstances people can die. It would be a slippery slope and many people who did not want to die could be affected."[70] An emphasis on stereotypical perceptions about the quality of life of persons with disabilities is regularly put forward by the Not Dead Yet UK Coalition, chaired by Baroness Jane Campbell who is also a Commissioner and Disability Committee Chair at the EHRC. The Coalition writes:

> Disabled people have become aware of the dangers associated with the call for assisted dying to be legalised. The idea that disabled people, including those who do not have long to live, are "better off dead" is not new. We believe individual disabled people's suicidal cries for help come from a lack of proper practical, emotional and medical support needed to live dignified lives, rather than from the "suffering" they experience as a result of a medical condition. Such loss of hope – which forces some to see death as their only option – is easily misinterpreted in a society that continues to see and treat disabled people as second class citizens. Individuals risk being easily exploited by the "right-to-die" movement or, worse, by family, friends and health care professionals. Their attitude is not compassionate – it is prejudiced and disablist.[71]

The DRC took a similar public position:

> The DRC takes very seriously the principle of autonomy expressed in the phrase "a right to die." However, we believe there is an overriding principle of a right to life. Alongside the wishes of people like Reginald Crew and Dianne (sic) Pretty, we hear the voices of disabled people who express a real fear that their lives will be put at risk if voluntary euthanasia or assisted suicide were legalized . . . At this point in time, in a climate where the lives of disabled people are not valued equally with those of non-disabled people, the DRC is not convinced that sufficient safeguards can be put in place to protect disabled people's right to live.[72]

---

[70] "Husband's Tribute to Diane Pretty," *BBC News*, May 13, 2002, http://news.bbc.co.uk/2/hi/health/1983941.stm (accessed May 13, 2002).

[71] Not Dead Yet UK Campaign Web site, http://www.livingwithdignity.info/ndy_aboutus.html (accessed January 21, 2007).

[72] Gooding, "The Application of the ECHR in British Courts."

The Commission made clear that "it is not making a general moral judgment on the legalization of voluntary euthanasia or assisted suicide, but is basing its view on the effect that such legalization will have on the lives of disabled people."[73]

As in Canada, right to die cases raise difficult issues for the disability rights movement. While activists put forward arguments regarding the importance of the principle of self-determination of disabled people, they also have had to emphasize the context within which this self-determination should be situated. The question of self-determination and provision of life-saving treatment reappeared in the courts several years later in the *Burke* case (discussed below). In this case, however, the claimant was coming from a fundamentally different perspective, and the strategic importance of the case was better harnessed by organizational actors in the disability lobby to put forward their message.

THE RIGHT TO LIFE AS A RIGHT TO TREATMENT: SEIZING AND REFRAMING THE ISSUE

Prior to the passage of the HRA, disability rights campaigners hoped that Article 2 of the ECHR, the right to life, would have a positive influence on policy toward withdrawal and provision of life-saving treatment. A report published by the DRC immediately before the implementation of the HRA argued:

> If a disabled person were refused treatment solely because of his/her disability (perhaps on the basis of assumptions about "poorer quality of life") this would almost certainly breach Article 2, together with Article 14... Article 2 will serve a useful role for disabled people in reinforcing their rights at a time when limited resources and technological advances may have otherwise put them under threat... It

---

[73] Ibid.

may have some impact on the allocation of resources to those need-
ing medical treatment in a life-threatening situation.[74]

Disability groups had expressed a number of concerns regarding
widespread, implicit perceptions in the medical profession of the quality of life of persons with disabilities, which they hoped Article 2 would
address. For example, the Down's Syndrome Association reported a
number of cases involving children with Down syndrome in which life-
saving treatment had been refused, allegedly on clinical grounds but
parents felt that the judgment may have been made by medical staff on
the basis of the child's perceived quality of life.[75] In another example,
the DRC report quotes the case of a company director with spinal
muscular atrophy who was admitted to hospital with a chest infection.
To her shock and dismay she found that a doctor had, without discussion, placed a "Do Not Resuscitate" notice on her medical notes
because her quality of life, according to the doctor, did not warrant
such intervention.[76] Growing expressions of concern and suspicion as
to the approach of the medical profession to the withdrawal and provision of life-preserving treatment for disabled people laid the backdrop
to a significant case in which the DRC tried to reframe the right to life
as a right to require treatment.

In *R (Burke) v. General Medical Council*, the Administrative Court
accepted a challenge to the legality of guidance documents issued by
the General Medical Council (GMC), the body regulating medical
practitioners, on the withholding and withdrawing of life-prolonging
treatments.[77] Leslie Burke, the claimant, had a congenital degenerative
brain condition, and he knew there would come a time when he would
lose the ability to swallow and would require the provision of artificial

---

[74] Ibid., p. 9.

[75] Ibid.

[76] Ibid.

[77] *Burke, R. (on the application of) v. General Medical Council & Ors* [2005] EWCA Civ
1003.

nutrition and hydration (ANH) by tube: in short, he was aware that there would come a time when he would be dependent on others for his care and survival. Mr. Burke was concerned that doctors would be able to make a decision on his behalf as to whether he would receive ANH on the basis of their own assessments of his quality of life as opposed to his own wishes. The GMC, in "Withholding and Withdrawing Life-prolonging Treatment: Good Practice and Decision Making," issued guidelines to doctors on matters to consider when deciding whether to withdraw ANH. Mr. Burke initiated a judicial review on the basis that the GMC guidance failed to give effect to the ECHR by making the wishes of patients (expressed at the time, if competent, or by advanced directive if no longer competent) determinative in the case of refusal to accept treatment, but not where the patient wished to continue with treatment. According to the claimant and the DRC, which intervened in the case, there was a disproportionate emphasis throughout the guidance documents on the right of a patient to refuse treatment in contrast to the right of the patient to require treatment. The claimant also maintained that the guidance failed to acknowledge "that it is the duty of a doctor who is unable or unwilling to carry out the wishes of his patient to go on providing the treatment until he can find another doctor who will do so" and failed "sufficiently to acknowledge the heavy presumption in favor of life-prolonging treatment."

The Administrative Court made six declarations of unlawfulness in the judicial review amounting to a ruling whereby patients' wishes should determine what was in their best interests, not doctors. The 2004 ruling was hailed as a landmark by disability rights campaigners and patients' groups.[78] However, the GMC appealed to the Court of Appeal, arguing that the ruling could put doctors in "an impossibly difficult position," obliging a doctor to provide treatment that the patient

---

[78] "Doctors Win Appeal Over the Rights of Terminally Ill," *The Guardian*, July 29, 2005, http://www.guardian.co.uk/society/2005/jul/29/health.medicineandhealth1 (accessed March 21, 2008).

demanded even if the doctor's professional view was that the treatment would not provide any benefit or would be futile.[79] Another significant controversy with the lower court's judgment was that it broadened the scope significantly from the relatively specific instance of decisions of ANH to medical treatment broadly conceived.

The DRC intervened in the Court of Appeal case to highlight its overarching concern that some decisions by medical professionals on whether disabled people should live or die are based on negative images and poorly informed assumptions. The DRC put forward three principles that it maintained should guide decisions to withhold or withdraw ANH: first, that the wish of a patient with capacity must be given effect; second, when a patient lacks capacity and there is a disagreement between the patient, medical staff, and/or other relevant people (including relatives) the matter should be referred to a court; and third, in other circumstances, the decision may be made by a doctor, whose approach should be that ANH should be provided where it would prolong life and be of benefit to the patient, unless their life – as seen from the patient's point of view – would then be intolerable. The policy implications of these principles are numerous; perhaps most significantly for this study, the second principle, ultimately not accepted, would have significantly increased the role of courts in deciding life and death matters.

In the end, the Court of Appeal concluded that the GMC's guidance was not unlawful and set aside the declarations made by the Administrative Court. The judgment states: "Mr. Burke's fears are addressed by the law as it currently stands and that declaratory relief, particularly in so far as it declares parts of the Guidance unlawful, is both unnecessary for Mr. Burke's protection and inappropriate as far as the Guidance itself is concerned."[80] Despite what they considered

---

[79] Ibid.

[80] *Burke, R. (on the application of) v. General Medical Council & Ors* [2005] EWCA Civ 1003.

disappointing results in the facts of the case, the DRC argued that the decision was nonetheless important because principles of patient autonomy and choice were recognized: a competent person's wishes must be respected (apart from a right to demand a particular treatment), and withdrawal of life-prolonging treatment contrary to a competent patient's expressed wishes could be considered murder.

In contrast to the minimal substantive policy implications of the *Burke* case, an analysis of the Court of Appeal decision highlights some mixed signals from the Court in regards to the use of strategic litigation for resolving complicated policy issues. First, there were a relatively large number of interveners that submitted arguments for the consideration of the Court.[81] In particular, the Administrative Court judgment explicitly praises the role of the Commission and of the use of interveners' submissions more generally.

> The DRC was able to deploy, to the great assistance of the Court, a particular and highly relevant informed expertise which none of the other parties could bring to the task in hand ... the important role that, in appropriate cases, bodies such as the DRC have to play in litigation, affording our courts the kind of valuable and valued assistance that courts in the United States of America have for so long been accustomed to receiving from those filing amicus curiae briefs.[82]

The involvement of interveners is a relatively novel phenomenon in the UK courts, whereas in Canada it is the main channel through which groups can become involved in legal action at the highest levels of the judicial system. It allows organizations to highlight the policy and societal implications of particular decisions for the benefit of the

---

[81] The Disability Rights Commission, The Official Solicitor to the Supreme Court, Catholic Bishops' Conference of England and Wales, The Secretary of State for Health, Patient Concern, Medical Ethics Alliance, Alert, British Section for the World Federation of Doctors who Respect Human Life, Intensive Care Society.

[82] *R. (on the application of Burke) v. General Medical Council* [2003] CO/4038/2003.

courts. However, in the *Burke* case, the higher court judgment firmly rejected the approach taken by the lower court in considering issues beyond those directly relevant to the case. Lord Phillips for the Court of Appeal writes:

> Mr. Francis QC, instructed by the Official Solicitor, submitted to us that Mr. Burke had performed a public service by enabling these wider issues to be debated. We do not agree. The judge himself observed that it was not the task of a judge when sitting judicially – even in the Administrative Court – to set out to write a text book or practice manual. Yet the judge appears to have done just that.[83]

DISABILITY AND THE POLITICS OF CAREGIVING IN THE EUROPEAN COURT OF JUSTICE

A point of controversy when the DDA was amended to be brought into line with the European Employment Equality Framework Directive was whether or not the directive would protect persons who were discriminated against on grounds of their association with persons with disabilities. Comparable common law jurisprudence protected those who suffered discrimination because of their association with persons of a particular racial group.[84] The DRC encouraged the inclusion of "associative discrimination," but a restrictive interpretation of the Directive was chosen instead.[85] Once the law reform route was closed off, there were discussions within the DRC of whether a judicial review for noncompliance with European law should be the next move. This

---

[83] Ibid.

[84] See, for example, *Zarczynska v. Levy* [1979], *Showboat Entertainment Centre Ltd v. Owens* [1984], and *Weathersfield v. Sargent* [1999].

[85] Disability Rights Commission, *DRC Legal Achievements*.

was rejected in favor of waiting to see whether a case would come along upon which to pursue strategic litigation.[86] That decision led to the first UK disability rights case, *Coleman v. Attridge Law*, to be heard by the ECJ.[87]

Ms. Coleman, who has a disabled son, left the Attridge Law firm, alleging that she was denied flexible working opportunities compared with parents of nondisabled children employed by the company. She claimed unlawful associative discrimination and unfair dismissal against her employer. Among the examples of discriminatory treatment that she alleges she suffered were that her employers refused to allow her to return to her existing job after coming back from maternity leave; they called her "lazy" when she sought to take time off to care for her son and refused to give her the same flexibility in her working arrangements as those of her colleagues with nondisabled children; she claims they said that she was using her child to manipulate her working conditions; they subjected her to disciplinary action; and they failed to deal properly with a formal grievance she lodged against her ill treatment.

During the proceedings, the Chairman of the Employment Tribunal referred a series of questions to the ECJ through the preliminary reference procedure to determine whether the wording of the DDA could be interpolated to cover associative discrimination.[88] This concept was explicitly excluded from the legislation, and yet there was a possibility that if the Directive were interpreted in a way to include the concept of associative discrimination then the DDA could be read in a purposive manner that would include protection from discrimination with those associated with persons with disabilities.

---

[86] Interview, August 8, 2007.

[87] *Coleman v. Attridge Law*, [2008] C-303/06.

[88] Under Article 234 of the Treaty of Rome, any national court, including employment tribunals, has the power to make a reference to the ECJ when the question involves interpretation of a Directive.

An interesting point of legal procedure emerged in this case, which could potentially have closed off the legal opportunity structure not just for disability rights litigants but all those relying on EU law, but in the end affirmed the power of all levels of national courts to refer decisions to the ECJ. After the Employment Tribunal's decision to refer questions to the ECJ, the respondents, Attridge Law firm, took the unusual step of appealing this decision to refer questions to the ECJ. The respondents argued that a reference should only be made where it was necessary to enable the Employment Tribunal to give judgment in this case. They contended that the domestic DDA cannot be construed in such a way as to include protection for associative discrimination and that by extension the reference was purely an academic exercise and should be revoked. The Chairman of the Employment Tribunal was persuaded that it may be possible to construe the relevant provisions of the DDA in such a way that it can be read to include associative discrimination if the concept is covered by the Directive. In the end, the Employment Appeals Tribunal dismissed the respondents appeal and accepted the arguments of legal counsel for Ms Coleman that it is not clear whether the Directive does or does not prohibit such associative discrimination, and the further argument that the DDA is capable of being interpreted so as to prohibit such discrimination if that is the meaning of the Directive.

In his opinion, issued in January 2008, the ECJ Advocate General (AG) relied almost exclusively on human rights considerations in formulating his interpretation of the Directive. In earlier cases before the ECJ in which human rights issues were considered, the Court and AGs had a tendency to at least allude to economic reasons for their judgments. The *Coleman* case may signal an increasing willingness on the part of the Court to suggest that domestic legislation should be interpreted in a purposive manner. The AG argues that:

> The Directive itself states in Article 1 that its purpose is "to lay
> down a general framework for combating discrimination . . . with a

view to putting into effect in the Member States the principle of equal treatment." The Court's case-law is clear as regards the role of equal treatment and non-discrimination in the Community legal order. Equality is not merely a political ideal and aspiration but one of the fundamental principles of Community law.[89]

However, despite the explicit assertion that equality is a driving force in Community law the economic argument is not completely absent. In a footnote to his opinion, the AG refuted an argument put forth by the UK government in the case that minimal standards suffice for implementation of the directive:

> There is a further reason which undermines the view of the United Kingdom. The equal treatment obligations that the Directive imposes may have costs, mainly for employers, and, to some extent, the imposition of those obligations entails a decision to socialise the costs through particular market mechanisms. This can be achieved in an efficient and equitable manner that does not distort competition only if those equal treatment obligations are interpreted and applied uniformly throughout the common market. If that were not the case we would be facing the risk of creating an uneven playing field in Europe, as the shape of the equal treatment obligations imposed on economic operators by Community law would not be the same throughout the common market but would depend on whether a particular Member State has chosen to outlaw a specific type of discrimination.[90]

The ECJ endorsed the AG's opinion by agreeing unanimously in July 2008 that Ms. Coleman had the right to claim discrimination by association if she was harassed and branded lazy for wanting the flexibility to look after her child. The ruling establishes for the first time that Europe's ban on employment discrimination is not limited to disabled

[89] Opinion of the Advocate General, Poiares Maduro delivered on January 31, 2008 in the case *Coleman v. Attridge Law*, [2008] C-303/06.
[90] Ibid.

people but extends to those responsible for them or with close connections. The ruling binds EU member–state courts only to extend employment protection to parents of disabled children. However, the AG's remarks, endorsed by the Court, send a signal that the principle should extend to all caregivers and may eventually do so. According to *The Guardian*, the EHRC and groups such as Carers UK will now press for British law to be altered to take the broad approach.[91]

CONCLUSIONS

The survey of landmark cases in this chapter demonstrates that the UK and European Courts have had an important influence on a wide range of disability-relevant policy issues. They have promoted a social model understanding of disability in a number of crucial employment, education, service provision, and human rights cases. It would not be an exaggeration to say that, in rejecting a purely formal approach to equality, the foundation for substantive equality for persons with disabilities has been largely achieved across many policy domains.

The purposive interpretations of relevant legislation in cases like *Archibald, Price, Ross,* and *Roads* are a significant achievement on the part of the individual litigants taking the case, their counsel, and, where relevant, the organizations backing them.[92] This element of strategic litigation in taking disability cases – "persuading" or "teaching" the courts that have never come across the social model before to develop a new kind of understanding – was a significant challenge. This is in contrast to the situation in Canada, where a substantive approach to

---

[91] "Carer Brings Hope to Millions with Landmark Win on Employment Rights," *The Guardian*, July 18, 2008, http://www.guardian.co.uk/society/2008/jul/18/socialcare .law (accessed November 1, 2008).

[92] *Archibald v. Fife*, [2004] IRLR 651; *Price v. UK*, [2001] 34 EHRR 1285; *Ross v. Ryanair Ltd and Stansted Airport Ltd*, [2004] EWCA Civ. 1751; *Roads v. Central Trains*, [2004] EWCA Civ 1541.

equality was developed in nondisability-specific cases that then paved the way for disability activists to influence the Court to adopt interpretations of legislation based on the social model of disability.

However, these victories have been balanced by some significant losses on a number of dimensions. First, the inability to convince the Courts that a right to life also constitutes a right to require treatment has meant that the quality of care, and in some cases even the lives, of persons with severe disabilities may still be contingent on the prejudices held by their medical practitioners. Second, a number of cases have been taken by individuals with less consideration of the impact decisions would have on disabled people more broadly. The right-to-die cases were not part of a wider strategic litigation effort, and the DRC had to become involved as part of a "damage limitation" strategy. This unpredictable nature of legal mobilization is an inevitable reality in the use of strategic litigation: immense amounts of time, effort, and resources may need to be channeled to avoid negative results in the courts or in publicity campaigns. Third, many disability activists express pessimism regarding the situation on the ground for persons with disabilities, arguing that discrimination is still rife and enforcement mechanisms are weak.

Another significant component of this survey has been gaining an understanding of the way in which the courts understand their own role as policy actors and courts as venues within which policy debates should or should not be happening. In some cases, judges have wholeheartedly embraced the powers inherent in the HRA and the EU legislation to ensure that important rights are protected, proper procedures are respected, and relatively novel legal techniques can be used to ensure equality (e.g., the use of an injunction in *Ford-Shubrook*). In the *Ross* case, the Court, by commissioning a report on accessibility to the courts from the DRC, demonstrated at least an interest in the question of physical access to justice for persons with disabilities. However, the courts' concern about access to justice, broadly construed, should not be overstated: the courts have not been whole-hearted participants in the policy process and, on several occasions, judges have demonstrated their reluctance to consider abstract issues, take a more proactive and inquisitorial role, give credence to the role of interveners in the process, and challenge the policy status quo on difficult issues even where logical inconsistencies have existed.

6

Conclusions: Litigation, Mobilization, and Social Movements

INTRODUCTION

The sociolegal implications of disability have changed enormously. In the late 1970s, disability rights were not only nonexistent, they were largely inconceivable. Policy makers and even the majority of people with disabilities themselves unquestioningly accepted that pity, charity, and paternalism, rather than rights provisions, were the most appropriate responses to the problems of poverty and social exclusion associated with disability. Thirty years later, the legal status of people with disabilities in Canada and the United Kingdom has been radically altered: the concept of disability is now considered as much the domain of citizenship and inclusion policy as welfare policy, and equality provisions are now constitutionally and statutorily entrenched.

The "rights revolution" in the realm of disability has been influenced by, and in turn has influenced, a significant change in the social construction of disability among crucial constituencies: specifically, a change from a medicalized, individual model of disability to a sociocontextual model. At the crux of the social model is the notion that "a disability is then not something that is just wrong with a person, but rather it is a site of difference that exposes hegemony and injustice in the normal workings of the world. The problem is the stairs, not the legs of the person who uses a wheelchair to get around."[1] This new understanding was developed and diffused by activists and disability studies academics to challenge the underpinnings of existing disability paradigms focused on rehabilitation and medicalized notions of the individual. This "meaning work" was undertaken within grassroots organizations of people with disabilities and led to the establishment of a rights-claiming social movement. In this way, activists radically shook up the way lawmakers and judges think about disability and how best to achieve equality for individuals with disabilities.

In this book, I have endeavored to assess areas of transformation and retrenchment in judicial understandings of the concepts of disability – and equality more broadly – and, where relevant, to gauge in a general sense the impact of organizational litigation on this judicial discourse. Second, I have sought to explore the conditions under which civil society organizations advocating disability issues are more likely to rely on strategic litigation to pursue their goals. The two goals are linked: in demonstrating how legal actions can transform or stagnate the conceptualization of equality in judicial discourses, we also then see how important the use of strategic litigation by disability rights activists becomes. Conversely, it is largely because of the proactive use of legal tactics by organizations that judges face questions of how disability should be conceptualized from a policy perspective.

In this concluding chapter, I draw together some of the major strands of my country-specific analyses to suggest broader comparative findings. In the next section, I present cross-national findings of the way in which judicial understandings of disability have evolved in Canada and the United Kingdom. I then highlight the similarities and differences in the empirical results of the case studies regarding social movement organizations and the use of strategic litigation. In the third

---

[1] Anna Kirkland, "Think of the Hippopotamus: Rights Consciousness in the Fat Acceptance Movement," *Law and Society Review* 42(2), 2008, p. 402.

section, I consider these results in the light of existing theoretical explorations of legal mobilization as well as the sociological–institutionalist perspective advanced here. In turn, I consider some of the implications of the empirical findings for theoretical understandings of legal mobilization by social movement actors. I explain how existing scholarly understandings can be amended in light of this new research. In the final section, I explore some of the limitations of this research and provide suggestions for future research directions.

THE COURTS, DISABILITY, AND EQUALITY: A CROSS-NATIONAL COMPARISON

Most studies of disability law have focused on the development of legislation, attempts to expand legal protections, and/or challenges of implementation and debates on how legislation should be interpreted.[2] This approach moves beyond purely legal analyses and examines judicial decisions in their sociopolitical context from an interdisciplinary perspective. To be clear, it is not a jurisprudential study, but the examination of disability case law in two countries represents an important contribution to the legal literature on disability law by demonstrating the impact of legal actions on judicial understandings of disability and its appropriate remedies. In both national contexts, we saw a clear development of a substantive understanding of equality in the sphere of disability issues. In comparing and contrasting major themes within the surveys of landmark decisions in the two case studies, some patterns are worth highlighting. I also draw attention here to the broader implications of these findings and directions for future research in the area of disability law specifically.

---

[2] Catherine Casserley, "The Disability Discrimination Act: An Overview," in Jeremy Cooper, ed., *Law, Rights and Disability* (London: Jessica Kingsley Publishers, 2000); Gooding, "Disability Discrimination Act: From Statute to Practice"; Mark Bell, *Anti-Discrimination Law and the European Union* (Oxford: Oxford University Press, 2002); Fredman, *Discrimination Law*.

First, the courts have broadly accepted key tenets of the social model of disability and have advanced a disability perspective in landmark equality decisions. Numerous cases and resulting judicial interpretations have demonstrated that equal treatment can lead in effect to inequality, whereas unequal treatment might be necessary in order to achieve equality.[3] Of central importance in early judicial interpretations of disability equality provisions in both countries was an affirmation of the positive duty to accommodate people with disabilities. Instead of simply requiring conformity to the able-bodied norm as a precondition for protection, legal protections in both countries now require adjustment of that norm. Whereas early cases in both countries focused on reasonable accommodation in the employment context, the concept has now been applied across a wide range of policy areas from education (the *Eaton* case in Canada and *Ford-Shubrook* in the UK) to service provision (*Eldridge* in Canada to *Ross* in the UK) and transport (*VIA Rail* in Canada and *Roads* in the UK).[4] The case of disability equality, as interpreted by Canadian and UK courts, provides a decisive challenge to notions of formal equality.

Although the development of the positive duty associated with disability in judicial interpretation and its influence across policy areas is remarkably similar across the two countries, there have nonetheless been significant differences in the course of this development. Key among these is that, in Canada, the concept of unintentional discrimination or adverse effect discrimination and the corresponding duty of employers to provide reasonable accommodations was initially developed in equality realms other than disability. The case of *O'Malley*

---

[3] Fredman, *Discrimination Law*, p. 2.

[4] *Eaton v. Brant County Board of Education*, [1997] 1 S.C.R. 241; *Ford-Shubrook v. St Dominics College*, [2003] MA315699, Manchester County Court; *Eldridge v. British Columbia (Attorney General)*, [1997] 2 S.C.R. 624; *Ross v. Ryanair Ltd and Stansted Airport Ltd*, [2004] EWCA Civ. 1751; *Council of Canadians with Disabilities v. VIA Rail Canada Inc*, 2007 SCC 15, [2007] 1 S.C.R. 650; *Roads v. Central Trains*, [2004] EWCA Civ 1541.

before the Supreme Court of Canada addressed the issue of discrimination on the basis of religion.[5] Similarly, the *Andrews* case, in which the Court enunciated a substantive model of equality, dealt with discrimination based on nationality.[6] In contrast, in the UK, the concept of reasonable adjustments was developed almost solely in the realm of disability issues and has later been used by scholars interested in antidiscrimination law in other areas, for example, in protections from discrimination based on pregnancy.[7]

A second notable trend is the similarity in the types of cases that garner broader public attention in contrast with those that receive little attention but which are nonetheless seen as landmark cases among the disability advocacy community. Among the Canadian cases discussed, it was the *Rodriguez* and *Latimer* cases on assisted suicide and the framing of the murder of a child with a disability as a "mercy killing" that sparked the most heated public debates and caused a significant degree of ink to be spilled in Canadian newspapers.[8] Among the UK cases examined here, the assisted-suicide issue was also at the forefront of public attention with the *Pretty* case.[9] Many activists and lawyers interviewed in both countries pointed out, however, that it is cases dealing with what might appear to be relatively mundane issues that lead to the most significant or widespread changes essential to enhancing the goal of inclusion for people with disabilities. In Canada, this is exemplified by the *VIA Rail* case, which dealt with complex transport regulations but addressed issues fundamental to the ability of Canadians with disabilities to participate in social and community life in the

---

[5] *Ont. Human Rights Comm. v. Simpsons-Sears*, [1985] 2 S.C.R. 536.

[6] *Andrews v. Law Society of British Columbia*, [1989] 1 S.C.R. 143.

[7] See Robert Wintemute, "When Is Pregnancy Discrimination Indirect Sex Discrimination?" *Industrial Law Journal* 27(1), 1998, pp. 23–36.

[8] *Rodriguez v. British Columbia (Attorney General)*, [1993] 3 S.C.R. 519; *R. v. Latimer*, [2001] 1 S.C.R. 3.

[9] "Law of Dying," *The Guardian*, November 1, 2008, http://www.guardian.co.uk/commentisfree/2008/nov/01/assisted-suicide-law (accessed November 1, 2008).

same way that other citizens do. Among the UK cases, the *A and B* case on manual lifting and handling by care workers also represented a controversy over a technically complex and relatively commonplace issue. The legal decision nonetheless touched on the issue of the dignity of people with disabilities as a component of human rights and was cited by experts as having widespread impact.

It is worth highlighting that, in both countries, decisions in the realm of life and death issues did not result in policy shifts: the cases are ultimately more notable for the continuity they engendered. It is, however, the promise – or danger – of change that has driven various activists or organizations to participate in these cases. The *Rodriguez* case represents an example of activists both pursuing change and intervening to prevent it: Sue Rodriguez took her case to the Supreme Court to try to achieve law reform on assisted suicide, whereas some of the main disability rights organizations participated as third-party interveners precisely because they feared that a change in the law would place Canadians with disabilities in a vulnerable position. The very notion of "landmark decisions," in current media and scholarly usage, tends to emphasize cases that successfully challenge the policy status quo. However, important cases supported by or participated in by disability rights activists have just as often been "maintenance cases" – those which protect against a regression in policy because adversaries advance arguments that threaten earlier legislative or judicial victories. These cases are just as significant as those that result in a major policy shift, and are arguably even more hard-fought by social movement actors.

DISABILITY RIGHTS ORGANIZATIONS
AND STRATEGIC LITIGATION

In Canada, many disability rights organizations have been active participants before the Supreme Court. It is clear that organizations advancing a disability rights agenda are major players in the Canadian justice system when it comes to the equality agenda. This does not suggest, however, that all organizations speaking on disability issues have used litigation: the examination of the Canadian National Institute for the Blind (CNIB) is a prime example of a high-profile organization that has forgone the opportunity to litigate. In the United Kingdom, strategic litigation has also been used to advance a disability rights agenda, but its development has taken a fundamentally different form from the Canadian case.

First, legal mobilization began much later in the UK than in Canada: regular and systematic participation in judicial venues only began in earnest with the establishment in 2000 of the Disability Rights Commission (DRC), a quasi-nongovernmental organization (NGO) with a dedicated legal department. The primary explanation for the differential timing of the take-up of strategic litigation across countries is the differing legal protections on which litigation could be based: the Canadian equality provisions came into force in 1985, whereas the Disability Discrimination Act and the Human Rights Act in the UK were established ten and thirteen years later, respectively. The introduction of legislation may have had an impact in two ways. At a formal level, individuals and organizations did not have explicit legal antidiscrimination protections on which to base claims until the mid-1990s. At a more symbolic level, the introduction of these protections may have played an important role in augmenting the degree of rights consciousness and legal awareness among people with disabilities.[10]

A second crucial cross-national difference is in organizational use of strategic litigation. In Canada, it is overwhelmingly organizations *of* people with disabilities – the Council of Canadians with Disabilities (CCD), the now defunct Canadian Disability Rights Council (CDRC), and the DisAbled Women's Network (DAWN Canada) – that have mobilized legally, with the Canadian Association

---

[10] Engel and Munger, *Rights of Inclusion.*

for Community Living, a family organization that has nonetheless adopted similar values to grassroots groups also playing an active role in the courts. In the UK, the use of legal action by the large NGOs varied during the time period studied: some groups, like the Royal National Institute of Blind People (RNIB), were early adopters of the use of legal action in campaigning efforts, whereas others had relatively little knowledge of, or interest in, the possibilities of using strategic litigation to complement campaigning activities. Grassroots organizations, by and large, did not mobilize legally (there have been but a handful of exceptions to this) but have been supportive of the DRC's test cases and regularly pushed the organization to be more vigorous in its enforcement efforts. The DRC has played a unique role in the disability sector in the UK. As an independent organization that was able to garner policy entrepreneurs, legal expertise, legitimacy and resources from across both grassroots organizations, and the traditional establishment, it has been the most active organization in promoting a disability rights agenda in the courts through a large number of strategic cases.

A third notable difference is the social movement impact of strategic litigation. In Canada, the ripple effect of organizational use of strategic litigation appears to have been much more significant. The case of the transformation of the identity associated with the change from the Canadian Association for the Mentally Retarded to the Canadian Association for Community Living after the successful victory in the *Eve* case is remarkable. This case also led to the establishment of People First of Canada, thus having a wider social movement impact. It also encouraged others to pursue legal cases. Similar impacts were not found in the UK country study.

Despite these significant differences, there are also some striking cross-national similarities in organizational approaches toward the use of strategic litigation. First, organizations using strategic litigation in both Canada and the UK developed their strategies in similar ways. Interviewees on both sides of the Atlantic pointed to the relatively unstructured beginnings of legal mobilization in their organizations with the later development of a more strategic approach. Early provision of legal advice and taking on of legal cases tended to favor a "we will help anyone who comes through the door" approach, whereas more recently organizations have begun to prioritize issues and proactively seek cases for test case litigation. Furthermore, organizations interested in using strategic litigation have actively sought to broaden the opportunities for legal mobilization. Both the DRC in the UK and ARCH Disability Law Centre in Canada have undertaken campaigning activity, both in the courts and through other channels, to enhance access to justice for people with disabilities.

A second cross-national similarity is that the opportunity to use litigation has not always been welcomed. Existing theories tend to neglect these situations where organizations would rather forego participation because of the costs (broadly understood) imposed by the use of this particular strategy. The diversion of organizational attention and resources that sometimes accompanies the use of litigation, such as in the *Latimer* case, can be frustrating for activists. In short, sometimes "opportunities" for legal mobilization are not welcomed by social movement actors.

The use of legal mobilization can also be difficult for the leadership to explain or "sell" to both the rank-and-file membership and the broader constituency. The DRC undertook extensive public relations efforts to explain the use of litigation as a policy-influencing strategy generally and to justify its involvement in particular cases more specifically. Similarly, a CCD leader highlighted challenges the organization faces in the Canadian context:

> I don't think the litigation actually mobilizes our constituency. I think litigation is actually a challenge to make understandable to our constituency. People get the fundamental issue. But when we get into the litigation we're into all kinds of legal-ese and interpretation. There is a real challenge to make litigation and the points being litigated understandable at the local level... So the ongoing challenge with litigation is to keep people understanding why we're

doing it, what are the issues at the centre and how does that relate to our understanding of human rights and equality from a disability perspective.[11]

A final point of comparison across the two country studies is skepticism among the activists and discrimination lawyers interviewed that legal victories translate into effective social change. For some, this skepticism is long-standing, whereas, for others, disappointment stems from the combination of euphoria after a judicial victory followed by a specific experience of a failure to effectively enforce a judicial decision. All activists and lawyers interviewed pointed to the limits of legal strategies and the necessity, when they are employed, of complementing them with other strategies, such as law reform, legal education, and public outreach.

EXPLAINING THE EMPIRICAL FINDINGS: THE LIMITS OF EXISTING THEORETICAL APPROACHES

How can we best explain both cross-national as well as within-country, cross-organizational variation in legal mobilization? One reason for the above-mentioned cross-country differences certainly lies in the realm of procedural law – or what can also be conceived of as the more formal components of "legal opportunity structure" – and the understanding among potential participants of the incentives and constraints to using legal action in pursuit of goals. A key distinction is that, whereas the Canadian Supreme Court is the final court of appeal, the UK is subject to judicial decisions beyond those pronounced by domestic courts: key decisions from the European Court of Human Rights and the European Court of Justice matter. This difference transforms the scope for legal change. The research here affirms the literature's findings that

---

[11] Interview, January 22, 2008.

international courts open up avenues for action when domestic opportunities may have closed, shifting the balance of power among domestic policy actors.[12] It also suggests that taking a test case before these Courts can have a much broader impact: for example, the decision in *Coleman v. Attridge* before the ECJ will have effect in the twenty-seven EU countries.

However, these supranational opportunities are complemented in the UK by institutional constraints on the domestic role of courts as well as signals from elements of the judiciary that they are unwilling to take on what they see as an "activist" role in decisions influencing policy. Paramount among the institutional constraints is the principle of parliamentary sovereignty, as expressed through limits on judicial review powers. Courts are unable to strike down primary legislation violating the Human Rights Act 1998. Instead, in the case of finding an Act that violates the European Convention on Human Rights, their role is limited to making a declaration of incompatibility. It remains up to parliament to rectify the violation. In contrast, Canadian courts can rely on the Charter to declare legislation invalid. However, in Canada, the extent of policy impact also depends on the type of case being brought: judicial review of an administrative or executive decision (for example, the *Eaton* case addressing the wishes of parents to keep their child with disabilities in a mainstream class instead of being placed in a separate class) leads only to a reconsideration of a particular decision, whereas constitutional challenges to a legislative regime (e.g., in *Eldridge*) can result in the overturning of wide-ranging policy decisions.

Another fundamental difference between the legal opportunity structures in the two countries relates to the ways in which organizational actors can participate in legal actions. In Canada, acting as a third-party intervener has been a primary method of interest group participation before the courts, and organizations in Canada

---

[12] Alter and Vargas, "Explaining Variation in the Use of European Litigation Strategies," Cichowski, *The European Court and Civil Society.*

have established standard operating procedures for participating in this way. In the UK, in the realm of disability issues, this method has been used but, thus far, only to a limited extent and only by the DRC.[13] This form of legal participation was introduced much later in the UK and has been exploited by organizations to a much lesser extent; it seems natural that there will be a period of adaptation to its usage both among the judiciary and potential participants. In short, factors such as legal bases, liberalized standing rules, and alternative methods of participating before the courts – in other words, elements of the legal opportunity structures – clearly matter. However, the within-country, cross-organizational differences suggest that opportunity structures alone cannot account for variation in participation in strategic litigation: the within-country groups compared in this book are all situated in similar opportunity structures but behaved differently in terms of their litigation activity. How then can we account for some of the within-country, cross-organizational differences and some of the cross-country similarities?

Resource mobilization explanations have also been put forward to account for variation in strategic litigation. Understandings of how organizations deploy resources may help to account for within-country, cross-organizational variation in the use of strategic litigation. In the UK, all grassroots activists interviewed cited the high cost of using litigation as the main factor accounting for their inability to use this as a strategy, buttressing resource mobilization explanations. This approach also explains, to a certain extent, patterns in the use of litigation in the Canadian case but not in the way that original formulations of resource mobilization theory might expect. These theories have tended to focus on the ability of groups to mobilize resources from their own constituency, whereas the Canadian case points to

---

[13] Other disability advocacy organizations have been slow to explore the possibility of intervening in cases.

the importance of the availability of resources external to the group. The reliance by many of the litigating organizations on the Canadian Court Challenges Program – public funding specifically earmarked to support groups pursuing claims to promote equality goals – has been paramount to their ability to participate in legal actions. The large majority of activists and lawyers interviewed in Canada pointed to the cutting of this program in September 2006 as a significant blow to the ability of organizations to continue to pursue cases. This demonstrates that, in most cases, resources matter to groups wishing to litigate, but material support for litigation does not necessarily come solely from within organizations.

Despite some evidentiary support for resource mobilization theories, this study has also demonstrated the incompleteness of these approaches when used on their own. First, the case of organizations choosing to litigate within the UK highlights this: traditional disability charities, which have far greater resources than grassroots groups, have had a very mixed approach to the use of strategic litigation. Some organizations, like RNIB and RADAR, have pursued test cases, whereas others, including those with the greatest financial resources, have foregone the use of litigation. The causal relationship between resources and strategy choice suggested by resource mobilization approaches falls apart here. Second, the pursuit of particular cases by some organizations also goes against the expectations of resource mobilization theories. CCD's commitment to the *VIA Rail* case, in the face of potential financial ruin and organizational collapse, suggests that other factors are at play in explaining the turn to the courts in some situations. Third, I have also shown that "resources" should not solely be considered as an independent variable in exploring the turn to litigation. Groups may develop resources with the specific goal of pursuing litigation strategies. The establishment of the CDRC by members of CCD and the later development by the latter of a fund devoted solely to pursuing test case litigation illustrates how resources may be reasonably considered a dependent variable in hypotheses where organizational commitment to a particular strategy is treated as the independent variable.

These weaknesses of opportunity structure approaches and resource mobilization explanations can be mitigated by an understanding of organizational agency, meaning frames, and social movement context to better account for the development of legal mobilization. While resource mobilizations and legal and politicial opportunity structure frameworks can help to explain the "why" of legal mobilization, the determinism of some of these approaches is questionable. These explanations implicitly suggest that, as soon as an organization's wealth surpasses a particular resource threshold, they will be more likely to use strategic litigation, or that as soon as opportunity structures open, groups will consider the use of legal actions. The findings of this study and the theoretical framework articulated here have shown that participating in litigation is anything but an automatic process.

To be sure, existing approaches move us part of the way forward in understanding why some groups actively participate before the courts and others do not. However, even in combination, they are not wholly satisfactory. For example, they cannot explain 1) why some of the best-resourced organizations eschew litigation, 2) why other organizations develop resources or lobby to change opportunity structures specifically to be able to participate in strategic litigation, and 3) the remarkable cross-national similarities in the evolution and spread of understandings of disability from the social model perspective within the community and the correlation of the adoption of this understanding with the use of strategic litigation. I argue that the theoretical approach advanced here, in complementing existing approaches, adds value in explaining some of these findings. The integration of these approaches allows for a better explanation of both the why as well as the how of legal mobilization and better captures the mechanisms at work in influencing strategy choice.

DISABILITY RIGHTS, LEGAL MOBILIZATION
THEORY, AND SOCIOLOGICAL–INSTITUTIONALISM

This book has sought to contribute to scholarly elaboration of theoretical approaches to explaining legal mobilization by engaging with the ideas and activities of the disability studies literature and the disability movement in two national contexts. Specifically, I have shown that an understanding of the ways in which movement organizations construct meaning frames matters – both through their own internal dialectical processes as well as through their relations with each other. In Chapter 1, I articulated two dimensions of sociological-institutionalism that could help explain strategy choice: the internal nature of social movement organizations as well as the external social movement context within which these organizations are nested. In this section, I revisit each of these dimensions and discuss how this theoretical approach sheds light on variation in the use of strategic litigation and how this approach, when combined with existing theoretical approaches, better explains the development of legal mobilization. Again, the elements of these two dimensions are interconnected, but I separate them here for analytical purposes.

Internal Factors: Organizational Identity, Logics
of Appropriateness, and Framing Processes

The shift from a medicalized, individual model understanding of disability to a social–contextual framework in both countries played a crucial role in establishing the legitimacy of the use of strategic litigation within the disability rights movement. The paradigm shift among disability activists in both countries resulted in a reconceptualization of people with disabilities and their relationship to society: they began to see disability as a citizenship and equality issue best addressed through the provision of rights. The reunderstanding of disadvantage as discrimination, related heightened levels of rights consciousness across the community, and shared vision of a barrier-free society on a cross-disability basis resulted in the use of litigation strategies possessing great legitimacy among adherents of both national movements. This paradigm shift can also help to explain the similar trajectory judicial discourse on disability has taken in both countries: activists have supported cases and advanced legal arguments based on a remarkably similar social model understanding of disability that transcends national differences. The relationship here between norms, action, and organizational strategy choice is one of influence not determinism. March and Olsen make clear that "while rules guide behavior and make some actions more likely than others, they ordinarily do not determine political behavior or policy outcomes precisely. Rules, laws, identities and institutions provide parameters for action rather than dictate a specific action."[14]

Again, in both countries, this conceptualization of disability spread from grassroots organizations to some, but importantly not all, of the traditional charitable organizations. The traditional disability establishment in the UK was much more resistant to change than the organizations examined in Canada, where charities tended either to adopt a social–contextual understanding of disability or moderated their claims of speaking on behalf of people with disabilities. The Big Seven UK charities have varied in their adoption of a social model understanding of disability, and this has correlated with their use of strategic litigation. This correlation allows us to make some claims regarding the influence of meaning frames in circumscribing "appropriate" strategies. The case studies of RNIB and Scope in the UK demonstrate how these meaning frames can diffuse through organizations or be met with resistance, and how they influence governance structures,

---

[14] James G. March and Johan P. Olsen, "The Logic of Appropriateness," *ARENA Working Paper 04/09*, University of Oslo, Centre for European Studies, p. 10.

representation of people with disabilities, the service-provision ethos, and policy priorities.

Relying on March and Olsen's assertion that organizational norms possess an almost inherent legitimacy which, through the power of "logics of appropriateness," dictate courses of action or the use of tactics which may seem irrational on a surface level, we can explain why some organizations and activists have supported the use of strategic litigation in the face of resource and opportunity structure hurdles.[15] My research has shown that organizations may even pursue litigation when this jeopardizes their material interests or threatens the very existence of the organization. The case of CCD and the *VIA Rail* action is an extreme illustration of this principle. There is, of course, also the counter-example of the BCODP grassroots body in the UK that has had funding problems threaten the very survival of the organization, such that strategy concerns become secondary.

The findings can also help in sociological–institutionalist theory building. Theorists have begun to consider how logics of appropriateness change and the conditions under which departures from path-dependent processes occur.[16] The findings of this study can shed some light on how organizational logics of action can be transformed. This book has explored some cases of bottom-up change in organizations, in both Canada and the UK, that can be generalized as falling into one of two categories of organizational transformation. First, there can be a change in the meaning frames of individuals already situated within an organization who act to diffuse new frames from within. An instance of this was the case of the group of consumers in the Canadian Association for Community Living who began to see themselves differently: as rights holders and citizens rather than objects of pity and recipients of charity and pushed the Board of the organization both toward funding

---

[15] Ibid.

[16] Ibid.; B. Guy Peters, et al., "The Politics of Path Dependency: Political Conflict in Historical Institutionalism," *Journal of Politics* 67(4), 2000, pp. 1275–300.

their legal intervention in the *Eve* case and later to change the name of the organization. These cases of "change from within" link in with the dynamic and mutually constitutive relationship between micro-level activists and the macro-level social movement organizational environment.

Second, individuals with differing meaning frames can join the organization and challenge the ideational status quo – what could be coined "change from without."[17] Individual activists can import competing meaning frames and act as "ideational (or norm) entrepreneurs" exerting agency in terms of pushing organizational learning processes.[18] This would describe, for example, the case of the radical disability rights leader who was recruited by a traditional charity, Scope, to help drive a change in the culture of the organization. This would also be an apt categorization of the blind activists who began to permeate the governance structures of the RNIB and transformed the organization.

These two types of import of meaning frames can also be further distinguished if considered from an organizational perspective. In the former case of Scope, the import was of an active, intentional nature, whereas in the case of the RNIB activists, the role of the organization can be considered passive. Individuals can also be brought within an organization and act as "strategy entrepreneurs" – those demonstrating agency and energy in promoting the use of particular tactics. Among interviewees from disability charities in the UK that had used strategic litigation, a significant number pointed to the role that particular

---

[17] James G. March, "Footnotes to Organizational Change," *Administrative Science Quarterly* 26(4), 1981, pp. 563–77.

[18] The literature on the role of norm entrepreneurs in international relations is particularly helpful here. See Martha Finnemore and Kathryn Sikkink, "International Norm Dynamics and Political Change," *International Organization* 52(4), 1998, pp. 887–917; Tanja A. Börzel and Thomas Risse, "When Europe Hits Home: Europeanization and Domestic Change," *European Integration Online Papers (EIoP)* 4(15), http://papers.ssrn.com/sol3/Papers.cfm?abstract_id=302 (accessed November 1, 2008).

individuals had played in bringing the use of a particular strategy to their attention – for example, the ability to act as a third-party intervener in cases. In all of these ways, individuals have demonstrated agency in diffusing ideational frames and raising awareness of particular strategies. In turn, it is the normative power of some of these ideas that encourages the exercising of agency by disability activists.

External Forces: The Organizational Environment and Social Movement Norms

This book has also demonstrated how interactions among organizations within a particular social movement can influence how ideas are disseminated, contested, and adopted, and how they influence and, in turn, are shaped by organizational strategy decisions. Analyses applying simple organizational ecological approaches have been helpful in exploring the content and intensity of relations among organizations: these dynamics reinforce, but also shape, organizational identities.

In the UK, the emergence of the grassroots movement, internal struggles over organizational style and values, and the growing dominance of the social model as the appropriate framework for understanding the concept of disability began to change the sector. It was particularly the social model's emphasis on privileging the voice of people with disabilities and the classification of organizations according to the *of* and *for* prepositions that began to define relationships between organizations all claiming to advocate on disability issues. The animosity, which more radical grassroots organizations have expressed toward the traditional disability charities, is a notable feature of the disability advocacy sphere. For a significant vocal minority of disability activists, the disability charities are embodiments of a paternalistic and disempowering understanding of disability. They have (at least until very recently) refused to work with these organizations, accept money from them, or acknowledge any legitimate role they might play in advocating on behalf of people with disabilities. Grassroots activists have blamed them for diverting public and governmental attention, as well as resources, away from organizations of people with disabilities.

However, social movement norms, or logics of appropriateness, began to create pressures on charities to change their campaign goals, governance structures, and service-provision ethos. Well-intentioned charitable organizations began to find the legitimacy of their ideological underpinnings and, in fact, their very existence challenged. In short, the disability sector's overarching logics of appropriateness began to exert pressures on organizations to change their policy priorities, governance structures, and service-provision philosophies. One of the results of this has been that, with the grassroots disability movement currently in a period of demobilization, the ideas and associated strategies are increasingly being considered and pursued by organizations with resources and, increasingly, with legal staff interested in the use of legal tactics in their campaigning work.

The nature of relations between Canadian disability organizations has been different. Despite some healthy skepticism on the part of people with disabilities, the evidence suggests that there are now relatively high (and increasing) levels of cooperation between traditional organizations and grassroots groups. Around the time of the Charter, disability-led organizations began to possess a relatively strong voice in the policy arena as well as in the courts. Cooperation, both within the disability community and with organizations from other movements, has been relatively common practice. These dynamics also have implications for resource mobilization explanations. Organizations can cooperate with the effect of sharing or offloading the costs of pursuing a particular strategy, such as DAWN Canada and the feminist organization the Women's Legal Education and Action Fund (LEAF), where the latter bears much of the cost of legal action.

In both national contexts, organizational divisions of labor, both substantive and tactical, have heavily influenced the shape of litigation activity. Organizational ecological approaches can better account for the variation in participation than existing approaches, such as resource mobilization and opportunity structure approaches, alone. The establishment of alliances can help to explain both cross-temporal and cross-organizational variation in the use of litigation. In the UK, this was seen most predominantly with the correlation between the establishment of the DRC and the decline in litigation activity by traditional organizations such as RNIB and RADAR. In Canada, examples of both tactical and substantive divisions of labor exist as well. For example, DAWN Canada has participated as an intervener before the Supreme Court of Canada to bring a feminist analysis to disability issues in cases where the CCD was also participating. To give another example, for a brief period in the late 1980s and early 1990s, CCD ceased their litigation activity and focused on lobbying, while the Canadian Disability Rights Council (CDRC) focused on legal mobilization. The shape of litigation activity across groups and over time is difficult to explain relying solely on existing theories: the organizational ecology approach adds explanatory value.

Evidence from both countries demonstrates that organizations are influenced by social movement dynamics and forces, and that this may shape variation in litigation activity across organizations and over time. This influence includes both the social movement of which an organization considers itself a part, as well as the example of other, similar social movements.[19] The theoretical implications of this are significant: groups are not situated within opportunity structures alone. Explanations focusing on political and legal opportunity structures, which make claims of generalizable patterns, will remain incomplete if they do not consider how interorganizational dynamics might affect the behavior of any single organization. It is worth reiterating that the approach focusing on social movement organizations themselves is not incompatible with theories emphasizing the importance of resource

---

[19] The example of disability activists in Canada emulating the tactics of the American civil rights movement and the Canadian feminist movement is notable.

mobilization and legal and political opportunity in explaining the conditions under which groups are more likely to turn to the courts. What the sociological–institutionalist account offers is a different, additional perspective on the dynamics of legal mobilization. What have been central here are the actors themselves and the agency they demonstrate while acting within institutional environments. Only by shifting the analytical focus in this way can we begin to fully understand the influence that resources and structures have. We also begin to see that they can be analyzed as dependent variables: collective actors, if their meaning frames encourage them to value the use of strategic litigation in and of itself, may take action to change structures and develop resources in order to pursue legal mobilization.

FURTHER ISSUES FOR DISABILITY STUDIES, LAW, AND POLICY

This book represents an exploration of an underexamined social movement and the complex political identities and interorganizational interactions within this movement. It has explored the experience of legal mobilization by the disability rights movement in two countries to establish the influence of meaning frames and intraorganizational relations on the likelihood of organizational use of strategic litigation. When considered together, the within-country and cross-national comparisons suggest a set of findings, outlined above, that highlight a common set of mechanisms influencing legal mobilization. However, the extent to which these findings are generalizable may be limited. As laid out in Chapter 2, the Canadian and UK cases were selected because of their relative comparability in terms of legal protections for people with disabilities and the existence of common law judicial systems that allowed for important legal opportunity structure dimensions to be held constant. A common assumption in the legal literature is that legal systems based on the civil code operate in such a fundamentally different manner that the impact on judicial doctrine, policy, and social movements themselves would also be radically different. Yet it is not unlikely that similar findings could be identified in other jurisdictions: the global spread of disability rights has been widely documented.[20] In order for the findings to be generalized to other national legal contexts, causal relationships would need to be traced and the impact of differences in procedural and substantive law would have to be accounted for in a rigorous fashion.

Several other areas ripe for future research can be identified based on the findings of this research and the theoretical implications discussed above. First, the comparative approach taken here has necessitated the exploration of the development of social movement politics and jurisprudence over time. This bottom-up perspective, placing activists and social movement organizations at the heart of the analysis, has driven which cases were examined in the legal surveys. This has necessarily meant that topical comparisons have been more shallow. The challenges faced in developing legal responses to transportation, immigration, education, employment, right to life, and access to justice issues are very different – not just across, but also within, countries. A number of questions emerge: Why do some issues rise to prominence across jurisdictions whereas others are country-specific? Do disability groups across countries find the same issues important and how can we explain issue hierarchies? Further cross-national reflection focused in a topical, rather than chronological, manner would go a long way in answering these questions.

Second, in the realm of disability studies and legal philosophy, research is beginning to probe existing understandings of equality and

---

[20] Katharina C. Heyer, "The ADA on the Road: Disability Rights in Germany," *Law and Social Inquiry* 27(4), 2002, pp. 723–62; Melinda Jones and Lee Ann Marks Basser, eds., *Disability, Divers-Ability and Legal Change* (The Hague: Martinus Nijhoff Publishers, 1999).

challenge fundamentals of the social model of disability and the duty to accommodate as it relates to a formal model of equality.[21] This concept has come under scrutiny in both scholarly literature and, more practically, in the Supreme Court of Canada. According to Shelagh Day and Gwen Brodsky, two prominent human rights lawyers who have regularly intervened before the Court, the judgment in a sex discrimination case, *Meiorin*, moves the Court's conception of discrimination to a different plane.

> The difficulty with this [accommodation] paradigm is that it does not challenge the imbalances of power, or the discourses of dominance, such as racism, ablebodyism and sexism, which result in a society being designed well for some and not for others. It allows those who consider themselves "normal" to continue to construct institutions and relations in their image, as long as others, when they challenge this construction are "accommodated".... Accommodation does not go to the heart of the equality question, to the goal of transformation, to an examination of the way institutions and relations must be changed in order to make them available, accessible, meaningful and rewarding for the many diverse groups of which our society is composed. Accommodation seems to mean that we do not change procedures or services, we simply "accommodate" those who do not quite fit. We make some concessions to those who are "different," rather than abandoning the idea of "normal" and working for genuine inclusiveness... In short, accommodation is assimilationist. Its goal is to try to make "different" people fit into existing systems.[22]

The development of this line of thinking could have enormous implications for the concept of equality in law and for conceptual understandings of the social model of disability.

---

[21] See, in particular, Shakespeare, *Disability Rights and Wrongs*; Kirkland, *Fat Rights*; Colker, *When is Separate Unequal.*

[22] Shelagh Day and Gwen Brodsky, "The Duty to Accommodate: Who Will Benefit?" *Canadian Bar Review*, 75, 1996, cited in *British Columbia (Public Service Employee Relations Commission) v. BCGSEU*, [1999] 3 S.C.R. 3.

Conclusions: Litigation, Mobilization, and Social Movements

Another area that could prove fruitful in the study of disability law and policy is the extent to which a rights discourse can lead to unseen and/or undesired rights assertions. For example, in the *Rodriguez* case, a single activist's use of an accommodation argument in advancing a right-to-die argument caused much disharmony in the movement in Canada. A second related area of political research is exploration of the notion and manifestations of backlash. "Backlash" refers to misinterpretation, hostility, or resentment toward those making rights claims.[23] Backlash has legal, societal, social movement, and political dimensions. One particular dimension meriting further attention is the importance of opposing social movements and their influence on strategy choice. I have tended to focus on cooperative relations among organizations because available evidence suggests that there has been relatively little collective action specifically opposing the notion of disability rights.[24] Research on other social movements, for example, the gay rights movement, has found that the ability of an organization to mobilize law is constrained by the conflict system surrounding those claims.[25] Didi Herman suggests that litigation by opposing social movements is part of a "struggle for interpretive authority" over a particular set of claims.[26] Similarly, Ellen Ann Andersen proposes that in the context of social movements and the law, future research should concern itself as much with adversaries as with allies.[27]

Finally, the undertaking of this future research could also benefit from the introduction of new methodologies to the field of law and society studies. One of the crucial findings of this study is that general heuristic devices claiming to explain legal mobilization across time,

---

[23] Linda H. Krieger and K. E. Carr, *Backlash Against the ADA: Reinterpreting Disability Rights* (Ann Arbor: University of Michigan Press, 2003).

[24] Burke, "The European Union and the Diffusion of Disability Rights."

[25] Andersen, *Out of the Closets*, p. 15; Didi Herman, *Rights of Passage: Struggles for Lesbian and Gay Legal Equality* (Toronto: University of Toronto Press, 1994).

[26] Herman, *Rights of Passage*, p. 126.

[27] Andersen, *Out of the Closets*, p. 210.

place, and social movements have been largely unsatisfactory on their own and when applied in a general manner: this may be, to some extent, the result of the positivism that has characterized much of political science and sociological theory, which is, as a result, increasingly being supplemented by alternative methodologies. One example of an alternative methodology is the use of discourse analysis, which provides a set of tools for understanding the rhetorical and ideational basis of social action.[28] I suggest here that, in order to more fully understand the role that ideas and meanings play in shaping social movement goals, relationships, and strategy decisions, one must understand the entire discourse within which ideas and meanings are embedded. Understanding the full implications of the "meaning work" around rights, undertaken by organizations, provides some exciting avenues for future research. By comprehending the full range of factors shaping the decision by social movement organizations to turn to the courts, we can both better understand the historic development of judicial understandings of equality and begin to envision the future role of civil society in court-led social change.

[28] Peters, *Institutional Theory in Political Science*, p. 115.

Bibliography

CASES CITED

Supreme Court of Canada Decisions

Ont. Human Rights Comm. v. Borough of Etobicoke, [1982] 1 S.C.R. 202

Ont. Human Rights Comm. v. Simpsons-Sears, [1985] 2 S.C.R. 536

Bhinder v. CN, [1985] 2 S.C.R. 561

E. (Mrs.) v. Eve, [1986] 2 S.C.R. 388

Andrews v. Law Society of British Columbia, [1989] 1 S.C.R. 143

R. v. Swain, [1991] 1 S.C.R. 933

Canadian Council of Churches v. Canada (Minister of Employment and Immigration), [1992] 1 S.C.R. 236

Central Okanagan School District No. 23 v. Renaud, [1992] 2 S.C.R. 970

Weatherall v. Canada (Attorney General), [1993] 2 S.C.R. 872

Rodriguez v. British Columbia (Attorney General), [1993] 3 S.C.R. 519

R. v. O'Connor, [1995] 4 S.C.R. 411

A. (L.L.) v. B. (A.), [1995] 4 S.C.R.

Battlefords and District Co-operative Ltd. v. Gibbs, [1996] 3 S.C.R. 566

R. v. Latimer, [1997] 1 S.C.R. 217

Eaton v. Brant County Board of Education, [1997] 1 S.C.R. 241

Eldridge v. British Columbia (Attorney General), [1997] 2 S.C.R. 624

British Columbia (Superintendent of Motor Vehicles) v. British Columbia (Council of Human Rights), [1999] 3 S.C.R. 868

British Columbia (Public Service Employee Relations Commission) v. BCGSEU, [1999] 3 S.C.R. 3

R. v. Ewanchuk, [1999] 1 S.C.R. 330

New Brunswick (Minister of Health and Community Services) v. G. (J.), [1999] 3 S.C.R. 46

Bibliography

Bese v. British Columbia (Forensic Psychiatric Institute), [1999] 2 S.C.R. 722
Orlowski v. British Columbia (Forensic Psychiatric Institute), [1999] 2 S.C.R. 733
R. v. LePage, [1999] 2 S.C.R. 744
Winko v. British Columbia (Forensic Psychiatric Institute), [1999] 2 S.C.R. 625
R. v. Darrach, 2000 SCC 46, [2000] 2 S.C.R. 443
Lovelace v. Ontario, [2000] 1 S.C.R. 950
Granovsky v. Canada (Minister of Employment and Immigration), 2000 SCC 28, [2000] 1 S.C.R. 703
R. v. Latimer, [2001] 1 S.C.R. 3
Nova Scotia (Workers' Compensation Board) v. Martin; Nova Scotia (Workers' Compensation Board) v. Laseur, [2003] 2 S.C.R. 504, 2003 SCC 54
Auton (Guardian ad litem of) v. British Columbia (Attorney General), [2004] 3 S.C.R. 657, 2004 SCC 78
Newfoundland (Treasury Board) v. N.A.P.E., [2004] 3 S.C.R. 381
Blackwater v. Plint, [2005] 3 S.C.R. 3, 2005 SCC 58
Nova Scotia (Minister of Health) v. J.J., 2005 SCC 12, [2005] 1 S.C.R. 177
Hilewitz v. Canada (Minister of Citizenship and Immigration); De Jong v. Canada (Minister of Citizenship and Immigration), 2005 SCC 57, [2005] 2 S.C.R. 706.
Tranchemontagne v. Ontario (Director, Disability Support Program), 2006 SCC 14, [2006] 1 S.C.R. 513
McGill University Health Centre (Montreal General Hospital) v. Syndicat des employés de l'Hôpital général de Montréal, 2007 SCC 4, [2007] 1 S.C.R.
Council of Canadians with Disabilities v. VIA Rail Canada Inc, 2007 SCC 15, [2007] 1 S.C.R. 650
Colaco v. Canada (Minister of Citizenship and Immigration), [2008] 2 F.C.R.D-10.

European Court of Human Rights Decisions
Botta v. Italy, [1998] 26 EHRR 241
Pretty v. UK, Application no.2346/02, [1998] 27 EHRR 163
Price v. UK, [2001] 34 EHRR 1285

Court of Justice of the European Communities Decisions
Grant v. South West Trains, [1998] ECR I-621
Coleman v. Attridge Law, [2008] C-303/06

UK Court Decisions
Mandla v. Dowell-Lee, [1983] 2 AC 548
The Queen (On the Application of A,B) v. East Sussex County Council, [2001] CO/4843/2001
Cruickshank v. VAW Motorcast Ltd, [2002] ICR 729, EAT

Bibliography

McNicol v. Balfour Beatty Rail Maintenance Ltd, [2002] ICR 1498

Heather, Ward and Callin v. Leonard Cheshire, [2002] EWCA Civ 366

Ms. B. v. An NHS Hospital Trust, [2002] EWHC 429 (Fam)

Essa v. Laing Ltd, [2003] ICR 1110, EAT

Ford-Shubrook v. St Dominics College, [2003] MA315699, Manchester County Court

R. (on the application of Burke) v. General Medical Council, [2003] CO/4038/2003

Archibald v. Fife, [2004] IRLR 651

Roads v. Central Trains, [2004] EWCA Civ 1541

Ross v. Ryanair Ltd and Stansted Airport Ltd, [2004] EWCA Civ. 1751

Burke, R. (on the application of) v. General Medical Council & Ors, [2005] EWCA Civ 1003

Igen Ltd v. Wong and two other cases, [2005] IRLR 258

Smith v. Churchills Stairlifts Plc, [2005] EWCA Civ 1220

GENERAL REFERENCES

Alter, Karen and Jeannette Vargas. 2000. "Explaining Variation in the Use of European Litigation Strategies: European Community Law and British Gender Equality Policy." *Comparative Political Studies* 33(4): 452–82.

Andersen, Ellen Ann. 2005. *Out of the Closets and Into the Courts: Legal Opportunity Structure and Gay Rights Litigation*. Ann Arbor: University of Michigan Press.

ARCH Disability Law Centre. 2005. *ARCH Celebrating 25 Years*. Toronto: ARCH Disability Law Centre.

Armstrong, Sarah. 2003. "Disability Advocacy in the Charter Era." *Journal of Law and Equality* 2(1): 33–91.

Barnes, Colin. 2002. "Disability, Policy and Politics." *Policy and Politics* 30(3): 311–18.

Bell, Mark. 2002. *Anti-Discrimination Law and the European Union*. Oxford: Oxford University Press.

Benford, Robert D. and David A. Snow. 2000. "Framing Processes and Social Movements: An Overview and Assessment." *Annual Review of Sociology* 26: 611–39.

Börzel, Tanja A. and Thomas Risse. 2000. "When Europe Hits Home: Europeanization and Domestic Change." *European Integration Online Papers* 4(15).

Bouwen, Pieter and Margaret McCown. 2007. "Lobbying versus Litigation: Political and Legal Strategies of Interest Representation in the European Union." *Journal of European Public Policy* 14(3): 422–33.

Bibliography

Brodie, Ian. 2001. "Interest Group Litigation and the Embedded State: Canada's Court Challenges Program." *Canadian Journal of Political Science* 34(2): 357–76.

Burke, Thomas F. 2004. "The European Union and the Diffusion of Disability Rights." In Martin A. Levin and Martin Shapiro, eds., *Transatlantic Policy-Making in an Age of Austerity: Diversity and Drift.* Washington DC: Georgetown University Press.

Campbell, Jane and Mike Oliver. 1996. *Disability Politics: Understanding our Past, Changing our Future.* London: Routledge.

Casserley, Catherine. 2000. "The Disability Discrimination Act: An Overview." In Jeremy Cooper, ed., *Law, Rights and Disability.* London: Jessica Kingsley Publishers.

Cichowski, Rachel A. 2007. *The European Court, Civil Society and European Integration.* Cambridge, UK: Cambridge University Press.

Cichowski, Rachel and Alec Stone Sweet. 2003. "Participation, Representative Democracy and the Courts." In Bruce E. Cain, Russell J. Dalton, and Susan E. Scarrow, eds., *Democracy Transformed? Expanding Political Opportunities in Advanced Industrial Democracies.* Oxford: Oxford University Press.

Colker, Ruth. 2009. *When Is Separate Unequal? A Disability Perspective.* New York: Cambridge University Press.

Commission of the European Union, Directorate-General V. 1996. *Mainstreaming Disability within EU Employment and Social Policy.* Brussels: DG V Services Working Paper.

Curtis, Russell L. and Louis A. Zurcher. 1973. "Stable Resources of Protest Movements: The Multi-Organizational Field." *Social Forces* 52(1): 53–61.

Della Porta, Donatella and Mario Diani. 2006. *Social Movements: An Introduction.* Oxford: Blackwell Publishing.

Diani, Mario and Doug McAdam. 2003. *Social Movements and Networks.* New York: Oxford University Press.

Disability Rights Commission. 2007. *DRC Legal Achievements 2000–2007.* Manchester: Disability Rights Commission.

———. 2007. *Evaluating the Impact of the Disability Rights Commission: Final Report.* Manchester: Disability Rights Commission.

Dowding, Keith. 1994. "The Compatibility of Behaviouralism, Rational Choice and 'New Institutionalism.'" *Journal of Theoretical Politics* 6(1): 105–17.

Eisinger, P. K. 1973. "The Conditions of Protest Behavior in American Cities." *American Political Science Review* 67(1): 11–28.

Endicott, Orville R. "Key Trends in Case Law Pertaining to Supports for Persons with Disabilities." Unpublished manuscript on file with the author. Toronto.

Bibliography

Engel, David M. and Frank W. Munger. 2003. *Rights of Inclusion: Law and Identity in the Life Stories of Americans with Disabilities*. Chicago: The University of Chicago Press.

Epp, Charles R. 1998. *The Rights Revolution: Lawyers, Activists, and Supreme Courts in Comparative Perspective*. Chicago: University of Chicago Press.

———. 1999. "The Two Motifs of 'Why the "Haves" Come out Ahead' and its Heirs." *Law and Society Review* 33(4): 1089–98.

Epstein, Lee and Joseph Kobylka. 1992. *The Supreme Court and Legal Change: Abortion and the Death Penalty*. Chapel Hill, NC: University of North Carolina Press.

Finnemore, Martha and Kathryn Sikkink. 1998. "International Norm Dynamics and Political Change." *International Organization* 52(4): 887–917.

Fredman, Sandra. 2002. *Discrimination Law*. Oxford: Oxford University Press.

Galanter, Marc. 1974. "Why the 'Haves' Come out Ahead: Speculations on the Limits of Legal Change," *Law and Society Review* 9(1): 95–160.

Gamson, William A. and David S. Meyer. 1996. "The Framing of Political Opportunity." In Doug McAdam, John D. McCarthy, and Mayer N. Zald, eds., *Comparative Perspectives on Social Movements*. New York: Cambridge University Press.

Gibson, James. 1978. "Judge's Role Orientations, Attitudes and Decision: An Interactive Model." *American Political Science Review* 72(3): 911–24.

Goffman, Erving. 1974. *Frame Analysis*. Boston: Northeastern University Press.

Gooding, Caroline. 2000. "Disability Discrimination Act: From Statute to Practice." *Critical Social Policy* 20(4): 533–49.

Goodwin, Jeff and James M. Jasper. 1999. "Caught in a Winding, Snarling Vine: The Structural Bias of Political Process Theory." *Sociological Forum* 14(1): 27–54.

Grewal, Ini, Sarah Joy, Jane Lewis, Kirby Swales, and Kandy Woodfield. 2002. *"Disabled for Life"? Attitudes Towards, and Experiences of, Disability in Britain*. London: DWP Research Report No. 148.

Hansford, Thomas G. 2004. "Information Provision, Organizational Constraints, and the Decision to Submit an Amicus Curiae Brief in a US Supreme Court Case." *Political Research Quarterly* 57(2): 219–30.

Harlow, Carol and Richard Rawlings. 1992. *Pressure Through Law*. London: Routledge.

Herman, Didi. 1994. *Rights of Passage: Struggles for Lesbian and Gay Legal Equality*. Toronto: University of Toronto Press.

Heyer, Katharina C. 2002. "The ADA on the Road: Disability Rights in Germany." *Law and Social Inquiry* 27(4): 723–62.

Bibliography

Hilson, Chris. 2002. "New Social Movements: The Role of Legal Opportunity." *Journal of European Public Policy* 9(2): 238–55.

Holyoke, Thomas T. 2003. "Choosing Battlegrounds: Interest Group Lobbying Across Multiple Venues." *Political Research Quarterly* 56(3): 325–36.

Jones, Melinda and Lee Ann Marks Basser, eds. 1999. *Disability, Divers-Ability and Legal Change*. The Hague: Martinus Nijhoff Publishers.

Kelemen, R. Daniel. Forthcoming. *The Rise of Adversarial Legalism in Europe*. Cambridge, MA: Harvard University Press.

Kirkland, Anna. 2008. "Think of the Hippopotamus: Rights Consciousness in the Fat Acceptance Movement." *Law and Society Review* 42(2): 397–431.

———. 2008. *Fat Rights: Dilemmas of Difference and Personhood*. New York: New York University Press.

Kitschelt, Herbert P. 1986. "Political Opportunity Structures and Political Protest: Anti-Nuclear Movements in Four Democracies." *British Journal of Political Science* 16(1): 57–84.

Koopmans, Ruud. 1999. "Political. Opportunity. Structure. Some Splitting to Balance the Lumping." *Sociological Forum* 14(1): 93–105.

Krieger, Linda H. and K. E. Carr. 2003. *Backlash against the ADA: Reinterpreting Disability Rights*. Ann Arbor: University of Michigan Press.

Kriesi, Hanspeter. 1995. *New Social Movements in Western Europe: A Comparative Analysis*. Minneapolis, MN: University of Minnesota Press.

Lawrence, Susan E. 1990. *The Poor in Court: The Legal Services Program and Supreme Court Decision Making*. Princeton, NJ: Princeton University Press.

Lempert, Robert O. 1976. "Mobilizing Private Law: An Introductory Essay." *Law and Society Review* 11(2): 173–89.

Mahoney, James and Gary Goertz. 2004. "The Possibility Principle: Choosing Negative Cases in Comparative Research." *American Political Science Review* 98(4): 653–69.

Malhotra, Ravi A. 2003. "The Duty to Accommodate Unionized Workers with Disabilities in Canada and the United States: A Counter-Hegemonic Approach." *Journal of Law and Equality* 2(1): 92–155.

Manfredi, Christopher P. 2004. *Feminist Activism in the Supreme Court: Legal Mobilization and the Women's Legal Education and Action Fund*. Toronto: University of British Columbia Press.

Manfredi, Christopher P. and Antonia Maioni. 2002. "Courts and Health Policy: Judicial Policy Making and Publicly Funded Health Care in Canada." *Journal of Health Politics, Policy and Law* 27(2): 213–40.

Bibliography

March, James G. 1981. "Footnotes to Organizational Change." *Administrative Science Quarterly* 26(4): 563–77.

March, James G. and Johan P. Olsen. 1989. *Rediscovering Institutions: The Organizational Basis of Politics.* New York: Free Press.

————. 1998. "The Institutional Dynamics of International Political Orders." *International Organization* 52(4): 943–69.

————. "The Logic of Appropriateness." *ARENA Working Paper 04/09.* University of Oslo, Centre for European Studies.

McAdam, Doug, Sidney Tarrow, and Charles Tilly. 2001. *Dynamics of Contention.* New York: Cambridge University Press.

McCann, Michael. 1994. *Rights at Work: Pay Equity Reform and the Politics of Legal Mobilization.* Chicago: University of Chicago Press.

McCarthy, John D. and Mayer N. Zald. 1977. "Resource Mobilization and Social Movements: A Partial Theory." *American Journal of Sociology* 82(6): 1212–41.

McColgan, Aileen. 2005. *Discrimination Law: Text, Cases and Materials.* Oxford: Hart Publishing.

Meister, Joan. 2003. "An Early DAWNing (1985–1994)." In Deborah Stienstra and Aileen Wight-Felske, eds., *Making Equality: History of Advocacy and Persons with Disabilities in Canada.* Concord, ON: Captus Press.

Morag-Levine, Noga. 2003. "Partners No More: Relational Transformation and the Turn to Litigation in Two Conservationist Organizations." *Law and Society Review* 37(2): 457–509.

Morton, F. L. and Avril Allen. 2001. "Feminists and the Courts: Measuring Success in Interest Group Litigation in Canada," *Canadian Journal of Political Science* 34(1): 55–84.

Naples, Nancy. 2003. *Feminism and Method: Ethnography, Discourse Analysis and Activist Research.* New York: Routledge.

Neufeldt, Aldred H. 2003. "Growth and Evolution of Disability Advocacy in Canada." In Deborah Stienstra and Aileen Wight-Felske, eds., *Making Equality: History of Advocacy and Persons with Disabilities in Canada.* Concord, ON: Captus Press.

Orren, Karen. 1976. "Standing to Sue: Interest Group Conflict in the Federal Courts." *American Political Science Review* 70(3): 723–41.

Park, Peter, Althea Monteiro, and Bruce Kappel. 2003. "People First: The History and the Dream." In Deborah Stienstra and Aileen Wight-Felske, eds., *Making Equality: History of Advocacy and Persons with Disabilities in Canada.* Concord, ON: Captus Press.

Peters, B. Guy. 2005. *Institutional Theory in Political Science: The "New Institutionalism."* London: Continuum Press.

Peters, B. Guy, Jon Pierre, and Desmond King. 2000. "The Politics of Path Dependency: Political Conflict in Historical Institutionalism." *Journal of Politics* 67(4): 1275–300.

Peters, Yvonne. 2003. "From Charity to Equality: Canadians with Disabilities Take Their Rightful Place in Canada's Constitution." In Deborah Stienstra and Aileen Wight-Felske, eds., *Making Equality: History of Advocacy and Persons with Disabilities in Canada*. Concord, ON: Captus Press.

Poulter, Sebastien M. 1998. *Ethnicity, Law and Human Rights: The English Experience*. Oxford: Oxford University Press.

Pritchett, C. Herman. 1948. *The Roosevelt Court: A Study in Judicial Politics and Values*. New York: MacMillan.

Public Law Project. 2001. *Third Party Interventions in Judicial Review: An Action Research Study*. London: Public Law Project.

Quinn, Gerard. 1999. "The Human Rights of People with Disabilities under EU Law." In P. Alston, M. Bustelo, and J. Heenan, eds., *The EU and Human Rights*. Oxford: Oxford University Press.

Rootes, Chris. 1997. "Shaping Collective Action: Structure, Contingency and Knowledge." In Ricca Edmondson, ed., *The Political Context of Collective Action: Power, Argumentation and Democracy*. London: Routledge.

Rubin, Eva R. 1987. *Abortion, Politics and the Courts*. Westport, CT: Greenwood Press.

Rucht, Dieter. 2005. "Movement Allies, Adversaries and Third Parties." In David A. Snow, Sarah A. Soule, and Hanspeter Kriesi, eds., *The Blackwell Companion to Social Movements*. Oxford: Blackwell Publishing.

Segal, Jeffrey A. and Harold J. Spaeth. 1993. *The Supreme Court and the Attitudinal Model*. New York: Cambridge University Press.

Shakespeare, Tom, ed. 1998. *The Disability Reader*. New York: Continuum.

_____. 2006. *Disability Rights and Wrongs*. London: Routledge.

Sikkink, Kathryn. 2005. "Patterns of Dynamic Multilevel Governance and the Insider-Outsider Coalition." In Donatella Della Porta and Sidney Tarrow, eds., *Transnational Protest and Global Activism*. Oxford: Rowman and Littlefield.

Smith, Miriam. 1998. "Social Movements and Equality Seeking: The Case of Gay Liberation in Canada." *Canadian Journal of Political Science* 31(2): 285–309.

_____. 2005. "Social Movements and Judicial Empowerment: Courts, Public Policy, and Lesbian and Gay Organizing in Canada." *Politics and Society* 33(2): 327–53.

_____. 2008. *Political Institutions and Lesbian and Gay Rights in the United States and Canada*. London: Routledge.

Bibliography

Snow, David A., Burke Rochford, Jr., Steven K. Worden, and Robert D. Benford. 1986. "Frame Alignment Processes, Micromobilization, and Movement Participation." *American Sociological Review* 51: 464–81.

Solberg, Rorie Spill and Eric N. Waltenburg. 2006. "Why Do Interest Groups Engage the Judiciary? Policy Wishes and Structural Needs." *Social Science Quarterly* 87(3): 558–72.

Stienstra, Deborah and Aileen Wight-Felske. 2003. *Making Equality: History of Advocacy and Persons with Disabilities in Canada.* Concord, ON: Captus Press.

Waddington, Lisa. 1999. "The European Community's Response to Disability." In Melinda Jones and Lee Ann Basser Marks, eds., *Disability, Divers-ability and Legal Change.* The Hague: Martinus Nijhoff Publishers.

Watters, Colleen. 2003. "History of Advocacy Organizations of the Blind in Canada: Two Stories." In Deborah Stienstra and Aileen Wight-Felske, eds., *Making Equality: History of Advocacy and Persons with Disabilities in Canada.* Concord, ON: Captus Press.

Wendell, Susan. 2006. "Toward a Feminist Theory of Disability." In Lenard J. Davis, ed., *The Disability Studies Reader.* New York: Routledge.

Williams, Bridget, Phil Copestake, John Eversley, and Bruce Stafford. 2008. *Experiences and Expectations of Disabled People.* London: Office for Disability Issues.

Wilson, Bruce M. and Juan Carlos Rodríguez Cordero. 2006. "Legal Opportunity Structures and Social Movements: The Effects of Institutional Change on Costa Rican Politics." *Comparative Political Studies* 39(3): 325–51.

Wintemute, Robert. 1998. "When Is Pregnancy Discrimination Indirect Sex Discrimination?" *Industrial Law Journal* 27(1): 23–36.

World Health Organization. 2001. *Rethinking Care from the Perspective of Disabled People: Conference Report and Recommendations.* Geneva: WHO's Disability and Rehabilitation Team.

Zemans, Frances K. 1983. "Legal Mobilization: The Neglected Role of the Law in the Political System." *American Political Science Review* 77(3): 690–703.

Zurcher, Louis A. and Russell L. Curtis. 1973. "A Comparative Analysis of Propositions Describing Social Movement Organizations." *Sociological Quarterly* 14(2): 175–88.

Index

Index

British Airport Authority (BAA), 8n
British Columbia
  (Attorney General), Auton (Guardian ad litem of) v., 65t, 96t, 110t, 132–136
  Bese v., 96t
  (Council of Human Rights), British Columbia (Superintendent of Motor Vehicles) v., 65t, 96t
  Eldridge v., 65t, 96t, 110t, 125–130, 250
  Orlowski v., 96t
  (Public Service Employee Relations Commission) v. BCGSEU, 65t
  Rodriguez v., 65t, 96t, 110t, 119–121, 132, 251–252, 271
  (Superintendent of Motor Vehicles) v. British Columbia (Council of Human Rights), 65t, 96t
British Council of Organisations of Disabled People (BCODP)
  disability charities and, 156–160, 184, 265–266
  funding of, 156t, 158, 159–160, 184
  history of, 153–155
  strategic litigation utilization by, 263
  strategy, 156–160, 173
Brodsky, G., 269–270
Burke, T. F., 209

Campbell, J., 149–150, 154, 158
Canada
  Accessibility for Ontarians with Disabilities Act (AODA) of 2005, 60t, 62, 101–102
  Canadian Human Rights Act (CHRA), 60t, 61
  Canadian Human Rights Commission, 61
  Charter of Rights and Freedoms, 48–49, 57, 57n, 59, 60t

Coalition of Provincial Organizations of the Handicapped (COPOH) (*See* Coalition of Provincial Organizations of the Handicapped (COPOH))
consumer organizations in, 54–55, 55n, 57
Council of Canadians with Disabilities (CCD) (*See* Council of Canadians with Disabilities (CCD))
Court Challenges Program, 74–75, 259
disability discrimination in, 36n, 36–37, 37n, 215–216
disability rights movement in (*See* Disability rights movement (Canada))
division of labor in the disability movement, 266–267
institutional constraints in, 257
as model, 43
Ontarians with Disabilities Act of 2001, 62
Ontario Human Rights Code, 60t, 61, 113–116
organizational actor participation in, 257–258
organizational cooperation in, 266
rights, implementation of, 127–129, 247
role of courts in, 217
Supreme Court (*See* Supreme Court of Canada)
Canada
  Canadian Council of Churches v., 65t, 96t
  De Jong v., 65t, 96t, 136–140
  Granovsky v., 65t
  Hilewitz v., 65t, 96t, 110t, 136–140
  (Minister of Citizenship and Immigration) v. Colaco et al, 139

Index

Index

Index

Index

Index

Index

Index

Index

5652594R00173

Printed in Great Britain
by Amazon.co.uk, Ltd.,
Marston Gate.